THE BATTLE FOR THE
SETTLE &
CARLISLE

JAMES TOWLER

D0243090

First published in 1990 by Platform 5 Publishing Ltd., Lydgate House, Lydgate Lane, Sheffield, S10 5FH

Printed in England by Icon Impressions Ltd., Yorkshire Street Mills, Yorkshire Street, Bacup, Lancs., OL13 9AF. All rights reserved.

James Towler & Platform 5 Publishing Ltd. 1990.

No part of this publication may be reproduced or transmitted in any form or by any means electronic, mechanical, photocopying, recording or otherwise, without the prior permission of the publisher.

This book is sold subject to the condition that it shall not, by way of trade or otherwise, be lent, resold, hired out or otherwise circulated without the publisher's prior consent in any form of binding or cover other than that in which it is published and without a similar condition including this condition being imposed on the subsequent purchaser.

ISBN 1 872524 07 9

CONTENTS

AUTHOR'S NOTE

This book tells the story of the eight year battle to save the Settle–
Carlisle railway line as it happened between 1981 and 1989.

Although essentially a personal record by one who was in the
middle of the action, I have endeavoured to present a comprehensive record of the events; from the decision to re-route the Nottingham–Glasgow service away from the line to the Government's
refusal to consent to British Rail's closure proposal.

In addition to drawing freely from my own experience and vast
accumulation of correspondence, memoranda and reports, I have
included extracts from the voluminous coverage by the media –
particularly the 'Yorkshire Post', 'Telegraph and Argus' and 'Craven Herald and Pioneer' – whose accounts so admirably captured
the mood of the battle at the time. However, unless otherwise
attributed, any views expressed are entirely my own.

I am grateful, too, for the support provided by colleagues on
the Transport Users Consultative Committees (TUCCs) for Yorkshire and North East England during my period as chairman, when
Settle–Carlisle was the most prodigious item on the agenda.

Thanks are also due to my wife Muriel, both for her support
whilst the battle was being fought and for her subsequent encouragement and assistance in drafting the narrative; and to the Platform 5 Organisation for their production skills in presenting this
episode of the Settle–Carlisle story.

Above all, I acknowledge my gratitude to all those who fought
to save 'England's Greatest Historical Scenic Route' and the 'Most
Magnificent Main Line in England'. It is to them that this book is
dedicated.

1

INTRODUCING THE TRANSPORT USERS CONSULTATIVE COMMITTEE (TUCC)

"In addition to joining a committee, I had also become a member of an exclusive quarterly luncheon club – complete with private bar!"

My first acquaintance with the Settle–Carlisle line was during the 1939–45 war. Friends of my parents had acquired a small hotel at Askham, near Penrith, and we spent a few days there during the summer of 1941. Being wartime, there was no petrol for holiday travel. So the journey was made by train from Leeds City station, probably on the 10.35 Leeds–Glasgow, although I remember little of the journey other than a vague recollection of alighting at Appleby in order to catch the local train on the North Eastern line to Penrith.

In 1945 when I was twelve, I became an enthusiastic collector of engine numbers. I was at a boarding school in Glossop, North Derbyshire, which was conveniently situated one mile from Dinting Junction on the Manchester–Sheffield line via Woodhead. Encouraged by the advent of the Ian Allan ABCs, a group of us would sprint along Dinting Road in the hope of seeing the early evening express trains from such far away places as Sheffield, Cleethorpes and even London itself.

From our vantage point on top of a cutting to the north of the station – from which we were banned by a rather officious porter! – we were able to witness the twilight years of Great Central motive power for Robinson Directors, B7s, J11s and 04s were the order of the day. Gresley was well represented, too; with Green Arrows, Sandringhams and the occasional Pacific, whilst the first of the Thompson B1s were being phased in. It was an interesting time to be about.

Like many youthful pastimes, my train spotting days were short lived. However, they proved of lasting benefit on two counts. They taught me my railway geography and how to find my way around a Bradshaw, the comprehensive timetable of the day. Throughout the Fifties and Sixties the railway played little part in my life, other than for business travel to and from London. Occasionally I would use the train for other journeys, to Newcastle or Liverpool for example. Very occasionally I travelled by rail to Glasgow, preferring the East Coast Main Line as one could get a good dinner on the down "Queen of Scots" – I'm an inveterate advocate of eating on trains.

During that 20 year period, I doubt if I used the Settle–Carlisle line more than two or three times. That it was a fine scenic route was taken for granted. However, having spent the first 25 years of my life living in the country, I also knew of the disadvantages of rural life, not least the lack of public transport. But what really irked me about the Settle route to Glasgow was the interminable time it took between Carlisle and Glasgow via Dumfries. The demise of the "Queen of Scots" followed by the withdrawal of restaurant car facilities from the "North Briton" and Settle–Carlisle trains persuaded me to discard rail for Scottish trips in favour of the car or plane.

By the early-Seventies, my long distance rail journeys, like those of many businessmen, were confined to travel to and from London; a trip I was making twice a month. In addition I had started using a local service to commute between offices in Leeds and Shipley. This was largely a matter of convenience, the much maligned DMU proving a godsend as it meant I could avoid the hassle of car parking in Leeds. I also used the Hull–Scarborough line during summer holidays, thus avoiding the congested coast road and parking problems.

This then was the situation in 1973 when, quite by chance, I became involved with a body called the Transport Users Consultative Committee or TUCC. Indeed, but for the fact I was opposed to Britain's membership of the Common Market, I doubt if I would ever have heard of them, let alone become a member and subsequently chairman of the TUCC which received most objections and held the longest public hearing into any railway closure proposal. Let me explain.

Whilst I have never been active in politics or, for that matter, a member of a political party, current affairs have always interested me. Ever since I was at school I've followed the political scene, from the days of Churchill and Attlee to the present time. During an average day I'll watch a couple of television news programmes and listen to innumerable radio bulletins. I cast my eye over four or five newspapers and also take a couple of weekly political journals, the 'Spectator' and 'New Statesman'. An MP once described me as being akin to a "19th century Whig with a radical edge," adding that I was proof that one should never put people into categories "because James Towler would defy anything you tried to put him in!" Be that as it may, I hope it establishes a certain detachment on my part.

Two years earlier, in the spring of 1971 when the Common Market issue was beginning to take off, I had been rushed into hospital with acute appendicitis. Since the Macmillan era, I had always questioned whether EEC membership was in Britain's best interests. From my sick-bed, with nothing to do other than read and listen to the radio, it struck me that the public were being subjected to an enormous hype by the media in general and the BBC in particular on the so-called 'benefits' of Common Market membership. Yet, the sums simply did not add up. Britain, as a net contributor, would not only end up subsidising its competitors; it would be subsidising competitors who were better off than itself.

My firm was a member of the CBI which had taken a strong pro-Common Market stance. So I suggested that they might be wrong. This didn't go down very well except with a minority of sage minded doubters like myself. Nevertheless, as a consequence of my interest, I was invited to join the CBI regional council; no doubt in the hope that it would shut me up. Needless to say, it didn't. I also joined a small anti-Common Market business lobby and got to know a number of MPs on both sides of the debate.

Towards the end of 1972, a circular from the regional CBI arrived on my desk stating they had been invited to nominate someone to the TUCC and asked for volunteers. Whilst not bursting with enthusiasm, I said that if no one else was interested, I was prepared to give it a go. I then proceeded to forget all about it. Therefore, it came as a surprise when, in the spring of 1973, I received a letter telling me that I had been appointed a member of the Yorkshire TUCC. Later I was to discover this was almost inevitable as I was the only CBI regional councillor who had responded to the circular!

TUCCs came into being under the Transport Act 1947, although that for Yorkshire was not established until 1952 when, writing on behalf of the Minister of Transport, Lt-Cmdr. J Gurney

Braithwaite MP, told the first chairman, Professor A N Shimmin, that:

"The Committee will provide an essential means through which expression can be given to the views and needs of the users of the British Transport Commission's services in a forum in which the Commission and the Executives can take their part, and against a background of statutory provision for discussion to be followed by effective action in those cases in which action is necessary. Should the occasion arise, the Minister will not for his part hesitate to avail himself of the opportunity which the Transport Act have given him to refer matters to you for your consideration."

Put more succinctly, the role of the TUCCs was to consider and make recommendations in relation to any matter affecting the services and facilities provided by the BTC. Under the Transport Act 1962, the British Railways Board was established to take over the railway interests of the BTC which was abolished. The revised duties of TUCCs were covered by Section 56 of the new Act (Appendix 1). This included the procedures applicable if British Rail proposed to close a station or line, when the TUCC was required to consider objections from users of services affected and report to the Minister of Transport on the hardship that would be caused if the station or line closed.

Those appointed to the TUCCs by government were from people nominated by local authorities, industry and commerce, trade unions, women's organisations and other representative bodies. The committee I had joined comprised 18 members, almost half of whom were local government councillors. The chairman, Mr W J 'Jim' Price, had been transport officer with the Yorkshire Area of the National Coal Board prior to his retirement. Before that he had been with the LNER for twenty years. A thespian of some repute, he had a canny eye for detail and an ability to bring a sense of occasion to issues which, in less capable hands, would have appeared mundane.

Although the chairman was a part-time appointment, there was a full time secretariat who handled the day to day work of the committee. During the Sixties, much of it related to the Beeching closures, but in recent years it had largely involved servicing complaints from the public. Most of these were resolved without recourse to the committee which met four or five times a year at the Royal Station Hotel in York.

When I received the agenda and supporting papers for my first meeting in June 1973, I remember thinking that it shouldn't take more than a couple of hours so I would be able to get back to Leeds in time for lunch. How wrong I was, for I had not appreciated that, in addition to joining a committee, I had also become a member of an exclusive luncheon club – complete with private bar!

Not, I hasten to add, that the hospitality provided by the state was abused. Nevertheless, after years of experience in trade associations and voluntary organisations, where any sustenance offered was strictly for cash, I felt I had landed on my feet. However, the taxpayer, who ultimately footed the bill, had no real grounds for complaint. TUCC members provided a wide range of experience and expertise and, apart from the chairman who was paid on the basis of one day a week, they received no remuneration.

Meetings were also attended by a British Rail 'liaison officer', in those days the chief passenger manager of Eastern Region, Bert Gemmell. Most issues discussed related to individual passenger complaints and in many cases the committee were able to persuade Mr Gemmell, an agreeable Scot, to provide a refund here or a free ticket there. Occasionally a more serious problem would arise which might result in British Rail, after much prodding from the committee, changing its procedure in some area of its activities. Overall, it was a friendly and largely harmonious forum at a time when the railway barometer appeared set fair.

Indeed, in retrospect the mid-seventies were halcyon days for British Rail. Timetables were augmented rather than cut, Mark 2 air conditioned coaches became the norm on the East Coast Main Line whilst prospects of the High Speed and Advanced Passenger Trains held promise of more good things to come. There was talk, too, of electrification of the sadly neglected Midland Main Line to Sheffield. Locally, DMUs were being refurbished and the new Passenger Transport Executives or PTEs were beginning to effect improvements in their areas.

Against this background Yorkshire TUCC members considered issues as varied as the perennial requests for additional stops at Marsden and Morley to the withdrawal of toilet facilities at Keighley. Colin Speakman, later to win acclaim for pioneering Dales Rail, pressed the committee to seek improved services to the Lake District by reinstating the main line platforms at Carnforth. Individual grumbles included a complaint about travel between Skipton and Glasgow, but it was nothing more than a ticketing error. Barbara Ashwin, who had joined the committee at the same time as me and who was later to prove an excellent deputy chairman, was concerned about a shortage of porters at York, whilst I had run into problems when the 09.40 Skipton-Leeds failed to connect into the "Yorkshire Pullman". No doubt it was all very interesting at the time, but it was hardly world shaking stuff.

Therefore when, in November 1976, British Rail announced it wished to close Filey Holiday Camp station, our work took on an extra dimension. The committee received 11 objections and held a public hearing in the ballroom of the Royal Hotel in Scarborough, at that time owned by Tom Laughton, brother of Charles Laughton the actor. British Rail's case for closure was presented by the divisional manager at Doncaster, Mr J J O'Brien. Objectors who presented evidence included spokesmen for Scarborough Borough Council, Filey Town Council and Bridlington Constituency Labour Party.

However, the most impressive case for retention of the Butlins station came from the only member of the public to speak, Manchester businessman Roger Smith. Scarborough-born and an old hand at fighting railway closures from the Beeching era, his ploy was to analyse the evidence submitted by British Rail in its 'Heads of Information' document and use it to turn the case for closure on its head. His presentation proved so effective that the hearing, which had been expected to finish by lunch, continued into the afternoon – much to the chagrin of British Rail's Mr O'Brien who had arranged for his chauffeur to collect him at one o'clock!

This closure proposal also led to a disagreement within the TUCC between the committee and the chair. It arose because members, including myself, felt their conclusion that there would be a 'degree of hardship' if the station closed had been watered down to refer only to 'inconvenience' in the draft report. After much telephoning amongst members, the matter was resolved and the original conclusion stood – a case of the committee rules, OK!

Shortly afterwards I was elected deputy chairman of the Yorkshire TUCC, taking over from Norman Bisby, a founder member who retired after 25 years service in June 1977. Quite why the choice fell on me, I don't know. But there were two factors in my favour. First my attendance at meetings was good – 100 per cent in fact. Second, and more important, I was one of the few members who regularly travelled by train. Rightly or wrongly, the committee was more representative of the public at large, of whom only about 10 per cent travelled by train, than of actual rail users.

My job was little more than a title. Jim Price was a resilient chairman so, apart from deputising for him at a British Rail electrification presentation, saying grace at a dinner attended by members of the Central Transport Consultative Committee or CTCC, the TUCCs 'parent' body, and being consulted on an extraordinary complaint regarding travel between Chesterfield and Moscow, I had little to do.

Nevertheless, I had detected a change of mood amongst members who looked to me to encourage a more consumer orientated outlook on the part of the committee. There were also two more closure proposals on the horizon, that for the Humber Ferry and associated rail links following the opening of the Humber Bridge and a complex issue of wrangling between local government and British Rail which threatened the Huddersfield–Sheffield line. Both were likely to prove far more taxing than Filey Holiday Camp.

However, the most significant event of the late Seventies was the General Election in June 1979 when the Conservatives led by Mrs Margaret Thatcher ousted Mr James Callaghan's Labour administration. Amongst the many targets in the sights of the new government were the nationalised industries and, even nearer to home, government sponsored quangos like the TUCCs.

This was the climate when, in September and much to my surprise, I was asked to succeed Jim Price who stood down after 26 years of diligent service to the Yorkshire TUCC, the last nine being as chairman. One did not need a crystal ball to realise I was intended as a stop-gap whilst the government decided what it was going to do with the TUCCs. Could they have done so, I believe they would have abolished them overnight. But this was not possible as legislation would be required and the Government had far more important priorities for the Parliamentary time at its disposal.

Nevertheless, there was no doubt that the future of the TUCCs was very much under threat at the time. The chairman of the CTCC left me in little doubt how he felt I should organise things. For a start, the cosy relationship between the Yorkshire TUCC and British Rail should end, a point stressed by a civil servant from the Department of Trade who expressed astonishment that my predecessor never issued any news releases. Fortunately these views concurred with those of members and myself. I felt it was time for the committee to show more initiative rather than just sitting back waiting for complaints to come in.

The committee I inherited was down to ten members, there being a number of vacancies. However, in view of doubts regarding our future – "The role of the TUCCs in protecting the consumers interest is currently under review but no decision on their future has yet been reached". (Mr Reginald Eyre MP, Under Secretary of State for Trade, 7th November 1979) – I did not press for additional members as I felt the existing committee more than competent to handle the existing work load. If nothing else, I was making a modest contribution to cutting Government expenditure.

I also decided there should be more emphasis on monitoring British Rail's quality of service in addition to following up complaints from individual rail users. These had only totalled 105 during the previous year which hardly justified employment of a full time secretariat (secretary plus typist), notwithstanding the complexity of many of the issues raised. In an endeavour to broaden the scope of the committee's work, I arranged for a series of talks on railway related matters to be given during lunch. If nothing else, it helped legitimise our 'luncheon club'!

We were fortunate, too, that our British Rail liaison officer at the time was Colin Driver, later to become director, freight sector. I not only liked him but, more importantly, could do business with him. Unlike so many within British Rail and other large organisations, he had a flair for discarding red tape, cutting corners and making quick decisions. He was well supported by divisional managers in Leeds, Sheffield and Doncaster.

As chairman of the Yorkshire TUCC, I became a member of the CTCC – a mix of TUCC chairmen and independent appointees. The CTCC was there to co-ordinate the work of the eleven TUCCs and deal with national issues. Socially, members tended to congregate into groups of common interest. Thus, those who were politically active gravitated towards others of the same party. Other areas of mutual interest ranged from the bench to cricket and, just occasionally, railways. It was on the latter subject that I teamed up with Barry Flaxman, the splendid chairman of the East Anglian TUCC whose detailed knowledge of almost every aspect of railway operation complemented my more modest and somewhat indefinable input as a frequent rail user.

Our initial subject of mutual concern related to the long neglected Midland Main Line where we were joined by C F 'Jim' Ward, the recently appointed chairman of the East Midlands TUCC. Our activities were not universally acclaimed by our colleagues and we were labelled 'The Gang of Three'! Nevertheless, our criticism of British Rail was invariably well founded. Moreover, we tended to rely on our own research, rather than on briefings provided by the TUCC secretaries who were seconded British Rail employees.

The question of secondment had always proved sensitive. I took the view expounded by Len Dumelow – the wiry CTCC secretary until his retirement in 1986 – and the more enlightened TUCC secretaries that any advantages of secondment were outweighed by the pitfalls. Someone put it to me that secondment was necessary so that the secretary could explain to members how the points worked! This struck me as a very weak argument.

Secondment also placed TUCC secretaries in an invidious position, especially if they were ambitious and hoped to return to British Rail to further their careers. In such conditions loyalties could be split and stretched to the limit. Some British Rail officers were not averse to using seniority when dealing with TUCC secretaries and there have been occasions when railway management have told the TUCC secretariat what to do. Not, I feel, the way an independent consumer watchdog should operate.

Indeed, there was the case in 1987 following Len Dumelow's retirement when a British Railways Board member sought to blackball the CTCCs choice of a new secretary. This, more than anything else, endorsed the case for discarding secondment once and for all. All TUCC and CTCC staff should be transferred to the civil service and forget that they were once railwaymen – or railwaywomen.

But I digress. To return to the Yorkshire TUCC of the autumn of 1979. Here I was fortunate in that the secretary, Norman Archer, had a conscientious and methodical approach to his work. Nor did he have any ambitions to return to British Rail, so he wasn't having to look over his shoulder all the time. Indeed, his abiding interest was bridge and he ranked as one of the leading players in the county.

Together we evolved a revised strategy for the committee. Norman would continue to run the office and handle complaints, although I would look in and cast my eye over them as they were a useful barometer on British Rail's performance, whilst I would do the travelling – by train, of course! – following up complaints, initiating projects and handling media enquiries. The first Yorkshire TUCC annual report was published in March 1980 whilst other initiatives that year included campaigns for HSTs on the Sheffield–St Pancras service, the opening of a new station at Slaithwaite and provision of a telephone at Scunthorpe station –

all of which eventually came to fruition.

During subsequent years we took up many issues, ranging from missed bus and rail connections on the Humberlink service to the disgraceful conditions at Halifax station. We pressed successfully for retention of the 'Great British Breakfast', argued strongly against cuts in services and rounded on the Serpell report for ignoring the interests of rail users. We also staged several public meetings and produced a number of special reports including a 'Train and Coach Comparison' based on our investigations.

By the beginning of 1980 things were beginning to move on the closure front. The anticipated breakdown in talks between British Rail and South Yorkshire County Council meant that a closure proposal for the line between Denby Dale and Sheffield was imminent, whilst the public hearing for the Humber Ferry and the rail links at New Holland was held on two consecutive days in September. We opened in Grimsby in the afternoon and, after an evening session, travelled to Hull by train and ferry where we resumed the hearing the following morning.

The withdrawal of the ferry was considered by most to be a foregone conclusion once the bridge opened and the committee only received 48 objections to the proposal. Nevertheless, there were people who felt strongly about the ferry and they presented a good case for its retention. Public interest appeared minimal, attendance at each session of the hearing never exceeding 20 whilst during our evening at Grimsby Town Hall we failed to muster double figures. So much for our drawing power! All the same it proved an interesting experience and a useful 'dry run' for the hearings that were to follow.

This then was the background to the position when, amid a climate of cutbacks and closures, the phrase 'Settle–Carlisle' first entered my vocabulary. Little did I realise that it would take quite a slice out of my life, too.

2

RIBBLEHEAD VIADUCT – REASON OR RED HERRING?

"I should say straight away that we have no desire, or at this time plans, to close the Settle–Carlisle line even though the numbers using the two intermediate stations at Settle and Appleby are comparatively few in number."

> Sir Peter Parker, Chairman of the British Railways Board, in a letter to the Rt Hon Denis Healey MP dated 4th November 1981.

In March 1981, the City of Sheffield published its report 'Priorities for Main-Line Electrification' which outlined an imaginative development programme for the following 15 years. It was an impressive, well argued and researched document based on an assumption that electrification could proceed at a rate of 100 route miles per year. It concluded, sensibly in my view, that priority be given to electrification between London St Pancras and Sheffield, and on through to Manchester via Woodhead, rather than to the East Coast Main Line.

The report stressed the benefits of the existing new Woodhead tunnel between Sheffield and Manchester. This had opened to electric express passenger services in 1954 but was closed to passenger traffic in 1970, ostensibly because its capacity was required for freight. By 1979 it was planned to close the route altogether. Needless to say, British Rail's handling of the Woodhead issue had attracted a great deal of criticism.

In totally rejecting any option which included use of the Woodhead route – "there is no justification whatever for it" – British Rail were particularly dismissive of the City of Sheffield's contention that trains linking London, the East Midlands, Sheffield, Manchester, Preston, Carlisle and Glasgow had commercial potential at least as good as the North East–South West route.

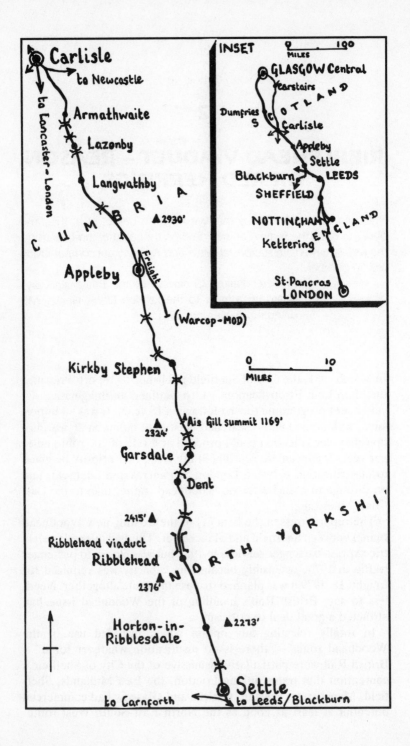

This was a strange response when you consider it subsequently introduced a service between London Paddington and Hull via Birmingham and Sheffield!

Although not directly a point at issue, Woodhead was seldom far from peoples minds during the public hearing into the first Huddersfield–Sheffield closure proposal in the spring of 1981. Simon Bain, in his definitive study of the Woodhead saga titled 'Railroaded' (Faber and Faber – 1981), recalls how he sat through the "interchange between public and officials, and wondered how it was that the 'embargo on what everyone wants to discuss' was still clearly in force." Nevertheless, 'Priorities for Main-Line Electrification', in which Woodhead featured so prominently, was a key part of the City of Sheffield's evidence at the hearing and was incorporated in the report the Yorkshire TUCC submitted to the Secretary of State for Transport.

The City of Sheffield's report was also considered by the committee as a separate issue at its quarterly meeting on 30th April 1981. It was at this meeting I also drew members attention to press reports that the Ribblehead Viaduct might have to be replaced or even closed. These had not unduly concerned me as, in my innocence, I didn't believe the only direct rail link between West Yorkshire and South West Scotland could be seriously under threat. Two weeks later I was to discover just how wrong I was.

I set off to the London Midland Region timetable presentation on 13th May with the intention of pressing for the early introduction of HSTs on the Midland Main Line between London and Sheffield as a prelude, I hoped, to complete electrification and deployment of the Advanced Passenger Train – as envisaged by the City of Sheffield. I was to return with something far more immediate and serious on my mind.

The presentation took place in the board room at Euston House, the London Midland Region's headquarters (now the British Railways Board's HQ) alongside Euston station. The objective was to brief representatives of the Department of Transport and the TUCCs on the timetable plans for the following year from May 1982. British Rail were represented by Brian Mander, the chief passenger manager of the London Midland Region, and Len Metcalf, the passenger services manager. A character called Humphrey Todd, who reminded me of someone in an Evelyn Waugh novel, also put in an appearance. It emerged he was from InterCity at the British Railways Board headquarters.

The meeting opened predictably enough. Brian Mander explained that the economic recession was having an adverse effect on train loadings and there had been a considerable downturn on earnings on all routes. Further cuts in services were inevitable. It appeared, too, proposals that the City of Sheffield should 'hire' an HST had been shunted into a siding as it had not been possible to agree terms.

Then came the shock news. Mr Mander announced that it was planned to re-route the Nottingham–Glasgow service from Leeds and the Settle–Carlisle line to run via Manchester and Preston. I immediately asked if this had any bearing on the condition of the Ribblehead Viaduct. Mr Mander replied that it had. I then pointed out that this would not only sever the direct link between West Yorkshire and Glasgow, it would also mean an end to through services between Leeds and Nottingham. Neither Mander nor Metcalf appeared to have realised the latter point.

In answer to my claim that the proposal represented a further step by British Rail to downgrade the Midland Main Line, Brian Mander said they felt very badly about the position. He claimed electrification of the Midland line to Sheffield remained top priority and that the Advanced Passenger Train would provide the most suitable form of rolling stock. Humphrey Todd chipped in to say the Midland route was a "problem area." British Rail had produced any number of investment schemes, yet each one had failed to convince the Department of Transport of its financial viability. So far as Sheffield–London was concerned, it simply was not competitive with the East Coast Main Line from Doncaster.

I left the meeting feeling very depressed and the following day I drafted a report for Yorkshire TUCC members outlining what I had learned. I also contacted our liaision officer, Colin Driver, expressing my concern at the proposed changes and asking what alternatives British Rail had in mind for Yorkshire passengers affected by them.

On 19th May 1981, David Heyward, the northern editor of 'New Civil Engineer' penned a feature page article in the 'Yorkshire Post' which opened:

"Rapid deterioration of the country's most exposed railway viaduct deep in the remote North Yorkshire Pennines could result in closure of the country's highest main rail line."

According to Hayward, fresh cracks were appearing "almost daily" in the 24-arch Ribblehead Viaduct and a £4.5 million replacement was urgently needed.

The article quoted British Rail's divisional civil engineer, Alan King, as saying: "We have spent over £600,000 on the viaduct in the last decade but have ended up with the structure in a worse condition than when we started. We can only continue maintaining it for another three years." Hayward's conclusion was that whilst the engineering solution to Ribblehead was relatively straightforward, the political decision to sanction construction of a new viaduct was "another story." He continued:

"British Rail must decide whether the line is at present worth major increased investment, and if so where the cash will come from. The route carries up to 40 trains a day and acts as an important diversion for the West Coast main line where track and ballast renewal will require regular weekend work for many years hence."

With this, coming top of the timetable presentation, it was high time I renewed my acquaintance with the Settle–Carlisle line. So the morning of Thursday 21st May found me amongst the 130 passengers on the 09.20 Leeds (ex 07.15 Nottingham)–Glasgow train en-route to Carlisle. The most interesting aspect of the journey was 40 people joined the train at Settle and 70 alighted at Appleby, including most of those from Settle. On my return journey, the 13.22 Carlisle (ex 11.50 Glasgow)–Nottingham left with almost 200 passengers. Another 40 joined at Appleby and 38 alighted at Settle.

In a subsequent report to my members, I concluded:

"On both the outward and return journey there appeared no appreciable speed restrictions over the Ribblehead Viaduct. The most striking feature of this line is that it is not only part of British Rail's InterCity network, it is also 'the most spectacular main line' and 'perhaps the finest scenic railway in England.' Those are not my words but come from British Rail leaflet (LM) 2/80.23m. I heartily endorse them!"

I was now faced with something of a dilemma. Whilst it was common knowledge all was not well with Ribblehead Viaduct and this could threaten services on the Settle–Carlisle line, the fact there were already plans to re-route the Nottingham–Glasgow service away from the line in less than a year was privileged information. Fortunately it wasn't long before British Rail's reputation for leaking like a sieve came to my aid as rumours surfaced that something was afoot regarding the Nottingham–Glasgow service.

This provided me with the clearance I required and on 11th June

I issued a carefully worded news release. It referred to the Yorkshire TUCC's concern regarding the future of rail services between
West Yorkshire and Scotland, following reports on the deteriorating condition of the Ribblehead Viaduct and a suggestion that
British Rail were considering re-routing the Nottingham–Glasgow
service via Manchester in May 1982. The release then posed a
number of questions: Would there be no InterCity trains between
Leeds and Carlisle via Settle? Would there be no direct service
between Leeds and Nottingham? And what would happen to Dales
Rail?

I pointed out that the Settle–Carlisle line provided the quickest
route between Leeds and Glasgow, and drew attention to the inter-
station traffic on the line, especially amongst holidaymakers. The
news release concluded:

"Indeed, there is considerable scope for expanding tourist traffic
on this line. It is acknowledged by British Rail as being 'the most
spectacular main line' and 'perhaps the finest scenic railway in
England'"

The release was taken up by several papers and local radio stations and an editorial in the 'Yorkshire Evening Post' of 15th June
stated:

"The Settle route, winding between Ingleborough and Pen-y-
Ghent, is one of Europe's most breathtaking. It offers much scope
for expansion in tourist traffic. There is no question that any suggestion of closing it would create a public outcry. But to keep it open,
that public will eventually have to pay, and so it should."

I had sent copies of the release with a covering letter to the two
MPs principally concerned in our area, John Watson (Skipton) and
Bob Cryer (Keighley), both of whom I knew from the days of the
Common Market debate and via my connection with Pennine
Radio, Bradford's independent local radio station of which I was
a director.

John Watson replied that he would "enthusiastically support"
any efforts which British Rail and the Yorkshire TUCC felt were
necessary to keep the line open. He continued:

"The Settle–Carlisle railway is not only one of the most historic
and scenic in the British Isles, it is also one of the most strategically
important and provides employment for a significant number of
people in my constituency. It is very widely used, too."

Bob Cryer – a railway enthusiast and founder member of the
Keighley and Worth Valley Railway – was equally positive. He

said he had already raised the matter in the House of Commons but had been told British Rail had not made any application to the Secretary of State for Transport for additional money for the replacement of the Ribblehead Viaduct. Therefore he had written to Sir Peter Parker, chairman of the British Railways Board, on the subject.

If nothing else, I'd got the public debate off the ground. Even more important was the fact that the politicians were interested. In the meantime I maintained pressure on British Rail and tried to discover what its plans were. Colin Driver reported that he had met his London Midland Region colleagues and discussed the implications of their proposals. The option he favoured was to re-route the Nottingham–Glasgow service via Barnsley, Huddersfield and Manchester as it would avoid any reversal movements at Sheffield. They were also considering a fast service between Leeds and Lancaster to connect into the West Coast Main Line by re-arranging the Leeds–Morecambe service.

There were stirrings at grass roots level, too. Two Dales Rail enthusiasts, David Burton and Graham Nuttall, called a public meeting in Settle on 27th June. It resulted in the formation of the 'Friends of the Settle–Carlisle Line Association' or 'FOSCLA' as it became known, to campaign for the retention of the line. It would be "absolute vandalism" if Ribblehead Viaduct was abandoned because of the cost of repairs, said Mr Nuttall, and Mr Burton added it was "a superb monument to 19th century railway engineering."

Assuming the re-routing of the Nottingham–Glasgow service was due, as I had been led to believe, to the condition of the Ribblehead Viaduct, I felt there was a slim chance that the Settle–Carlisle line could be saved. Daunting though the task would be, it was by no means the only crumbling structure in the north of England. Others, like York Minster, had been saved from the ravages of the elements and time by a combination of public funds and private subscription. So why not Ribblehead? Then came a bombshell!

British Railways Board chairman Sir Peter Parker, in a letter to the Rt Hon Michael Jopling MP (Westmorland), confirmed the proposals to re-route the Nottingham–Glasgow service via Manchester. However, a service would also be provided between Leeds and Carlisle "to cater for the local traffic." Then the real surprise. Sir Peter said the condition of the Ribblehead Viaduct should be seen as a "separate issue" from the timetable changes, although "nonetheless a very serious one." He continued:

"Current estimates are that we will require to spend £6 million on the viaduct alone as part of the cost necessary to put the line into a condition which will ensure its long term future...It is hard to see how expenditure of this magnitude can be justified in this route at present – certainly no submission for authority to replace or repair the viaduct has been prepared, although the matter is still under consideration and you may rest assured we shall carefully study all the options."

This was the first of many letters Sir Peter was to write in similar vein. He told Bob Cryer (20th July) that proposals to re-route the Nottingham–Glasgow service were "based entirely on commercial grounds" and would "create valuable new links" between the East Midlands and Lake District "with very little time penalty" for long distance travel. And, in answer to John Watson (4th September), Sir Peter agreed that £6 million for the repair of the Ribblehead Viaduct was a great deal of money and continued:

"Our Civil Engineers hesitate to put a precise life span on Ribblehead, but intimate that even with interim expenditure of £150,000 a year, it is unlikely to be possible to keep it in operational condition for more than another three to five years."

On 2nd September, I met the London Midland Region's Brian Mander and Len Metcalf in York under the auspices of Colin Driver in the hope of discovering exactly what they had in mind for West Yorkshire users of the Settle–Carlisle line. Unfortunately, they had no draft timetables for the alternative services and whilst Mr Mander accepted my contention that Leeds generated more traffic on the Nottingham–Glasgow service than any other station, he was not prepared to reconsider the decision to re-route it via Manchester. He claimed they would save £2½ million a year in train costs alone – a figure I found hard to believe. So I asked what the savings would be if the Settle–Carlisle line was closed. He replied that he didn't know.

As the line remained inextricably linked with the Ribblehead Viaduct, I suggested the Nottingham–Glasgow service should continue to run via Settle so long as the viaduct was safe. To re-route it via Manchester would undermine the case for repairing or replacing it. This, in turn, could spell a quick death to the proposed DMU service between Leeds and Carlisle. Mander dismissed this suggestion.

I then asked whether it would be more sensible for British Rail to initiate closure proceedings for the Settle–Carlisle line at once, thus avoiding the charge of 'closure by stealth' – a phrase, whilst often attributed to me, was first used in a railway context by Dr Hugh Porteous of the Sheffield Passengers Association. Such a move would prevent the re-routing of the Nottingham–Glasgow service until such time as the TUCCs had considered the proposal and reported to the Secretary of State for Transport who would make the ultimate decision. Unfortunately, Mr Mander was not prepared to buy it.

Finally, I asked for an assurance in writing from the London Midland Region general manager, Mr J J O'Brien – the same Mr O'Brien I'd encountered at the Filey Holiday Camp station closure hearing – that there was no connection between the re-routing of the Nottingham–Glasgow service and the possible closure of the Settle–Carlisle line; a point I subsequently confirmed by letter. All in all it had not been a particularly useful meeting and the atmosphere – on both sides – had been pretty frosty.

September also saw the first letter in 'The Times' about the problems facing the Settle–Carlisle line. Mrs Beata Connell of Appleby recalled the line's centenary celebrations in 1976 and the more solemn event two years later when a memorial service was held at Appleby station to commemorate the death there of "that staunchest of railway enthusiasts, Eric Treacy, late Bishop of Wakefield and an inveterate lover of the Settle–Carlisle." Mrs Connell outlined the threat to the line as a result of British Rail's decision to re-route the Nottingham–Glasgow service. She concluded:

"And yet, Sir, it would surely be a national tragedy if this line were to die of inanition. The Settle–Carlisle is a main line, but it is more than that: it is a living tribute to the skill, courage and sheer vitality of your Victorian ancestors (I say "your" because I am Hungarian by birth and upbringing). If ever there was a justifiable public work the preservation of the Settle–Carlisle must surely be it."

On Saturday 10th October, FOSCLA held a public meeting in Settle. I attended as an observer. It was a bright sunny autumn day and there were well over 200 people on the 12.30 to Glasgow when it left Leeds. I wondered how many were off to the meeting. Sadly, very few as only four alighted at Settle. Nevertheless, of those, three of us made our way to the Victoria Hall where there were 38 present at the start of the proceedings. Not a bad turn-out.

Certainly Cabinet Ministers have spoken to far smaller gatherings.

FOSCLA chairman David Burton and secretary Graham Nuttall were on the platform, as was Graham's dog Ruswarp – an amicable collie named after a station on the Whitby line who later achieved considerable media fame! Whilst there was no doubt their inatiative and enthusiasm was supported by those present, doubts were expressed from the floor as to whether the chairman and secretary plus "the chap in Appleby" had sufficient experience and organisational clout to mount a campaign to save the line.

It wasn't long before the 'professionals' present, including John Watson, Mrs Clare Brooks – the prominent Liberal who had run him a close second in the 1979 General Election – and her sister Councillor Beth Graham began to influence the meeting. Councillor Graham particularly stressed the importance of getting all the local authorities involved, especially those in West Yorkshire. The outcome was the formation of a steering committee to augment FOSCLA and get it established on a more businesslike footing. Amongst those who stepped forward were Mrs Brooks, Councillor Graham and John Watson's popular agent, Gerry Thorpe.

I came away feeling that, at last, things were beginning to gell; although FOSCLA would find British Rail a formidable opponent. Whilst FOSCLA was to grow and subsequently outpace David Burton and Graham Nuttall, all those who use and love the Settle–Carlisle line owe them a debt of gratitude for their dedication and enthusiasm which got the campaign off the ground in the first place.

The following week Colin Driver arranged a meeting in Carlisle so Yorkshire TUCC members could travel on the Nottingham–Glasgow service and engage in discussion with the London Midland Region's Brian Mander and Len Metcalf regarding the 1982 timetable and the future of the line. Prior to the meeting we had set out our views on the situation in a memorandum which we had submitted to the London Midland Region.

We arrived at Carlisle to discover that Mander had pulled out at the last minute whilst Len Metcalf didn't have the details of the timetable we had come to discuss! He dismissed most of the points we raised in our memorandum and at the meeting, including our plea for some market research on the potential of the Settle–Carlisle line. "We don't have any money for it," he claimed. He did, however, give an assurance that the future of the line would not be prejudiced by the decision to re-route the Nottingham–Glasgow service.

The only amusing aspect of the largely abortive discussion was that Len Metcalf's train back to Euston was running 40 minutes late. So we 'railroaded' the hapless railwayman on to the 13.22 back to Leeds and forced him to experience at first hand the service he proposed to truncate. Fortunately the train was well loaded with 210 on board and, to his credit, he took it all in good fun.

The next piece of excitement was generated by none other than the Secretary of State for Transport, Mr David Howell. FOSCLA secretary Graham Nuttall had been in prodigious correspondence with MPs regarding the re-routing of the Nottingham–Glasgow trains. Amongst those he had written to was Industry Minister Sir Keith Joseph who had passed on the letter to Mr Howell. In his reply of 3rd November, the Transport Minister stated:

"British Rail's decision to re-route the Nottingham–Glasgow service arises from the deteriorating condition of the Ribblehead Viaduct."

Well! Well! This was a turn up for the book as it completely contradicted what Sir Peter Parker had been telling MPs. So who was kidding who?

It wasn't until 25th November, when John Watson initiated an excellent Adjournment Debate in the House of Commons on the 'Settle–Carlisle Railway (Closure)', that the question was finally answered. In addition to useful contributions from Bob Cryer, Robert Adley (Christchurch and Lymington), the well known rail buff, and Christopher Price (Lewisham West), a Yorkshireman brought up in the Settle area; Michael Jopling also spoke up for the line. This was unusual as Chief Whips don't usually participate in debates. It was left to the Under Secretary of State for Transport, Mr Kenneth Clarke, to admit that the letter which had been sent to Sir Keith Joseph had been written in error on advice which was mistaken. "We have since been assured categorically by British Rail that the decision to re-route the Nottingham–Glasgow service had nothing whatever to do with the condition of the Ribblehead Viaduct," he told the House. Yet doubts remained.

The following day the Yorkshire TUCC held its quarterly meeting. Members were not impressed at the London Midland Region's handling of the Settle–Carlisle issue and I was asked to write to the general manager, Mr J J O'Brien, and make the following points:

    1)   The planned Leeds–Carlisle service, which was now to be

loco-hauled should be merged with the Carlisle–Dumfries–Glasgow service, thus retaining a through service between Leeds and Glasgow.

2)   National Express had introduced a new express coach service between Leeds and Glasgow.

3)   Talk of 'attractive new travel opportunities' for those in Lancashire and the East Midlands was unlikely to placate West Yorkshire which provided over 40 per cent of the loadings on the existing Nottingham–Glasgow service.

I also asked for confirmation in writing that the re-routing of the Nottingham–Glasgow would not prejudice the future of the Settle–Carlisle and warned him the whole issue could develop into another classic 'closure by stealth' case.

Throughout the second half of 1981, the controversy surrounding the re-routing of the Nottingham–Glasgow service and the future of the Settle–Carlisle line surfaced in the media, due largely to the initiative of FOSCLA members. Moreover, journalists knew a good story and this looked likely to run for some time. Settle–Carlisle devotees were also putting pen to paper in letters to the Yorkshire TUCC objecting to the proposed changes. By the end of the year we had received 27 letters which represented 13 per cent of all the complaints received during 1981.

Even more importantly, people were writing to their MPs who, in turn, usually passed the correspondence on to British Railways Board chairman Sir Peter Parker. Following the embarrassment as to whether the re-routing was for commercial reasons or due to the condition of Ribblehead Viaduct, Sir Peter's stance was to endorse the commercial decision and present a gloomy view of the prospects for the line due to capital expenditure required to maintain it. Even so, he continually stressed there were no plans to close it.

For example, in his reply to The Rt Hon Denis Healey MP (Leeds East) who had taken up the case on behalf of Graham Nuttall of FOSCLA, Sir Peter wrote on 4th November:

"We can, of course, appreciate Mr Nuttall's concern, but I should say straight away that we have no desire, or at this time plans, to close the Settle–Carlisle line even though the numbers actually using the two intermediate stations at Appleby and Settle are comparatively few in number."

This position was repeated time and time again so that, even as late as June 1982 in a letter to Mrs Barbara Castle MEP, Sir Peter continued to maintain there were no plans to close the line:

"Once again, let me stress that our recognition of the changing role of the Settle–Carlisle line does not imply we are anxious to ensure its closure. At present we have no plans in that direction."

Nothing could be clearer than that, or so it would seem, for in the light of what was subsequently disclosed it was an extraordinary statement to say the least. However, back in 1981 and as the year drew to a close, perhaps the final word should go to Mr R W Croft of Bath who, in a letter to me, asked:

"What is British Rail's precise argument for re-routing the Nottingham–Glasgow services via Manchester? Like the argument advocated to close the main line between Matlock and Chinley, it was a case of that famous bit in 'The Mikado' of 'merely corroborative detail lending artistic verisimilitude to an otherwise bald and unconvincing narrative."

3

'FACTS' and FICTION

"The re-routing of the through Nottingham–Glasgow service would in no way prejudice the future of the Settle–Carlisle line."
                                    J J O'Brien, General Manager, London Midland Region, March 1982

Taking stock of the Settle–Carlisle situation at the beginning of 1982, my overriding feeling was one of utter frustration. When I had first learnt of the proposal to re-route the Nottingham–Glasgow service, my initial reaction had been one of indignation because it would mean that, for the first time in over 100 years, there would be no express through service between Leeds and Glasgow; nor, come to that, between Leeds and Nottingham. That it should occur at a time of economic recession only made it appear worse.

For over six months I'd been trying to extract from British Rail details of the alternative services it proposed for West Yorkshire users, yet I was little the wiser. Then there was an underlying feeling that British Rail were being less than frank about the whole issue, a point demonstrated by the 'mix-up' surrounding the reasons behind the re-routing of the Nottingham–Glasgow service. First we were told it was because of the condition of the Ribblehead Viaduct, then it was said the decision was solely for commercial reasons and had nothing to do with the viaduct. As if that wasn't enough, we then had an action replay of both explanations!

My suggestions to defer the re-routing pending market research and consultation with local authorities had been dismissed out of hand. So, too, was my proposal that the projected Leeds–Carlisle service be combined with that between Carlisle and Glasgow via Dumfries so as to retain a through Leeds–Glasgow service. In desperation I sought a meeting with London Midland Region general manager Jim O'Brien. I invited him to join me for lunch at Bentley's, the well-known West End fish restaurant. He didn't respond. Perhaps he didn't like fish!

Nor could I look to other TUCCs for much support. Of those directly involved, Scotland appeared disinterested whilst the East Midlands and the North Western positively welcomed the re-routing of the Nottingham–Glasgow service to provide a direct link between their areas at Yorkshire's expense. That Appleby would suffer seemed to be of no concern to the North West TUCC. Only Barry Flaxman of the East Anglian TUCC had any time for the Settle–Carlisle line. But then he was the only TUCC chairman who had a detailed knowledge of railways and how they operated.

Throughout I had kept our British Rail liaison officer, Colin Driver, *au-fait* with my abortive correspondence with his London Midland Region colleagues. Indeed, their apparent unwillingness to 'come clean' with regard to Settle–Carlisle was in stark contrast to the co-operation the Yorkshire TUCC and myself enjoyed with Eastern Region at that time. Colin was one of the few people within British Rail who seemed aware of the complex and sensitive nature of closure propsals, something he had deployed well when I had handled the controversial Huddersfield–Sheffield case.

He had also proved his worth in another example of London Midland Region ham-fistedness regarding the Dore Curve closure proposal in 1981. This was the Yorkshire end of a complex package which also included the line between Philips Park No. 1 Junction and Ashburys West Junction to the east of Manchester and involved a summer Saturdays only Blackpool–Leicester train. In this instance British Rail discontinued the service before they published their statutory notice of intent. This scant regard for the statute did not pass unnoticed by Dr Hugh Porteous of the Sheffield Passengers Association and the service was re-instated pending completion of the closure procedure.

In its 'Annual Report 1981' published in February 1982, the Yorkshire TUCC referred to "certain irregularities" in the London Midland Region's handling of the Dore Curve case. More importantly it stressed the concern regarding the proposed re-routing of the Nottingham–Glasgow service and continued:

"Although British Rail stated that its decision to re-route the service was made for commercial reasons and would not prejudice the future of the Settle–Carlisle line, the Committee remained sceptical, especially as the proposed alternative services for Yorkshire passengers (who represent over 50 per cent of the users of the present service) appeared ill-drafted and inadequate."

Not all was doom and gloom. On the credit side, the debate on the future of the Settle–Carlisle line was in full flow. MPs were involved and the user group – FOSCLA – was beginning to make its presence felt. Local authorities had begun to take an interest, too. For example, in Leeds Councillor Neil Taggart (Labour) had won all-party support for a motion calling on the council to make the strongest possible representations to British Rail about the re-routing and the threat to the Settle–Carlisle line.

At FOSCLA's first annual general meeting in Skipton on 16th January 1982, chairman David Burton reported that membership stood at 350, including several from the Continent and one in Australia. Members questioned the figure of £6 million quoted by British Rail as required for the repair of the Ribblehead Viaduct. In reply, secretary Graham Nuttall said he had been "reliably informed by railway sources" that £4 million was nearer the mark.

The following month British Rail issued a paper confirming a "major change" in the pattern of InterCity services from the East Midlands (Nottingham/Sheffield) and Leeds to Glasgow. There were no surprises. The existing Nottingham–Glasgow service of three trains in each direction would run via Manchester and Preston and be combined with the Manchester–Glasgow service from 17th May 1982. During the winter the service would be cut to two trains each way, with the third just running between Nottingham and Preston.

The paper explained how withdrawal of the overnight services between Nottingham and Glasgow in 1977 had led to such an improvement in the financial results as to allow the daytime service to be uplifted to three trains each way. However, various economic factors, starting with the steel strike, had led to a continuing decline in the passenger business and the service had gone into deficit. This had accelerated with the general economic recession.

It continued:

"The total loaded passenger train mileage sponsored by the London Midland Region has been progressively reduced to reflect the fall in passenger journeys as well as to put the InterCity business on course for the targets set by the Department of Transport as those worthy for further investment both for modern resources and further electrification. To have applied similar percentage reductions individually to the Nottingham–Glasgow service and to the Manchester–Glasgow service commensurate to the decline in their profitability would have left an unacceptable service on both routes. It became clear that by re-routing the East Midland to

Glasgow service via Manchester the combined demand of the two areas was sufficient to support a continuing through service albeit by one route instead of two."

The paper added that the new service would create through journey opportunities from the Nottingham and Sheffield areas to Central and North Lancashire and the Lake District in "comfortable Mainline InterCity Coaching Stock and will prove an attractive bonus to the route's potential. Alternative services with one change will exist for Nottingham–Leeds and Leeds–Carlisle–Glasgow intermediate business as a result of the diversion away from that route."

I cannot say I was particularly impressed by all this gobbledegook, parts of which read more like a political manifesto. Perhaps it was phrased to impress MPs rather than existing users of the Nottingham–Glasgow service. It made no direct reference at all to the Settle–Carlisle line. Overall, it cut little ice with the Yorkshire TUCC because Leeds and West Yorkshire fared so badly.

So far as Leeds was concerned, it meant the withdrawal of through trains to Glasgow and Nottingham plus the reduction by one third of trains on direct route to Carlisle via Settle. Extended journey times plus the hassle of having to change en-route, at Carlisle or Lancaster for Glasgow, or at Sheffield or Derby for Nottingham, added to the inconvenience.

Nor would Sheffield and South Yorkshire fare much better. Apart from June, July and August, the through service between Sheffield and Glasgow was cut by one third and discontinued altogether on Sundays. Journey times, far from being improved, were slightly extended – the current best Sheffield–Glasgow time of 5 hours 8 minutes increasing to 5 hours 16 minutes. As for Rotherham, it lost out altogether. The only plus point was the new through service between Sheffield, North West Lancashire and the Lake District. But if this was such a potentially rich market it could have been exploited as a separate service. Above all, British Rail had done nothing to dispel fears regarding the long term future of the Settle–Carlisle line.

One man who had no doubt was Mr I Bentley, a guard based at Leeds. In a letter published by British Rail's own 'house' newspaper 'Railnews' in March 1982, he claimed the re-routing "was nothing more than a devious way to eventually close the whole Settle–Carlisle line." He went on:

"The proposed replacement service of two trains a day each way between Leeds and Carlisle is nothing more than a pathetic attempt to pacify the travelling public. I am aware that Ribblehead Viaduct is in need of repair and urge the British Railways Board to press the Government for funds to pay for this. They must be told in no uncertain terms of the importance of keeping open this valuable link. Meanwhile, management should be improving services over this line and attracting more revenue – not running it down. It seems the BRB aim to close this line by stealth. I hope I am wrong."

I hoped he was wrong, too; but rather doubted it. In a response printed immediately below his letter, a 'passenger department spokesman' stated:

"The real 'closure by stealth' is the loss of services and quality arising from inadequate funds. British Rail has no wish to see parts of the system close, but Ribblehead Viaduct is vulnerable as it needs major expenditure and must compete with other priorities for the limited funds available."

Funny how British Rail kept using Ribblehead to support its case in view of the categorical assurance that the condition of the viaduct had nothing to do with the re-routing which was said to be solely for commercial reasons. Nevertheless, top marks to the editor of 'Railnews' for publishing Guard Bentley's letter.

Throughout the spring of 1982 I seemed to be involved in a continuous round of meetings and consultations regarding the Settle–Carlisle line. However, the first and perhaps most significant was one I did not attend. It was convened by British Rail for the benefit of MPs whose constituencies were on the line – John Watson (Skipton), Michael Jopling (Westmorland), William Whitelaw (Penrith and Border) and Ron Lewis (Carlisle) – and was held in London on 10th March.

Later John Watson told me that Tom Brazier, the divisional manager at Preston who was responsible for the line, provided some pretty horrendous figures and said quite definitely, though confidentially, that they were planning to close it. The case against the line appeared so strong that the problems of Ribblehead were almost an irrelevance.

At the end of March the London Midland Region general manager, Jim O'Brien, eventually found his pen. Responding to a succession of my letters, he replied on 30th March:

"Let me assure you again that, despite the rumours, no decision has been made to propose the withdrawal of passenger services cession of my letters, he replied on 30th March:

"Let me assure you again that, despite the rumours, no decision has been made to propose the withdrawal of passenger services from the Settle–Carlisle line. I endorse the statement made by my representative at the Yorkshire TUCC committee meeting on 19th October 1981 that the re-routing of the through Nottingham–Glasgow service would in no way prejudice the future of the Settle–Carlisle line. If closure were to be proposed – and no decision has been reached on this – the issue for the TUCCs would be that of hardship. This is not affected by the diversion of the through services which may cause inconvenience but not hardship."

Welcoming his assurance, I replied pointing out that his assessment of inconvenience and hardship was subjective, just as my own was. I added that the Yorkshire TUCC remained convinced that the re-routing of the Nottingham–Glasgow service would adversely affect the vast majority of its users.

On 5th April I went to Preston for an informal meeting with divisional manager Tom Brazier. He handed me an eight page document 'Settle–Carlisle Line: The Facts' which he had given to the MPs the previous month. Like so many British Rail papers, it was somewhat selective when it came to the facts. For example, a financial evaluation included £45,000 for passenger revenue generated by Appleby and a further £72,000 from charters, but excluded the £48,000 I understood to be applicable to Settle. I couldn't believe they really thought that all Settle users would transfer their patronage to Giggleswick, a mile away on the Morecambe line. Then there was no reference at all to revenue generated by through travellers between Leeds and Carlisle who represented the vast majority of users. Using selective figures it was not difficult to come up with an annual expenditure of £1,965,000 against revenue of £426,000 (of which £309,000 was from freight) – a loss of £1,539,000. A case of creative accounting?

Nevertheless, it was a useful meeting. Without saying it in so many words, both Brazier and his passenger manager David Harrison left me in little doubt that they planned to close the Settle–Carlisle line and nothing, short of a miracle, could save it. The only glimmer of hope was the role of the line as a diversionary route for the West Coast Main Line between Preston and Carlisle. Brazier said they were still awaiting completion of an internal feasibility study on alternative diversionary routes. I left feeling very depressed about the whole issue. However, they had brought a

burn – a popular dining rendezvous just within the Lancashire border – proved less fruitful. For a start British Rail fielded a fresh
team following a merger of the Manchester and Preston divisions.
Tom Brazier had left for pastures new at the British Railways Board
where he was said to be 'on special assignment', invariably a prelude to retirement. In his place was Trevor Anderson, the divisional
manager in Manchester whose empire had been extended to include Preston and encompassed the Settle–Carlisle line. He was
accompanied by his public relations man. Also present were David
Burton and Graham Nuttall of FOSCLA and Robert Foster, a
Skipton solicitor well known in railway circles as a timetable expert
who advised John Watson on railway matters.

I had been under the impression there was to be a second showing
of the audio–visual presentation provided two months earlier to
the group of MPs. This was not so. Instead we were all given a
copy of the 'Facts' document. I had already digested this and came
armed with a long list of questions. However, Anderson was most
reluctant to respond or discuss anything in any depth other than
to repeat the O'Brien stance that no decision had been reached on
the future of the Settle–Carlisle line. This was not what Tom
Brazier had told John Watson and the other MPs nor what he had
implied to me the previous month.

Throughout the meal Anderson continued to be evasive and the
evening only came to life when David Burton said he understood
British Rail would be putting in for closure of the line to become
effective from 3rd January 1983. This must have touched a raw
nerve as Anderson became quite upset. He kept pressing us on
our interests in the line and why we were there. I retorted that the
reasons should be obvious. Quite apart from the fact that British
Rail had extended the invitation, Messrs Burton and Nuttall wished
to save ' the most spectacular main line in England' – "and jolly
good luck to them" – whilst my interest was purely statutory. There
was no answer to that.

All that remained for me to do was to forward Anderson my
questions in written form, which I did the following day along with
my 'bread and butter' letter for what I had felt was a largely abortive
evening.

A get-together the following week proved more fruitful, or so I
thought at the time. At the invitation of Jim O'Brien, I joined
fellow TUCC chairmen Barry Flaxman (East Anglia) and Jim Ward
(East Midlands) on what was programmed as a 'General Manager's

Saloon Trip with TUCC Chairmen'. This was initiated by Barry Flaxman so we could discuss with O'Brien and his colleagues outstanding issues regarding the 1982–83 timetable, with particular regard to the Midland Main Line and the re-routing of the Nottingham–Glasgow service.

British Rail had planned the programme with meticulous care. I shudder to think how much it all cost. The one coach – general manager's saloon – train left St Pancras with Jim O'Brien, his chief passenger manager Brian Mander and Barry Flaxman. The chief operating manager for the London Midland Region, John Gregory and Jim Ward joined at Derby whilst Colin Driver, representing Eastern Region, and myself got on at Sheffield, just in time for an excellent lunch which was taken on the saloon 'stabled' in a siding.

The train then continued via Leeds and Settle to Carlisle. Here we were whisked off in a fleet of cars to the String of Horses, the residential inn at Heads Nook noted for its plush bathrooms, where we stayed overnight. The following morning it was back to Carlisle where the general manager's saloon was attached to the rear of a re-routed Glasgow–Nottingham train. This was undoubtedly the life although it was by no means all high living as there was much hard discussion round the saloon's conference table.

Our host Jim O'Brien was generally considered to be one of British Rail's high flyers. A management trainee from the 1960 intake, he was appointed divisional manager at Doncaster in 1975 and deputy general manager of the Western Region in 1977 prior to taking over as supremo of the London Midland Region. A tall, slim, softly spoken man whose disarming manner tended to conceal a ruthless approach to his work. He was married to a daughter of Sir Henry Johnson, chairman of the British Railways Board between 1968 and 1971.

On the future of the Settle–Carlisle line, O'Brien stated that no decision had been made. It no longer ranked as an InterCity line, having been transferred to 'Other Provincial Services' with the re–routing of the Nottingham–Glasgow service. Freight traffic was declining and the overnight parcels trains could be re-routed. The line's importance for diversions remained but even here there were other possibilities. Whilst he accepted there was scope for further economies, like the reduction of shifts from the current three (24 hours) to one, the savings would be insignificant when set against the overall cost of maintaining the line which, quite apart from the question of the Ribblehead Viaduct, was uneconomical.

Jim O'Brien said he did not want to close the line. He felt it had two assets – its role as part of the country's national heritage and its unrivalled scenic beauty. These were possible angles to exploit in seeking funds to retain the line. He added that the track bed was good but signalling presented problems.

On the question of the Ribblehead Viaduct, O'Brien accepted that singling might help; although it would be expensive and he was not keen on the idea. He confided that he had paid £5,000 for an independent survey but declined to disclose its contents, other than to say he was prepared to sell them to Barry Flaxman for £2,500. Needless to say there was no taker!

I argued that if the line were to be retained, it required a firm commitment to its future from British Rail. There was enormous scope for developing tourist and recreational traffic. Rail enthusiasts should be encouraged to become practically involved in the upkeep of the line. However, this would be fruitless if British Rail were not fully committed to the Settle–Carlisle line. One could not expect people to put their cash up-front to save it if British Rail planned to syphon off donations to support developments of the Advanced Passenger Train (APT) – the current 'in' project at that time.

When I alighted from the general manager's saloon at Sheffield I felt faintly encouraged. Whilst Jim O'Brien had given little away, he had expressed more enthusiasm for the Settle–Carlisle line than his subordinates Trevor Anderson and Tom Brazier. Moreover, O'Brien was the first senior British Rail executive I'd spoken to who had recognised the positive assets of the line, not least the heritage and tourist potential. Even so, I was not sure what to make of it all. The spurious figures in 'The Facts' document – something O'Brien didn't dwell on other than to emphasise the fixed costs required to keep the line open – suggested British Rail might wish to opt out of any commercial debate as they considered it to be cut and dried. Then, who would advocate the case for the line in its widest context? Certainly not British Rail as they did not consider themselves to be in the conservation business.

Summarising my thoughts in a letter to John Watson on 19th May, I wrote:

"Being a sceptical type of bloke, I am bound to wonder if British Rail's ploy of understating the commercial value of the Settle–Carlisle line and its importance as a link between Yorkshire and Scotland isn't part of a deliberate policy to hasten its demise."

This seemed to be John's view, too. The following day a report in the 'Yorkshire Post' referring to 'The Facts' document quoted him as saying:

"I believe British Rail wants to close the line and this is a softening-up process, a bit like shadow boxing, so that when the closure proposal is announced it will come almost as a relief."

Notwithstanding the selective nature of the document, it served a useful purpose if only to concentrate the minds of those campaigning to save the line. I found it useful, too; although my advocacy for its retention had to be more tacit and behind the scenes. This was because the view at the time was the TUCCs should be strictly impartial when considering contentious issues in view of their statutory responsibilities, especially when it came to potential closure proposals.

Nevertheless, 'The Facts' and the presentation of them added fuel to my overall scepticism regarding British Rail's handling of the issue. Using their document as a frame, I contrived to fill in some of the gaps in order to come up with a paper which showed the Settle–Carlisle line in a rather better and more realistic light. I forwarded a copy to John Watson who felt my historical perspective helped to discredit British Rail's intention and agreed that the financial evaluation offered by railway management was weak and needed to be challenged as strongly as possible.

The next move came from John himself. On return from a visit to the United States at the beginning of July, he asked Graham Nuttall of FOSCLA and myself to meet him so we might exchange notes and discuss tactics. At my suggestion he extended the invitation to include Roger Smith, whose experience of fighting railway closure would be useful. The meeting took place on a Friday evening at John's Skipton home and was, in effect, a mini 'council of war'. After reviewing every aspect of the situation we were under no illusions that we were up against a formidable opponent in British Rail and that the odds were heavily stacked against us.

It was agreed that John would continue to exert pressure at Parliamentary and Governmental level, stressing doubts regarding the validity of much of the material in 'The Facts' document and emphasising the political sensitivity of the Settle–Carlisle line. We would all highlight the heritage angle of the line together with its outstanding scenic attractions and tourist potential.

4

THE 15.37 AND ALL THAT!

'New and Improved Services between West Yorkshire and Glasgow'
Heading of British Rail News Release dated 13th May 1982

Whilst the planning and strategy of the campaign to save the Settle–Carlisle line was gathering momentum behind closed doors, what was happening on the line itself? What was the impact of the re-routing of the Nottingham–Glasgow service away from the line? How had it affected train loadings (the number of passengers) on the 'new' service between Leeds and Carlisle, designated by British Rail as being primarily for the 'local traffic' – that is to say to and from Settle and Appleby? And what of the service advocated for InterCity travel between Leeds and Glasgow via Lancaster?

It should be remembered that, as British Rail's excellent promotional leaflet so admirably put it:

"The Settle and Carlisle is no obscure branch line meandering through gentle countryside but a main-line railway built to take its trains over the hills at speed."

Since it opened in 1876, the passenger service had comprised of express trains between London, the East Midlands, Yorkshire, Carlisle, Glasgow and Edinburgh; and local services between Hellifield and Carlisle. In addition there was a wide range of freight traffic.

Throughout most of its history, express services on the line comprised two overnight sleeping car and four daytime trains in each direction. The sleepers ran to and from London St Pancras, one serving Edinburgh and the other Glasgow; as did the two named daytime services – 'The Thames–Forth Express' (later renamed 'The Waverley') and 'The Thames–Clyde Express'. There were lunchtime departures from St Pancras to Glasgow St Enoch and vice versa, plus a morning Leeds–Glasgow train and its afternoon return.

Local services were more fragmented. There were three trains in each direction between Hellifield and Carlisle. These were augmented by morning and afternoon trains in each direction between Hellifield and Garsdale, and between Appleby and Carlisle. By the early 1960s some of the local trains had been combined. Thus there was an afternoon working in both directions between Bradford and Carlisle which stopped at all stations – including Manningham and Frizinghall. The journey took some 3 hours 48 minutes.

The first station to close on the Settle–Carlisle line was Scotby, 2.3/4 miles from Carlisle, in 1942. Crosby Garrett, Ormside and Cotehill closed in 1952 and Cumwhinton in 1956. In 1963 British Rail proposed to discontinue the local services and close all the remaining stations on the line, including Settle and Appleby, although the line would continue to be used by express trains. However, following receipt of reports from the Yorkshire and North Western TUCCs, the Minister of Transport vetoed the proposal on the grounds of the hardship that would be caused to users. A further proposal in 1968 proved more successful and 12 of the stations involved – Horton-in-Ribblesdale, Ribblehead, Dent, Garsdale, Kirkby Stephen, Long Marton, Newbiggen, Culgaith, Langwathby, Little Salkeld, Lazonby & Kirkoswald, and Armathwaite – were closed in 1970. Neither of the proposals appeared to have generated much interest at the time, probably because the line itself was to remain open.

British Rail's report 'Network for Development' (1965) had included the Hellifield–Horton and the Kirkby Stephen (North Eastern)–Warcop–Appleby–Carlisle sections as freight lines. Whilst this report was coy on the subject of passenger line closures, it was understood that British Rail saw no future for the Settle–Carlisle line as a through route nor, indeed, for any passenger services to the north and west of Skipton. Despite these conclusions and the subsequent electrification of the West Coast Main Line (WCML) through to Glasgow, the Settle–Carlisle line remained part of the InterCity network. Amongst the reasons expanded for this by British Rail were that the Transport Act 1972 and Ministerial statements had indicated that Government policy did not favour rail closures, whilst the line had a diversionary role for WCML services.

Although services between London and Edinburgh/Glasgow via the Settle–Carlisle line were discontinued during the late 1970s, they had been replaced by three InterCity trains in each direction on weekdays between Nottingham and Glasgow via Sheffield,

Leeds, Settle and Appleby. There was also a Sunday service of one train in each direction. In addition the Dales Rail service ran on selected weekends during the summer, largely for the benefit of hikers and ramblers. This, then, was the scenario when the Nottingham–Glasgow service was re-routed away from the line in May 1982 and replaced by a 'local' service between Leeds and Carlisle plus a hotch-potch of connections at Lancaster.

When it became apparent that the future of the Settle–Carlisle line was likely to become a live issue, I made a point of doing a little research of my own; first on the Nottingham–Glasgow service, travelling on the trains and, more importantly, checking the loadings, and later on the replacement services. Contrary to some observations made by British Rail, the Nottingham–Glasgow service was relatively well patronised; albeit that there were, as one would expect, considerable seasonal variations with the heaviest loadings in the summer.

Down departures to the north from Leeds were well spread at 09.20 (07.15 ex-Nottingham), 12.30 (10.20 ex-Nottingham) and 18.07 (16.00 ex-Nottingham); as were the up departures from Carlisle at 09.25 (06.55 ex-Glasgow), 13.22 (11.50 ex-Glasgow) and 18.20 (15.50 ex-Glasgow). The first and last departures ran by the traditional Glasgow & South Western route via Dumfries and Kilmarnock whilst the 'midday' trains, which were the best supported, used the quicker direct route via Carstairs.

My spot checks between May 1981 and May 1982 indicated that average loadings on the 09.20 from Leeds were:

	Join	*Alight*
Leeds	125*	–
Keighley	16	4
Skipton	10	7
Settle	25	5
Appleby	8	31
Carlisle	–	137†
Total	**184**	**184**

*   Includes passengers from the south through Leeds.
†   Includes passengers travelling through to Scotland.

The particularly good figures for Settle and Appleby were indicative of the seasonal traffic between the two stations plus support by British Rail's 'Merrymaker' party outings.

The 12.30 from Leeds, the busiest train on the Settle–Carlisle line, left with an average of 245 passengers and the 18.07 with about 90, of who some 50 (more on Fridays) travelled north beyond Skipton. Loadings from Carlisle worked out at about 80 on the 09.25, 240 on the 13.22 and 120 on the 18.20. Whilst these were by no means Britain's best loaded InterCity trains, there were many others plying the network carrying far fewer passengers.

Following the re-routing of the Nottingham–Glasgow service away from the Settle–Carlisle line on 17th May 1982, the picture changed. The new down 'locals' departed from Leeds at 08.57 and 16.01 (later re-timed to 16.05). My first journey on the 08.57 was made on the Wednesday of its first week. It comprised a Class 31 locomotive hauling four of the most ancient Mark 1 coaches imaginable. The detailed loadings were:

	Join	*Alight*
Leeds	35	–
Keighley	4	9
Skipton	10	2
Settle	9	1
Appleby	3	1
Carlisle	–	48
Total	**61**	**61**

Not a particularly happy omen for the future. However, loadings did improve and throughout the rest of 1982 the average number of passengers joining the 08.57 at Leeds on weekdays was 52; not too bad in the circumstances.

The volume of loadings on the 16.01 was more difficult to define. Whilst the train was often quite full when it left Leeds, it provided an all stations commuter service to Skipton as well as a through service to Carlisle. Thus when I used it one Wednesday in September, it departed from Leeds with 95 passengers and picked up many more at Keighley only to discard many of them at Skipton. At Settle 25 alighted. Nevertheless, there were 52 of us on the train as it clattered across the Ribblehead Viaduct.

I never had the opportunity to use the 10.00 up service from

Carlisle (although I am reliably informed that on its second day it left Carlisle with only 13 passengers!), the least well supported of the four Settle–Carlisle line trains. However, I did get to know the 15.37 from Carlisle particularly well. This also stopped at all stations between Skipton and Leeds, a frustrating experience when one was in a hurry to get home. Throughout the duration of the May 1982 timetable, I made 11 weekday journeys on this train. The average loadings were:

	Join	Alight
Carlisle	94	–
Appleby	7	3
Settle	7	13
Skipton	5	18
Keighley	5	6
Crossflatts	0	0
Bingley	1	2
Shipley	2	5
Leeds	–	74
Total	**121**	**121**

Timekeeping was excellent – as it should have been given the enormous amount of slack in a timetable which allowed 31 minutes between Settle and Skipton (down trains only required 18 minutes) plus a 6 minute stop at Skipton. As a consequence trains were stopping at Skipton for 15 or more minutes. The up journey also called for 15 minutes between Skipton and Keighley whereas the down journey only took 12 minutes. It was as if the timetable had been designed to make the journey as slow and unattractive as possible as a part of British Rail's 'closure by stealth' policy.

So much for the new 'local' service. But how were the public responding to the new InterCity connection via Lancaster which British Rail had the temerity (or cheek!) to describe as a "new and improved service between West Yorkshire and Glasgow"? Not very well if my own experiences were anything to go by.

I first sampled it on a Thursday early in June. On paper it looked most attractive, the 12.00 Leeds–Morecambe fast with stops at Keighley, Skipton, Carnforth and Lancaster. Here the connection was made into the 'Royal Scot' (ex 10.45 from Euston). There were 85 of us on the distinctly shabby 4 car 'Trans-Pennine' Class 124 DMU as it left Leeds three minutes late, the delay being largely due to the protestations from a passenger (not me!) who could not believe his ears on being told it was the Glasgow train. The journey proved uneventful until we came to Hest Bank Junction between Carnforth and Lancaster. Then the fun began!

The train took a 'wrong turning' having being signalled into Morecambe by mistake! As there was only a six minute connection at Lancaster, this was no laughing matter. There was consternation amongst those who realised something was wrong. "What time will we get to Carlisle?" "Will I miss my connection to Dumfries?" "They should never have taken off the Nottingham–Glasgow trains." And, of course, "I'm going to write to Sir Peter Parker about this!"

To his credit, the guard took it all in good grace and, at my suggestion, arranged for the signalman at Bare Lane box to 'phone Lancaster to ask them to hold the connection'. So, after a brief yet totally unexpected sojourn in Morecambe, it was back the way we came to Bare Lane and round the loop to Lancaster. We arrived at 14.03 just as a northbound train was pulling into the station. Then it was a case of up and over the footbridge at the double, not much fun for a party of Saga passengers I had befriended.

The situation was not made easier by the fact that the Lancaster station staff seemed unaware of our plight. Then the confusion was all the greater as not all northbound trains went to Glasgow. It transpired that this particular train was not the late running 'Royal Scot' which formed the 14.48 from Lancaster but an earlier late running train, the 13.34 departure to Stranraer which was good enough for me and my Saga friends and actually departed at 14.08. Such experiences are particularly good for TUCC chairmen as they emphasise in a way no letter could just why the vast majority of people prefer to travel on through trains rather than having to change en-route. It was a pity Sir Peter Parker and some of his minions had not been present, too. For had they been there they would have got the message from their customers loud and clear.

Indeed, the problem of late running on the WCML was one of the major reasons why the Lancaster connection proved so unattractive. Of my first four journeys by this route, only one arrived at Carlisle within 5 minutes of its advertised time. The other three were 10, 18 and 42 minutes late. Nor was it much fun getting on the train at Lancaster only to find it so crowded that there were no seats – a frequent occurrence during the summer of 1982.

In a report to the Yorkshire TUCC, I summarised my conclusions of the new services thus:

1) The direct route via Settle was quicker (with scope for improvement) and more reliable.

2) Northbound passengers only had a cross platform change at Carlisle whereas they had to contend with the footbridge at Lancaster.

3) There was a considerable degree of public resentment at the withdrawal of through trains between West Yorkshire and Glasgow.

4) Although the Lancaster route with its departures from Leeds timed at 09.33, 12.00 and 17.12 was designed to attract former users of the Nottingham–Glasgow service, the public had yet to be convinced of its credibility.

Members unanimously endorsed my views. They also expressed concern at British Rail's failure to market the Settle–Carlisle line which, although acknowledged as the finest scenic route in England, was not promoted in Leeds and West Yorkshire where the greatest market potential existed. I had already taken up this issue, both with British Rail and the English Tourist Board as I felt the latter organisation might be able to help.

The Yorkshire TUCC also supported proposals it had received from T V Frankland, a rail user and enthusiast from Derby. He had submitted a revised timetable for the Settle–Carlisle line on the basis that it would be the main feeder into the WCML, leaving the Leeds–Morecambe line to concentrate on its traditional local traffic.

Mr Frankland outlined his proposals – incorporating departures from Leeds at 08.57, 11.57, 14.37 and 18.05, and from Carlisle at 08.45, 11.45, 15.10 and 18.40 – which would operate with the two sets of stock allocated to the current service of two trains in each direction. He stressed the following advantages:

1) More productive use of rolling stock – it doubled the daily mileage of the two sets of stock.

2) Faster overall journey times between Leeds and Glasgow than the present service.

3) Improved comfort and facilities for passengers.

4) A service of four trains each way giving a better spread of

service than the former Nottingham–Glasgow service.

5) A wider choice of connections at Carlisle.

6) Much improved access to Settle and Appleby.

7) Encouraged travel on the Settle–Carlisle line and increased revenue for the route.

Whilst maintaining its view that there should be a through service between Leeds and Glasgow, the Yorkshire TUCC endorsed the Frankland proposals as being vastly preferable to the existing service. I had already sent a copy to the London Midland Region. Therefore, I was encouraged when I received a reply from Brian Mander accepting that Mr Frankland's suggestions were "worthy of consideration" and saying that they would be fully evaluated. Did this represent a change of heart on the part of British Rail?

Sadly the answer was no. The 'evaluated' response proved to be almost entirely negative. Taking but one simple example, Mander stated with characteristic clarity:

"The minimum turnround time at both Carlisle and Leeds is 30 minutes. This is infringed on one occasion (by only 5 minutes) in the Frankland proposals but by implication on more occasions."

Then he dismissed Frankland's improved connectional advantages with a curt:

"From 1983, however, Mr Frankland's plan would be less advantageous than the scheme we have tabled, because the revised Anglo-Scottish pattern destroys one of his Glasgow services in each direction."

As Frankland himself put it, the 30 minute turn-round was fairly tight but no more so than in many areas of British Rail operations. As for references to the proposed 1983 services, these were nonsensical as his timetable was framed around the present service. "It is pointless to condemn my proposals on the basis of a timetable which I have not seen," he retorted, adding his disappointment at the standard of British Rail's response which seemed to be a collection of comments in no particular order, some of which were conflicting. "I found some of the paragraphs very difficult to understand at all!," he concluded.

I agreed. I suppose that, at the end of the day, it was just another case of 'if the will was there' and when it came to the Settle–Carlisle line, British Rail simply didn't want to know.

Nor did we appear to fare any better with the English Tourist Board. Here, too, the initial response from chairman Michael Montague had been encouraging. He was seeking information from the Yorkshire and Humberside Tourist Board as to how closure of the Settle–Carlisle line would have an economic effect and the extent of adverse consequences to tourism so that he could consider an appropriate reaction.

However, when that reaction was subsequently received, I considered it singularly inappropriate. Mr Montague replied:

"It is suggested to me that if the line were to close, it would be possible to provide an alternative service via Morecambe. Should that be the case, there could be two losses. Firstly, there might be no rail service from Appleby to Leeds, though a bus service would be likely. In the event of a bus service, this might satisfy the requirements of day-trippers and local residents. Secondly, there would be the loss of opportunity to see the magnificent countryside on the Settle–Carlisle route of the train.

The argument which we would have to put to British Rail would be that the level of use of this service for sight-seeing only, rather than sight-seeing plus transport, is high. I am doubtful as to the extent to which we might be able to support such a case.

British Rail, which comes in for a lot of disparaging comment generally, always seems to me to be more strongly committed to the future of tourism than is generally appreciated. They engage in special joint promotions, take a great interest in some services, and study always future opportunities as they relate to tourism. All this, however, has to be done cognisant with the responsibilities placed upon them by Government.

Unless there is advocacy of a commercial nature, I do not identify a line of argument which could be pursued with the expectation that it might gain a positive response."

'Thank you for nothing', was my immediate response. Indeed, I don't think Sir Peter Parker could have come up with a better answer.

5

STAY OF EXECUTION

*"There is no change in the situation regarding the Settle–Carlisle line
– we are still collating information."*

J J O'Brien, General Manager, London Midland Region, 25th November 1982.

By the autumn of 1982, I had been chairman of the Yorkshire TUCC for three years. Notwithstanding the heavy work load, including the complex Humber Ferry and Huddersfield–Sheffield closure proposals plus a growing number of public complaints regarding rail services, it had been a period of relative stability so far as the working of the committee was concerned. Now, quite apart from Settle–Carlisle, there were other storm clouds on the horizon.

The most immediate was that our secretary, Norman Archer, had decided to take early retirement after over forty years service with the railway. He had joined the LNER in 1941 and, following service with the railway unit of the Royal Engineers, had been based at Malton. After his secondment to the Yorkshire TUCC in 1963, he had been involved in almost fifty 'Beeching' closure proposals. Whilst neither a campaigning consumerist nor a rail enthusiast – he once told his local newspaper that he had no favourite line, but if he had it would be "the last mile home!" – his conscientious, methodical approach coupled with an eye for detail had been the bedrock on which the committee rested.

The impact of Norman's retirement was compounded by the fact that ill-health had forced the committee's excellent typist Rene Philippo, who had been a tower of strength, into retirement. This double blow was not helped by British Rail's terms of secondment which meant that, in order to accommodate these early retirements, we could only recruit from staff who were redundant within British Rail. This was not, I felt, the right way to get the best person for the job, let alone attract a highflyer.

In the event we were faced with a short list of one. Given these circumstances, it was no surprise that our new secretary proved a fish out of water. It was not the fault of the individual, who found himself in the classic square pin in a round hole situation, but of the system itself and said little for consumer protection. The public deserve something better. The net result was that I found myself taking over more and more of the committee's work. For example, after preparing for and chairing meetings, I then had to write the minutes. Mind you, there were some advantages in this – at least I could ensure that all my best lines were included!

This was just the start of my problems. There had been changes within British Rail, too. Earlier in the year we had lost our splendid liaison officer as Colin Driver had moved up to become deputy general manager of the Eastern Region. His replacement Fergus Gibson, an amiable, soft spoken Scot came from the chief passenger manager's post in Glasgow. No sooner had he begun to get the hang of things in York than he was up and away back to Scotland to resume his old role.

Our next liaison officer was Ivor Warburton, who took over as Eastern Region chief passenger manager after a spell as overseas tourist manager at the British Railways Board. I quickly got the impression that he intended to 'sort us out' and shunt the Yorkshire TUCC into a siding out of harm's way. Neither members nor I were prepared to go along with this so it looked as if we were in for a bumpy ride. Whereas Colin Driver had always extended a genial bonhomie, the Warburton stance was completely unpredictable. It reminded me of the billing given to the celebrated 1950s Hollywood film star Jane Russell – 'mean, moody and magnificent'!

Meetings with British Rail which in the past had been generally affable became decidedly testy on both sides. I cannot say I enjoyed them. Indeed, on one occasion I actually lost my temper – a rare event! Nevertheless, not everyone was unhappy. One member told me that he looked forward to the battle of words between Warburton and myself. He said it added to the interest of the meetings. I wouldn't have put it that way myself. Another member said he had it in mind to throw Ivor out of the window! He was joking, of course. Nevertheless, it gives some idea of the air of confrontation at the time.

Recalling these incidents with the benefit of hindsight, I like to believe that amidst all this there developed a mutual respect between Ivor and myself. That he had a brilliant brain there was no doubt. He had graduated from Cambridge with an MA in mathematics and oriental studies. One certainly had to do one's homework before engaging him in argument. Whilst I was no match against his intellect, I had – or so I am told – a certain stubbornness which enabled me to stand my corner. When our paths were to cross in later years there were no recriminations. Indeed, we found that we agreed on a great many railway issues.

In addition the TUCCs faced something of an onslaught from the Government on two separate fronts. First, as part of a probe into 'quangos', the Department of Trade had published a consultation document 'Consumer Interests and the Nationalised Industries' which concluded there should be smaller yet more effective consumer bodies. One of the ideas it fostered was that a single TUCC should cover the whole of British Rail's Eastern Region – a daunting task if ever there was one.

The second issue which concerned us was the Government's decision to set up the 'Review of Railway Finances'. One didn't need a crystal ball to anticipate its conclusions. These were likely to include recommendations for a smaller rail network coupled with substantial reductions in the level of the Public Service Obligation (PSO) subsidy. Such moves could only lead to further cutbacks in the standards of service for passengers. Add to this the fact that the committee was beginning to feel the impact of some of the more eccentric innovations coming from sector management, and you will appreciate that the latter half of 1982 was a far from easy time for the Yorkshire TUCC and myself.

Following a bit of a lull during the summer, things had started to move again on the Settle–Carlisle front. On 10th September there was the 'Rural Transport in the Yorkshire Dales' seminar at Bolton Abbey. It was staged by the Yorkshire Dales Society, an independent voluntary organisation designated amongst other things to "work with existing statutory and voluntary bodies to achieve common objectives" in order to project its "fundamental concern for the well being of the working community within the Dales." The driving force behind the organisation was its secretary Colin Speakman, the founding father of Dales Rail.

Colin is a born enthusiast. Anything he becomes involved in he undertakes with the zeal of an evangelist; hence the success of Dales Rail. Therefore, it had come as no surprise that he had been amongst the first to come to the aid of the Settle–Carlisle line.

Moreover, he had contacts, too.

The seminar attracted some 50 participants, including Paul Watkinson, British Rail's divisional manager at Leeds, and David Burton of FOSCLA. Even more significant was the fact that the session titled 'The Settle–Carlisle Line – A Rural Railway in Crisis' was chaired by John Watson MP. My role was to provide what Colin described as the 'keynote talk' and I took the theme that the line was "perhaps the finest scenic railway" and "the most spectacular main line in England" – quoting freely from British Rail's own leaflet 'Highlights of the Settle & Carlisle Line' which appeared to have been withdrawn from the travel centres and information offices.

I then rebuked British Rail for its failure to promote the line and stressed that the scope for publicising it was enormous. After calling for co-operation between British Rail and local authorities, an improved timetable based on the 'Frankland proposals', and an extra stop at Garsdale on summer Saturdays, I concluded by saying that, most of all, the line needed a firm commitment to its future from British Rail itself.

John Watson endorsed my views and said the line should be retained and developed as a major part of the rail network, part of our national heritage and as a major tourist attraction which also served local needs. For British Rail, Paul Watkinson said that no decision had yet been taken regarding the line's future. He spoke of the "grave financial crisis" facing British Rail and its difficulty in meeting Government targets. Indeed, I got the impression that most of those present looked upon closure of the line as a foregone conclusion, although there was a ray of hope when a spokesman for Cumbria County Council "strongly supported retention of the line for tourist and local needs."

The following week I was asked by Ivor Warburton to attend an 'informal meeting' in York. Also present was Leeds divisional manager Paul Watkinson and Norman Blackstock, the Eastern Region's InterCity manager. They intimated that the closure proposal for the Settle–Carlisle line was imminent and could be expected before Serpell was due to report (on railway finances) in November. In addition, all North East–South West services to and from Leeds were to be re-routed from the Midland Main Line via Goose Hill (Normanton) and Wath Road to the Wakefield Westgate–Moorthorpe line. This represented yet another classic example of 'closure by stealth' as it would mean only a couple of summer seasonal trains would continue to use the Midland route.

At the quarterly Yorkshire TUCC meeting on 23rd September, I asked Ivor Warburton if rumours I had heard that through freight services were to be re-routed away from the Settle–Carlisle line were true. He replied that this was none of our business. That was nonsense and the deputy chairman, Barbara Ashwin, told him so. "Anything that could affect the future of the line was relevant to the work of the committee," she said. Nevertheless, Warburton agreed to check claims that the 'Highlights of the Settle & Carlisle Line' leaflet had been withdrawn because it was under threat. He also said British Rail would consider the suggestion that trains should stop at Garsdale on summer Saturdays.

The next day I had an evening meeting with members of FOSCLA. It was held on an informal 'off the record' basis. I had no qualms about this. For some time I had been conscious that, whilst TUCCs were meant to be impartial or neutral when it came to closure proposals, in reality the balance was strongly weighted in favour of British Rail. One factor was that TUCCs were in continuous contact with British Rail personnel. Indeed, we had got to know many of them well. When I presided over the Humber Ferry closure proposal I was on first name terms with most of the British Rail team yet I didn't know a single objector.

Likewise when it came to the first Huddersfield–Sheffield public hearing. Here, too, I had known most of the British Rail people but, apart from Richard Wainwright MP and David Smith of the City of Sheffield, I didn't know any of the objectors from Adam. Whilst the committee had come through relatively unscathed, I still recall the tension and, indeed, hostility from row upon row of objectors when we opened in Sheffield; many of whom looked upon TUCCs as being British Rail stooges. Therefore, when it came to the Settle–Carlisle closure proposal, which looked as if it could become the most hotly contested of all time, I was determined that, come the day, we would be on equal terms with both sides.

Whilst I had already met FOSCLA chairman David Burton and secretary Graham Nuttall on a number of occasions, this was the first opportunity I had had to meet members of their committee and informally brief them on the closure procedure. I spelt out its A to Z, from publication of the Section 54 notice giving advance warning of the proposal right through to the submission of the TUCC report to the Secretary of State for Transport who would make the ultimate decision. It was only right that FOSCLA should be put in the picture. For whereas British Rail knew what it was all about, FOSCLA were new to the game. Therefore fair play indicated they should be as well informed as their opponents as to how the Yorkshire TUCC handled closure proposals.

The meeting took place in a private room at the Skipton Conservative Club. In addition to Messrs Burton and Nuttall, others present included Peter Walton, the photographer from Kirkby Stephen whose work I knew and admired, Ian Taylor of Bentham, whose company made extensive use of Settle station's Red Star parcels facility for the despatch and receipt of agricultural machinery spares, and Geoffrey Dickinson, a rail enthusiast and solicitor who practiced in Colne.

I explained that, whilst the Section 54 notice published in 'The Times' and 'The Daily Telegraph' represented the starting pistol of the closure proposal, it was British Rail's Section 56 notice a month later which FOSCLA would need to act on. This would be published in local newspapers and give full details of the proposal and indicate how users or representatives of users should lodge their objections with the TUCCs. I stressed that FOSCLA should aim to get as many objections as possible which should concentrate on the hardship closure of the Settle–Carlisle line would cause. To assist them I had drafted a sample Section 56 notice to show how I thought it would be worded.

Then I outlined the procedure the Yorkshire TUCC would adopt in considering the objections, how British Rail would submit a 'Heads of Information', a copy of which would be sent to each objector together with the TUCC's 'Summary of Written Objections' and the responses to them by British Rail. Recalling Roger Smith's track record of demolishing British Rail's case on the strength of its own 'Heads of Information' and responses to the objections, I said they should not be short of ammunition.

My next move was to fix an early meeting with John Watson. I had already tipped him off that a decision on the Settle–Carlisle from British Rail was imminent so it was arranged I would attend one of his Saturday morning surgeries in Skipton on 30th September. His agent, Gerry Thorpe, who was acting as a liaison between John and FOSCLA, was also present. I outlined the TUCC procedures, much as I had to FOSCLA the previous week. John confirmed that his London contacts had intimated that an announcement from British Rail regarding the future of the line was expected shortly. He was writing an article for the 'Craven Herald

& Pioneer', the local newspaper, which would update readers and
alert them of the TUCC procedures.

John's article was excellent. He opened by stating there was a
strong rumour that British Rail would be initiating closure proceedings in January 1983 – a little later than I had anticipated. Explaining that the case for closure was entirely financial, he quoted figures
from 'The Facts' document which, he asserted, were "highly available to challenge", quoting the example that no account was taken
of the £48,000 generated each year by Settle station.

On Ribblehead Viaduct, he observed that it was built in 1874
and that a hundred years later it was still considered to be in first
class condition. Now it was supposed to be falling down. He could
not understand why a solid and worthy viaduct should apparently
deteriorate so rapidly but that was what British Rail said had happened.

After spelling out the mechanics of the closure procedure I had
given him, he concluded:

"I personally hope we can do everything possible to keep the
line open.The Government gives British Rail £800 million a year,
largely to fund the social and amenity value of lines like the Settle
and Carlisle. The line provides access and some local employment.
Above all, however, it rightly occupies a privileged place in our
cultural heritage. It is the highest railway line in England and also
the most scenic. Its construction was a task of terrifying human
ordeal and its appearance is irreplaceable. In fact if British Rail
were to be rather more enthusiastic about these aspects of the line
and rather less concerned about its immediate mathematics then
the line could ultimately prove to be profitable after all."

I was greatly heartened on reading this. With the unequivocal
backing of people like John Watson, the Settle–Carlisle line was
in with a chance, albeit a slim one.

Indeed, John's support was all the more valuable because he
was a Conservative MP and, as such, carried more influence with
the Government. A solicitor, he had also worked in industry and
was a director of John Waddington's, the printing and packaging
conglomerate best known for its games, including Monopoly. To
the left of the party, and at one time Edward Heath's personal
assistant, he was elected member for Skipton in 1979. Described
by Andrew Roth in his 'Parliamentary Profiles' (1979) as a "top-
notch liberal newcomer" who "knows everyone", John Watson is
also blessed with a sense of humour as epitomised by his entry in

'Who's Who' which lists his recreations as "walking, running, standing still."

The next development of any consequence came on 12th November at a meeting of the Central Transport Consultative Committee addressed by John Welsby, the sector director for Provincial Services which, of course, included the Settle–Carlisle line. During the discussion that followed, I asked whether any Section 54 closure notices would be published before the Serpell Report came out – now expected in January. He replied that, whilst there might be the odd closure of a short section of line which did not include any stations, he did not envisage any major closures.

Afterwards, over a pre-lunch drink, he told me that whilst the Settle–Carlisle line was undoubtedly "a problem" he did not envisage a closure proposal being introduced "before a General Election." This was a turn-up for the book and represented a complete contradiction of what I had been told by Eastern Region two months earlier. Whilst Welsby was not prepared to expand on what he had said, I could only assume that the British Railways Board had overruled plans to go ahead with the closure because of the inept way the issue had been handled from the beginning and the political rumpus which would follow the announcement of formal closure proceedings.

The following day I alerted John Watson of British Rail's change of strategy, saying that it appeared the line had been given a stay of execution rather than a reprieve. He agreed and said it was "rather good news". In a press release welcoming British Rail's change of heart, he stated:

"Of course, nothing fundamental has changed. The line is still losing money and Ribblehead Viaduct is still in a poor state of repair. The new decision seems, however, to be a ray of hope. If British Rail can now be persuaded to promote the line properly, to include it more realistically in their traffic plans and to judge its financial performance more fairly, then we still have a sporting chance of postponing its closure indefinitely."

The issue was taken up in the 'Yorkshire Post' on 17th November by the paper's astute and well informed transport correspondent, Alan Whitehouse, who wrote:

"One possible reason for the U-turn is that the Settle–Carlisle line – it links Leeds with Glasgow – has become a very political railway. It is held up by the pro-rail lobby as an example of all that is wrong with British Rail, a cash-starved system which is slowly but surely wearing out.

Additionally, the route passes through the constituencies of two leading Tory MPs, Mr William Whitelaw, the Home Secretary, and Mr Michael Jopling, the party's Chief Whip.

Observers have been speculating that the Conservatives would not relish the political backlash caused by the closure of such a major rail route. If they win the next General Election, however, it is suggested that the position could change overnight."

At local level, there was no doubt that senior British Rail managers were far from happy that closure plans had been deferred. At the Yorkshire TUCC meeting the next day, it was a somewhat testy Ivor Warburton who said that, as soon as he had read the 'Yorkshire Post' report, he had contacted the British Railways Board who confirmed there would be no closure proposals before Serpell reported "at the end of November." I remarked that there must be some misunderstanding as Serpell was not expected until January. Moreover, both John Welsby and the 'Yorkshire Post' had specifically referred to the impending General Election which was up to eighteen months away, although it was expected early rather than late.

Until that General Election it appeared to be a case of politics rule – OK! As for British Rail, the official stance was confirmed to me by London Midland Region general manager Jim O'Brien at the end of November: "There is no change in the situation regarding the Settle–Carlisle line – we are still collating information." And so the matter rested – for the time being at any rate.

6

THE GATHERING STORM

"One of Britain's most scenic railway lines, the Settle to Carlisle route, is to close – in spite of British Rail denials that no decision on its future has been taken."

Alan Whitehouse in the 'Yorkshire Post' of 18th March 1983

Throughout 1982 the shadow of impending closure had loomed over the Settle–Carlisle line. However, by the beginning of 1983 something of a lull had set into the Settle–Carlisle saga. Unless British Rail were to make another U-turn, there would be no closure proposal before the General Election, confidently expected in June or early autumn. As a consequence, the fight to save the line took something of a back seat, certainly so far as the politicians were concerned, until the election was out of the way.

I wasn't altogether sorry as the Yorkshire TUCC were preoccupied with a number of other issues. First of these was the much leaked Serpell Report. It didn't impress either the committee or myself and turned out to be something of a damp squib. Indeed, about the only person to have a good word for it was Lord Beeching who told the 'Yorkshire Post's' Alan Whitehouse that the 1,600 mile option was "the maximum-sized network I would have recommended." The major weakness of the Serpell report was that its terms of reference were restricted to railway financing. There was nothing about the requirements of passengers, let alone the public at large. Far from providing a cure-all for British Rail's problems, all it came up with was a series of options for cutting back the network. These were politically unacceptable, especially in an election year.

The danger of Serpell's more ludicrous options, like cutting the network from 11,000 miles to just 1,600 miles which appealed to Lord Beeching, was that they could be used as a ploy to gain acceptance of a less drastic pruning of the network, say down to two-thirds its present size. Then people might accept that it wasn't going to be as bad as they had first thought. Even so, it would still mean goodbye to the Settle–Carlisle line and many others to boot. That the report received an almost universal thumbs-down and was discarded to the attic, if not the dust-bin, does not alter the fact that, at the time, it had an unsettling influence and undermined the case for the railway.

Then there were diversions on another front. Ever since the Conservative Government was elected in 1979, there had been a question mark over the TUCCs and other nationalised industry consumer 'quangos'. Now our sponsors, the Department of Trade, had come up with its 'Strategy for Reform'. This accepted that there was a need for TUCCs and similar bodies for gas and electricity, but costs had to be cut. This was likely to lead to a reduction in the number of TUCCs which could result in those parts of the London Midland Region – including the Settle–Carlisle line as far as the middle of Blea Moor tunnel – being transferred to the North Western TUCC.

Nor was the Settle–Carlisle line the only closure proposal on the cards.British rail confirmed to me that it planned to axe the section of the Midland Main Line between Goose Hill (Normanton) and Wath Road (near Rotherham) together with the Oakenshaw Junctions near Wakefield. Although only used by two summer seasonal services – a Luton–Scarborough and a Bradford–Paignton – plus a Fridays only Portsmouth Harbour–Leeds following the re-routing of the North East–South West services, it was also an important diversionary route. Moreover, like the Settle–Carlisle, it was once part of the Midland Railway which gave it an added significance. Add to this that we still had secretarial problems at the York office, so my hands were pretty full.

Nevertheless, I managed to get our 'Annual Report 1982' out in February. It made grim reading. Complaints regarding British Rail services were up a massive 85 per cent and one third related to timetable changes. Needless to say the re-routing of the Nottingham–Glasgow service headed the list. Whilst some complaints were largely motivated by concern for the future of the Settle–Carlisle line, many lent chapter and verse to the inadequacies of the alternative route via Lancaster. Amongst those who had sampled it were Philippa Simpson, a local government officer from Leeds, and botanist Peter Shaw of Baildon; both of whom were later to take a prominent role in the battle to save the line.

In addition to writing to British Rail, MPs and the Yorkshire TUCC, many people were also contributing to correspondence columns in their local newspapers. I recall an editorial in 'The Cumberland and Westmorland Herald' which lambasted British Rail management as "worn out" and of having "no new ideas, no enthusiasm and no hope for the future." This provoked a reply from divisional manager Trevor Anderson who refuted that he was old, tired, worn out or without ideas or enthusiasm. 'Herald' readers thought otherwise and launched an avalanche of questions on British Rail's handling of the Settle–Carlisle issue.

The subsequent lack of response from British Rail prompted Mr G D Walker of Ravenstonedale to remark that Mr Anderson seemed to be "sulking in his tent" as the divisional manager had shown no sign of further life. "Is it," posed Mr Walker, "that he thinks that masterly inactivity will drive his critics into silence or, more likely, that he has no cogent reply to make?" That said it all!

February also saw FOSCLA's Annual General Meeting at Skipton Town Hall. Over 60 members were present to hear the new secretary, Colne solicitor Geoffrey Dickinson (who had been drafted to beef-up the administration, Graham Nuttall having become assistant secretary) forecast that, following the Serpell Report, 1983 would be the "crunch year" for railways in general and the Settle–Carlisle line in particular.

There was no doubt that FOSCLA were beginning to get their act together although the task that faced them was still daunting. They had about 800 members, including several overseas, and had also teamed up with the Railway Development Society, a national pro-rail umbrella organisation which enjoyed all-Party political support and was dedicated to the retention, improvement and greater use of the rail network. A series of public meetings were planned along the line and in Leeds whilst one of Settle's more famous residents, TV personality Russell Harty, had agreed to become FOSCLA's president.

Of one meeting held in Appleby on 19th February, FOSCLA newsletter No 8 records:

"To fill in the audience with further details, the chairman of FOSCLA strode to the platform introducing himself as 'Mr David Burton – man of action!' In a fighting speech he said we were all 'having the wool pulled over our eyes' over the state of Ribblehead Viaduct. He revealed that in this great technological age British Rail inspected Ribblehead Viaduct with a pair of binoculars, that

Ribblehead Viaduct had been repaired at a cost of £½ million shortly before British Rail claimed it needed £6 million spending on it, and that at Easter the line would be taking all the traffic from the West Coast Main Line because of bridge works. Ribblehead Viaduct was supposed to be in a bad state yet it has proved perfectly adequate recently to take enormously heavy loads. The Chairman said that a Chartered Engineer's tests on a section of Ribblehead Viaduct confirmed the opinion that WE ARE BEING CONNED!"

Fighting stuff, and characteristic of the FOSCLA chairman.

On 17th March press reports stated that the RDS and FOSCLA claimed that British Rail would start closure proposals in May, irrespective of whether a General Election was imminent or not. This was immediately denied by a British Rail spokesman who stated that, whilst a study of the line was in progress, no decision had yet been reached. He added that no time had been set for the study and nobody knew when it would be completed.

However Alan Whitehouse, writing in the 'Yorkshire Post' the following day, said that two separate sources at British Rail head-quarters had told him that this was just a "smokescreen". A decision had already been taken to close the line but no one would confirm it officially. It was just a case of deciding when to announce the first stage of the closure proceedings. One informant told Whitehouse that the pressure was on British Rail to defer announcing the closure and say nothing until after a General Election.

The first tangible example of RDS/FOSCLA co-operation came at the end of March with the publication of a special four page leaflet headed 'Settle–Carlisle is Threatened'. After summarising the position in considerable detail, the leaflet concluded: "The Settle to Carlisle line is an asset. British Rail must keep and develop that asset as part of a modern, attractive rail network playing a greater part in the nation's transport system."

At a news conference in Leeds on 28th March, which I attended as an observer, RDS national committee member Trevor Garrod told journalists that a list of objectors was being compiled so that its protest could be quickly orchestrated if British Rail put in for closure. "We want to see people from all over the country protesting about it," added Mr Garrod.

He was strongly supported by Mr Frank Edwards, a local official of the National Union of Railwaymen, who said British Rail were attempting to close the line "by stealth." He maintained passengers were being driven away from the line by the poor quality of services on it. "We have seen this sort of rundown on other lines before they have closed," claimed Mr Edwards who added that the alternative Leeds–Glasgow service via Lancaster was most unsatisfactory.

Of even greater significance, the local authorities – by nature cautious bodies, especially at officer level – were beginning to lend support for retention of the Settle–Carlisle line. In April, Cumbria County Council issued invitations to North Yorkshire, West Yorkshire and Lancashire County Councils to a meeting to consider mounting a campaign against closure of the line. Meanwhile, in Parliament on 11th April, Mr Reginald Eyre MP, for the Secretary of State for Transport, told rail buff MP Robert Adley that British Rail were "currently undertaking a study of all aspects of the Settle–Carlisle line with a view to determining its long–term future."

On Saturday 7th May, Craven District Council held a public meeting at the Victoria Hall, Settle, at which local MP John Watson, prospective candidates Mrs Claire Brooks (Liberal) and Mrs Margaret Billing (Labour) together with myself spoke from the platform. Messages of support were received from Home Secretary William Whitelaw MP (Penrith and the Border), Government Chief Whip Michael Jopling MP (Westmorland) and Ron Lewis, the Labour MP for Carlisle. As John Watson had said earlier, the Settle–Carlisle line had become a very political railway.

Following the speeches, the meeting agreed that the British Railways Board be called upon to:

● commission an independent survey of the problems surrounding the Ribblehead Viaduct and the possible costs of a solution;
● to present a full set of passenger, freight and financial statistics to representatives of local authorities before considering issuing any closure proposal;
● to consider means by which the usage of the line could be increased by more energetic marketing and promotion.

The meeting also called on the local authorities involved to be asked to provide for the appointment of a consultant to make an independent investigation of the case for retention of the line.

So far, so good. And as spring progressed into early summer, attention became diverted by national politics and the 1983 General Election on 9th June, at which the Conservatives were returned with an increased majority. Although the Settle–Carlisle line did not become an election issue, simply because at local level there was all-Party support for its retention whilst nationally British Rail continued to maintain that "no decision had yet been made," attention returned to the line immediately afterwards when, as a consequence of Mr Whitelaw's elevation to the House of Lords, there was a by-election in the Penrith and The Border constituency.

For some time I had been impressed at the way Geoffrey Dickinson had taken to his role of FOSCLA secretary. It was useful to have a keen legal mind in such a hot seat. We had established our own 'hot line', rather like that I used to enjoy with Colin Driver when he was our British Rail liaison officer. Quite apart from anything else, I looked upon it as an 'insurance policy' for the Yorkshire TUCC when it came to the Public Hearing as we would need the goodwill and co-operation of FOSCLA to get through it.

Therefore, it came as no surprise when Geoff sought my views on whether FOSCLA should put up a candidate in the Penrith and The Border by-election on 28th July. Although the idea had considerable publicity potential, I had my doubts and advised against it. Single issues, even those as emotive as the Settle–Carlisle line, rarely dominated elections and they could have ended up with mud on their faces, especially if their candidate polled fewer votes than the ubiquitous Lord Sutch of the Raving Monster Looney Party!

In the event the Settle–Carlisle line became one of a number of issues – the major one being the necessity of the by–election in the first place! Thus it was possible to claim, if not prove, that David Maclean's support for the line enabled the Conservative's to just hold the seat, whilst the achievement of Michael Young in reducing a Tory majority of over 15,000 to a mere 552 owed much to his advocacy of the line.

Of more lasting importance was a meeting which had taken place in Settle a month earlier. Here, under the auspices of Cumbria County Council, an organisation of local authorities opposed to closure of the line had been established. After considering the impact of closure on the local communities, the problems caused by the re-routing of the Nottingham–Glasgow service, job losses, the loss of part of the country's national heritage, and the potential for future development; it was agreed there were three options: to accept the inevitability of closure; to await a closure proposal and then object; or to take the initiative to seek help and possible outside funding. To their eternal credit they plumped for the third.

Following the Penrith by-election, it seemed only a matter of time before British Rail would start formal closure proceedings for the Settle–Carlisle line. But what of business on the line itself at that time? From 16th May the new timetable had led to a number of changes, the most significant being the re-timing of the celebrated 15.37 from Carlisle to 16.35 which also, much to my delight, ran 'fast' between Skipton and Leeds, stopping only at Keighley. However, 29 minutes was allowed between Settle and Skipton for a journey which was invariably done in 18 minutes. Still, it was a modest improvement on the 31 minutes of the previous timetable even though the net result was that the scheduled two minute stop in Skipton was one of 10 minutes or more.

Such timetabling eccentricities, on which I spent many hours of largely fruitless discussion and correspondence, never cease to amaze me. For example the timetable allowed 37 minutes between Carlisle and Appleby, a time that was virtually unattainable in view of long established speed restrictions. A time of 40 minutes would have been far more realistic. Yet British Rail, in its infinite wisdom, seemed unable to grasp this and continued to provide too little time between Carlisle and Appleby and far too much time between Settle and Skipton. Such decisions only undermine the integrity of the timetable.

Moreover, these incomprehensible timings lent considerable weight to suggestions that they were part of a deliberate ploy to make the remaining services on the line unattractive in the hope of persuading passengers to undertake the longer, more circuitous route via Lancaster. Even so, the direct service via Settle continued to offer a faster, more reliable service for Anglo-Scottish journeys than the Lancaster option. Here problems were exacerbated as the 12.35 from Leeds now connected into 'The European' (Harwich Parkeston Quay–Glasgow/Edinburgh) which had the worst punctuality record of any train on British Rail. Anticipating this, I managed to persuade London Midland Region to put a special Lancaster stop into the 11.45 Euston–Glasgow when 'The European' was running more than 20 minutes late – which was quite often!

I had less success with the FOSCLA proposal that the morning Leeds–Carlisle and the afternoon return working should stop at Garsdale on summer Saturdays. Ever since I'd taken it up British Rail had come up with a variety of excuses to reject the idea. First they said there was no demand for such a stop, which was possible. Then they said the timetable could not accommodate it, which was nonsense. Subsequently they fell back on the tale that, as there

were no lighting facilities at Garsdale, the Railway Inspectorate
would not agree to trains stopping; seemingly oblivious to the Dales
Rail trains which stopped there and the fact that during the summer
the Almighty provided the lighting.

The latest explanation proved quite an eye-opener. As the Leeds
Division Passenger Marketing Officer put it in a letter to me:

"Last summer (1982) the Saturday trains were so well loaded to
the extent that my colleagues at Preston are likely to withdraw
Saturday promotional fares on these services. The alternative to
this of course is to increase the accommodation but you will be
aware that the coaching stock demand on summer Saturdays pre-
cludes any strengthening of these services. I am, therefore, unable
to proceed with this suggestion at present but will bear it in mind
if an opportunity arises in the future."

In other words, the Settle–Carlisle line was so popular on Saturdays that any extra patronage attracted by stopping trains at
Garsdale simply could not be accommodated!

This confirmed my own observations. For whilst immediately
following the re-routing of the Nottingham–Glasgow service, loadings were little to write home about, a year later things were looking
up. Overcrowding had become commonplace on weekdays during
the summer as well as on Saturdays. A class 31 locomotive plus
four Mark 1 coaches had insufficient capacity to match public demand, a point that didn't go unnoticed by British Rail who, to their
credit, managed to rustle-up an extra coach.

There was no doubt that the 'Settle–Carlisle' had become a marketable product, although British Rail were doing little to exploit
it. In reality the public were responding to a steady flow of news
items and photographs in the media – Ribblehead Viaduct made
a splendid picture providing you had five columns to accommodate
it. Then in the correspondence columns, from 'The Times' to the
humblest local weekly, the case for the line was being eloquently
expanded. Whereas in the past travel on the line had been part of
longer journeys to and from Scotland, now a significant new market
had been tapped of people who were travelling simply because it
was the Settle–Carlisle line.

On Wednesday 17th August 1983, FOSCLA convened a meeting
in Leeds of interested parties to "discuss the future of the Settle–
Carlisle line which is likely to be the subject of a closure notice in
the not too distant future." It hoped to form a group comprising
the local authorities and those persons and organisations who

would be affected by the closure in order that they might co-ordinate their efforts in opposing any closure proposal and press for
the retention and development of "this vital trunk link".

According to the notice calling the meeting, the question of the
Ribblehead Viaduct "which is said to be in a state of near collapse
but it has been rumoured that this is not the case" would also be
discussed. FOSCLA felt that the record should be "put straight"
by commissioning an independent survey. Rather surprisingly, I
felt, British Rail had been invited to attend in order that they might
be acquainted of the "strength of feeling." As it was, they didn't
turn up; which was probably as well as the meeting had all the
stamp of a 'council of war' and British Rail were the enemy.

There were about twenty of us present that afternoon seated
round a large table in a private room at the Griffin Hotel. Some
I knew, others I recognised, but a good half were strangers to me.
FOSCLA chairman David Burton opened the proceedings in a
low-key style. After welcoming us, he handed over to Geoff Dickinson, the secretary, who summarised the rundown of the Settle–
Carlisle line during the past two years. The meeting was then
thrown open and, going round the table, all present gave their
views on the problems facing the line and the possible solutions.

Dr John Whitelegg of North Lancashire and Cumbria Transport
2000 expressed total opposition to any closure. His colleague Peter
Horton warned that whichever TUCC organised the Public Hearing would be in for a rough ride. He felt sorry for the chairman
who would face "scenes reminiscent of the motorway enquiries of
the 1960s as well as having to listen to at least a thousand individual
and corporate objectors." So much for my 'insurance policy'!

Then it was my turn. I said the truth of the matter was that
British Rail were simply not interested in the Settle–Carlisle line.
The high flyers within British Rail were those whose prime aim
was to cut costs – irrespective of the inconvenience and hardship
this would cause to their customers. Therefore they had no commitment to the line and I expected closure proposals would start within
a matter of weeks. After outlining in detail the closure procedure
in accordance with Section 56 of the Transport Act 1962, I said
that I was of the opinion that users of Dales Rail, steam specials
and Red Star parcels would rank as valid objectors. I stressed, too,
that whilst the TUCC role was to consider hardship, this should
not discourage people from raising other issues which the TUCC
could draw to the Minister's attention.

Councillor Beth Graham of Settle spoke next. Her council was, of course, totally opposed to any closure proposal. So, too, were Craven District Council, represented by Richard Tulloch, and Bradford Metropolitan District; although neither was able to commit any cash for a Ribblehead survey fund at that time.

John Carr, head of public transport for West Yorkshire Metropolitan County Council, said they had supported Cumbria County Council's initiative in examining ways of developing the line. He was concerned that if the Settle–Carlisle line closed, the West Yorkshire PTE could be faced with all the costs of supporting services to Keighley and Skipton.

For Cumbria County Council, Peter Robinson, group leader in the planning division, reported on the organisation formed by the local authorities opposed to closure of the line. They were meeting British Rail on 2nd September and would report back to representatives of the councils at the beginning of October. This was good news. I had felt for some time that local authority involvement was essential if the line was to be saved. For whilst FOSCLA had the grass roots enthusiasm, the councils had the political clout plus access to funds and resources which, although modest when set against overall council expenditure, were far in excess of anything FOSCLA had at its disposal.

Richard Atkinson for Kirklees (Huddersfield) and a spokesman for Rotherham confirmed that their councils were fully opposed to closure. There were further rallying calls from Graham Nuttall, Philippa Simpson and Brian Sutcliffe, all of FOSCLA, whilst Denis Bradbury, the sage secretary of the RDS in Yorkshire, remarked that British Rail had got itself in a tangle over closure proposals in the past and could well do so again when it came to Settle–Carlisle.

Then Dr W Eastwood, a consulting engineer, gave an assessment on the state of Ribblehead Viaduct. He felt the problem was one of stress, although the weight of the trains passing over the viaduct were so light in comparison with the weight of the structure itself that they were of little consequence.So far as a survey was concerned, it would help if British Rail made known the results of its investigations. Even with British Rail's full co-operation a survey could cost anything up to £20,000. "You get the type of survey you pay for," he added.

In the discussion that followed, I detected a degree of reservation towards each other on the part of both the councils and the users groups. For a start the former were used to working with British Rail whereas relations between railway management and FOSCLA were on the chilly side. As someone who represented neither councils nor user groups at the meeting, I suggested that each should concentrate their efforts on doing what they did best as the battle to save the Settle–Carlisle line would have to be fought on all fronts.

John Carr of West Yorkshire took up this point. He suggested that FOSCLA's more limited resources would be better spent on seeking public support and collecting evidence for the TUCC Public Hearing, leaving the councils to concentrate on the survey. This was agreed. Meanwhile it was arranged that each side would keep the other informed as to what progress they were making on their respective fronts.

As I left the meeting, one of the FOSCLA representatives handed me a folder and asked if I had seen it. It contained a typewritten report running to about 70 pages under the insignia of the General Manager of the London Midland Region and was titled 'The Case Study for Closure of the Settle–Carlisle Route'. I replied that it was new to me and asked if I could keep it. He said I could.

When I got home I settled down to read it. The report was a thoroughly professional, if somewhat one sided assessment of the Settle–Carlisle line and the alternatives to it and expanded many of the points in 'The Facts' document which British Rail had released earlier on a limited basis. Therefore it came as no surprise to read its main conclusion: "That a clear case exists for complete closure of the Settle–Carlisle line."

As I ploughed through the report there were a number of points which particularly caught my attention. Under the heading 'Timescales' it stated:

"If it is decided to close the Settle–Carlisle route it is estimated by the Chief Operating Manager that all through traffic can be diverted with the 1982 timetable change. However, the timescale of the TUCC closure procedures could take up to a further two years and hence the likely date of closure would be May 1984."

Under a sub-heading 'The Need for Urgency', the report referred to the "developing opportunities for growth in the East Midlands–North West InterCity passenger market" while at the same time catering "adequately" for passengers from the East Midlands to Scotland. There was a telling addition which read:

"Although a residual Leeds–Carlisle local service will still be operated, this development has the effect of diverting InterCity

passenger services from the Settle–Carlisle route and concentrating
them on the West Coast Main Line"

Surprise! Surprise! And there was more to come.

On the 'Current Traffic Position', the report stated that "although loadings on the two mid-day services were reasonably
good," the load factors on the rest of the services had been "mod-
erate to poor." This had "contributed to a commercial decision to
re-route the service from the 1982 timetable via Manchester," leading to a resource saving of three sets of coaches.

Stating the obvious that no local service was operated, as Settle
and Appleby were served by the Nottingham–Glasgow service, the
report noted:

"However, from 1982 it will be necessary to operate a service
from Leeds to Carlisle each way daily to avoid the need to institute
formal closure proceedings for the line."

This was just a legal stop-gap to avoid delay in the re-routing
exercise.

Under 'Interface with Outside Bodies' it was recorded that Cumbria County Council's 1980/1981 Public Transport Plan stated that
it would oppose any reduction in the basic rail network and encourage moves to develop rail services to cater for tourists and visitors
to the area.

As for 'Other Interested Groups', I saw that I had rated a mention as:

"The Yorkshire Area TUCC Chairman has issued a press release
(11 June 1981) in which he expresses his 'growing concern' regarding the future of rail services between West Yorkshire and Scotland
via Settle and Carlisle."

It continued that other organisations with an interest in the future
of the line could include various enthusiast groups as well as conservation and preservation organisations like the Ramblers Association. In addition it was expected that the local and national press
would take a "close interest in developments, particularly if the
rail unions mounted any form of campaign to retain the line."

As I studied the report late into the night I became increasingly
incensed. It was not because of what was in it, for there was little
that was new or unexpected. It was simply because of the date of
the report – August 1981. So much for all the assurances to MPs
and lesser mortals from British Railways Board chairman Sir Peter
Parker downwards that there were "no plans to close the Settle–
Carlisle line." If this wasn't a plan I'd have liked to have known

what was! Then what of Jim O'Brien's statement that "the re-routing of the Nottingham–Glasgow service would in no way prejudice the future of the Settle–Carlisle line"?

So much for British Rail's honesty and integrity. However, as I put the report on one side and poured myself a large whisky to calm my anger, little did I know of the bombshell that was to explode the following day.

7

THE FATEFUL DECISION

"British Rail's master plan to axe the Settle–Carlisle line was drawn up two years ago behind a shroud of denials that closure was even contemplated."

Alan Whitaker in the Bradford 'Telegraph & Argus' 29th August 1983.

The morning of Thursday 18th August dawned bright and clear. It was going to be a nice sunny day. After an early breakfast, I settled down in my 'office' at home – a small yet convenient room with everything to hand which used to be the porch – to work on some accounts. I had discarded the report which had so angered me the previous night to a bottom drawer and my mind was far removed from British Rail and the Settle–Carlisle line when the phone rang. It was Paul Watkinson, the divisional manager at Leeds. What, I wondered, was brewing?

I soon found out as Paul came quickly to the point. Later in the day the British Railways Board would be telling the railway trade unions that it intended to proceed with proposals to close the Settle–Carlisle line. He felt I should know as I was likely to become involved "quite quickly." I thanked him for taking the trouble to let me know. At least it was nice to learn the news first hand from the 'horses mouth' rather than reading it in the press – or a leaked report!

Then it was just a case of waiting for the action to begin. It wasn't long before I received the first of many telephone calls as journalists picked up the story and sought my views. I had prepared a statement some time earlier for such an eventuality which I hoped would take me over the tight rope I was obliged to walk when dealing with the issue. After a couple of minor amendments it simply stated:

"The news comes as little surprise, yet it is characteristic of British Rail's timing that the decision has been announced just after they have issued a new leaflet promoting the line. I have no doubt there will be a lot of objections by users to the proposed closure of the line. In addition to providing the quickest journey from West Yorkshire to Carlisle, Glasgow and South West Scotland, people came from all over the country and even abroad to travel over what British Rail describes as the 'greatest historical scenic route and the most spectacular main line in England'."

I have to confess the fact that British Rail had issued a new promotional leaflet extolling the attractions of the line a matter of days before they announced they intended to go for closure added a certain piquancy to the occasion. Both the BBC and Yorkshire Television were on to me for copies of the leaflet and I was happy to oblige. That evening I took part in a rather acrimonious discussion with Paul Watkinson on BBC's 'Look North' during which I had found it necessary to remind him that the final decision as to whether the line closed rested with the Minister of Transport and not British Rail.

Needless to say British Rail's public relations people – or 'Public Affairs' as they preferred to be called – had pulled out all the stops to put a favourable gloss on things. Their news release headed 'Rationalisation of Rail Infrastructure', a title hardly likely to hold the front page, stated the Corporate Plan for 1983–88 envisaged no basic change in the network. Then they attempted to sweeten the pill by emphasising that complete closure would only affect the route between Ribblehead and Appleby, the rest of the line (between Settle Junction and Ribblehead, and Appleby and Carlisle) would remain open for freight traffic. Big deal!

The release continued:

"The present through services between Leeds and Carlisle will continue and be re-routed via Carnforth with additional calls at Giggleswick, Carnforth, Oxenholme and Penrith. Diversion via Carnforth will increase journey times by an estimated 10–15 minutes, but this routing will open up attractive through journey opportunities between West Yorkshire and the Lake District."

"Closure of the line will give an annual saving of £600,000 and will obviate the need for expenditure of £9 million on renewal and maintenance over the next 5 years. This figure includes some £5 million for the replacement of Ribblehead Viaduct."

Reaction to British Rail's statement was as expected. The media – press, television and local radio – were largely sympathetic to the views of those opposed to the closure of the line, although I don't recall any seasoned journalist about at the time giving those opposed to closure better odds than for a 33 to 1 outsider.

Apart from my own observations, those of Geoff Dickinson, the FOSCLA secretary, were extensively reported. He recalled that the Government had said that it would not countenance any major route closure. Yet the Settle–Carlisle line was a major route and its closure would be "a clear breach of an election promise." Dickinson said FOSCLA were angry with British Rail who had stated for two years that it had never been their intention to close the line "while we have been saying they have been running down the line as a prelude to closure – this proves it!"

As things began to hot up I was concerned that my own position was in danger of becoming untenable. Any commitment I had as an impartial, neutral referee between British Rail and those opposed to closure of the line had been completely undermined by the continual evidence of deceit and deception deployed by British Rail since the Settle–Carlisle case came to light in May 1981; culminating in the discovery that the 'Case Study' for the closure of the line, which lay locked in my desk, was dated August 1981. It was the date on that report that proved the last straw and destroyed any illusion I might have retained about the 'Mr Nice Guy' image of senior British Rail management.

For two pins I would have publicly blown my top, opted out of my part time – albeit becoming increasingly full time – role as Yorkshire TUCC chairman and thrown in my lot with FOSCLA. Yet common sense persuaded me that this was not the route to take. If I had any contribution to make to the Settle–Carlisle debate, it would be more effective under the banner of the statutory TUCC rather than in the trenches alongside the FOSCLA dragoons.

In many respects, British Rail's announcement had come as something of a relief. The lines of engagement had been drawn and the battle could now commence. All the indications were that there would be a great deal of flack flying about and I was likely to be in the middle of it. Then there was the 'Case Study' report burning a hole in my desk. There was little I could do about it. Yet I found it hard to believe I was the only person FOSCLA had given a copy to. It would not be long before the media or an MP got to learn about it. In the meantime there was work to be done.

First I felt we owed all those who had written to the Yorkshire TUCC expressing concern about the future of the Settle–Carlisle line – and there were about 120 of them – an update on the position. So I drafted a summary detailing the procedure we proposed to adopt and asked the secretary to send it to them along with an extract of the relevant part of Section 56 of the Transport Act 1962. If nothing else, it meant those who had felt strongly enough to write to us would be as *au-fait* with things as we were.

For over a year I had been endeavouring to obtain an answer to the list of questions I had put to Trevor Anderson, the divisional manager responsible for the line, following my meeting with him in May 1982. At the end of July – before the announcement of the proposal to close the line – he had responded to my umpteenth 'chaser' saying that "it would be best if we met you in the near future." So a meeting was fixed for 24th August at London Midland Region headquarters in London.

Since my last meeting with them regarding the Settle–Carlisle line, there had been some changes amongst the senior regional personnel. Passenger manager Brian Mander had taken a post with the British Railways Board. In his place was Ian Brown, a youngish chap who displayed an enthusiasm for railways and shared my interest in train loading counts. He opened by expressing regret at the delay in answering my queries. These had now been overtaken by events but the answers would be covered by British Rail's 'Heads of Information' document which set out the formal case for closure.

As I was able to extract some details about the time scale British Rail had in mind for the closure proposal, it wasn't a completely wasted journey. They had still to consult the railway trade unions and relevant local authorities, so the statutory Section 54 notice giving advance warning of the impending closure proposal – which was simply a legal formality in this instance was a public announcement had been made on 18 August – would not be published before the end of September or early October. This meant that the key Section 56 notice, which was the starting gun for objections to be sent to the TUCCs, could be expected around Christmas or the New Year – a neat ploy on the part of British Rail as people would be preoccupied with other issues at that time. I warned them that this would not go unnoticed.

Then I raised the question of users of Dales Rail and steam specials. Ian McCubbin, the divisional passenger manager in Manchester standing in for Trevor Anderson who was on holiday, quickly replied that these services fell outside the provisions of the Act. I said that I doubted if his interpretation of the statute was correct and warned him that it was likely to be vigorously challenged. Somehow I felt my warning fell on deaf ears.

Ian Brown confided that they would probably use the closure proposal as an opportunity to publicise the difficulties facing British Rail in providing services at a time of financial constraint. I didn't respond, although the suggestion struck me as half baked and naive. One could hardly envisage people taking kindly to a 'poor British Rail' scenario expounded by smooth voiced public relations – sorry, public affairs – officers at the same time as they were trying to deprive them of their favourite railway. I doubted, too, if British Rail were really aware of the strength of public feeling regarding the Settle–Carlisle line.

As I left the meeting and walked to King's Cross to catch the train back to Leeds, my overriding impression was that whilst British Rail had been planning to close the Settle–Carlisle line for over two years – a fact endorsed by the leaked 'Case Study' – they had only just started to get their act together so far as the actual mechanics of the closure proposal itself was concerned.

That night I drafted out a report to my Yorkshire TUCC members outlining the main points to emerge from the meeting. It concluded:

"Had British Rail taken the committee's advice and put in for closure of the Settle–Carlisle line when it was being used by the Nottingham–Glasgow service, I believe they could have avoided much of the rancour that will undoubtedly be directed towards them; especially as this will rank as a classic 'closure by stealth' case.

Feelings are likely to become more enraged if the details of a 'leaked' British Rail document titled 'The Case Study for Closure of the Settle–Carlisle Route' become widely known. It is not so much the contents, nor indeed the title, that gives cause for concern but the fact that it is dated August 1981.

This suggests that assurances given by British Rail to this committee in 1981 and throughout 1982 that closure proposals were not envisaged, that the future of the line would not be prejudiced by the decision to re-route the Nottingham–Glasgow service and that there would be no 'closure by stealth', were lacking in candour.

It certainly endorses the policy of the Committee throughout this period to have treated the whole issue with a degree of scepticism."

And there my case rested, for the time being at any rate.

The next event of significance occurred the following Sunday

evening. I had just settled down to watch television when I received
a telephone call from Alan Whitaker, a reporter on the Bradford
'Telegraph & Argus'. I had met him on a couple of occasions and
knew he had a keen interest in railways, whilst he was a devotee
of the Settle–Carlisle line which he used to attend Carlisle United's
home games.

He asked if I knew anything about 'The Case Study for Closure
of the Settle–Carlisle Route'. I replied that I was aware of it. It
appeared that Alan had been given a copy whilst one was on its
way to John Watson. This was good news. Alan then asked what
were my views on it. I said there was not much I could say other
than I was angry because repeated assurances from British Rail
that there were no plans to close the line appeared to be little more
than a pack of lies or, as I was speaking on the record, were "lacking
in candour."

The following day Whitaker blew the gaffe. Under the banner
headline 'Secret BR plan lifts lid on Settle line', his report opened:

"British Rail's masterplan to axe the Settle–Carlisle line was
drawn up two years ago behind a shroud of denials that closure
was even contemplated.

A secret BR document leaked to the 'Telegraph & Argus' shows
that the re-routing of the last InterCity services last summer was
the start of the closure plan.

This confirms the suspicions of campaigners battling to save the
line who have repeatedly accused BR of deliberately running down
services in a 'closure by stealth' exercise."

He then summarised the major conclusions of the case study,
emphasising that the re-routing of the Nottingham–Glasgow service in May 1982 only left a minimum passenger service until TUCC
closure procedures had been completed. This, said Whitaker,
clearly implied that removal of the through InterCity services would
reduce the number of objectors thereby providing a stronger case
for closure. A good point. His piece concluded with my "lacking
in candour" remark and a footnote that British Rail were "unavailable for comment." I cannot say I blamed them!

On the strength of this I formally wrote to the general manager
of the London Midland Region, enclosing a copy of the 'Telegraph
& Argus' report and asked if it was true; and, if so, how he equated
it with the assurances provided to MPs, the Yorkshire TUCC and
others that there were no plans to close the line and the re-routing
of the Nottingham–Glasgow service would not affect the line's fu-

ture.

Not surprisingly, the newly appointed general manager Malcolm Southgate – Jim O'Brien had been despatched upstairs to the British Railways Board – didn't want any truck with my queries and passed them on to his hapless chief passenger manager, Ian Brown, who replied:

"I cannot trace the document referred to in the Bradford 'Telegraph & Argus' report, although clearly we did review a number of different options for the Settle–Carlisle route prior to reaching a decision in August to seek closure of the line."

I responded expressing my astonishment that he could find no trace of the document, especially as his predecessor (Brian Mander) had contributed a major input, and asked if he would like me to try and get him a copy! Needless to say he didn't take up my offer. Whilst correspondence like this seldom achieves much, it did go a little way to relieve my overall sense of frustration at the whole way British Rail had handled the Settle–Carlisle case.

It wasn't as if this was my only problem at the time. Far from it. Eastern Region had a queue of closure proposals lined-up. In addition to Goose Hill–Wath Road – a significant part of the Midland Main Line between Leeds and Sheffield – there was Goole–Gilberdyke due to the cost of repairs to Goole swing bridge and half-a-dozen or so curves in the Leeds, Wakefield, Halifax and Huddersfield areas. Then, to cap it all, there was to be a re-run of the Huddersfield–Sheffield proposal. This had developed into a most bizarre situation and was fast becoming a farce, except for those who relied on the service. To put the seal on it, British Rail had – with a characteristic sense of timing – formally initiated closure proceedings just two days after launching a publicity campaign to promote the line!

Thus it was a far from placid Yorkshire TUCC which met for its quarterly meeting on 22nd September. I had always made it a policy to keep the committee informed as to what was happening on important issues between meetings and although members occasionally baulked at the amount of paperwork, I believe they appreciated being kept in the picture. As a consequence our meetings, although occasionally lively, were free of any acrimony amongst members or between them and the chair. We were a happy ship. Indeed, I cannot recall any issue during my eight years as chairman when, after due deliberation, we did not reach a unanimous decision.

By contrast our relationship with British Rail was less smooth. This was inevitable if we were doing our job properly, especially at a time when they were engaged in a series of cutbacks which were clobbering rail users. Nor did British Rail make it any easier for themselves by presenting some of these changes as if they were improvements – as in the case of the withdrawal of through services between Leeds and Glasgow. As a consequence there were many heated arguments with the British Rail representatives as the committee did not see its role as being a 'rubber stamp' of railway management decisions.

So far as Settle–Carlisle was concerned, the relationship had become even more strained, not least because the leaked 'Case Study' indicated that all the assurances British Rail had provided regarding the future of the line had proved to be untrue. Therefore members left me in no doubt of their indignation at Ian Brown's response to my letter to the general manager. Irrespective of whether the document could be traced or not, the London Midland Region had made no attempt to answer the question relating to their earlier assurances.

The minutes of the meeting recorded:

"Members unanimously concluded that, whilst the situation vindicated the committee's scepticism towards the issue; it was a matter of great concern that British Rail appear to have misled the committee and others by a chapter of unanswered questions, half truths and, in some instances, lies with regard to their proposals for the line. Nevertheless, the committee were aware that, irrespective of what had happened in the past, they had responsibilities under the Transport Act 1962 which they would undertake to the best of their ability."

Strong stuff to come from one of those watchdogs people were always claiming to be toothless.

The meeting also considered the mechanics of the closure proposal. The actual line between Settle Junction and Carlisle Petterill Bridge Junction passed from the area covered by the Yorkshire TUCC to that covered by the North Western TUCC at the boundary between North Yorkshire and Cumbria which happened to be in the middle of Blea Moor tunnel. Therefore objections to the closure proposal could be lodged with either TUCC or, indeed, both. There was a provision in the Transport Act 1962 so that in such cases the committees could report jointly or agree that consideration of the objections and submission of the report be delegated to the committee which appeared to be principally concerned.

Yorkshire members and myself were in no doubt we were the committee principally concerned, if only on the basis of the interest we had shown in the Settle–Carlisle line. By contrast, our North Western colleagues had displayed little interest in the line other than welcoming the re-routing of the Nottingham–Glasgow service away from it! And whilst I had informally suggested to the North Western chairman, Mrs Olive Clarke, that we would be prepared to handle the proposal should her committee wish, I had detected a distinct lack of enthusiasm from across the Pennines.

Indeed, many of my members shared my doubts regarding the extent of the North Western committee's commitment to the interests of rail users. "You get the impression they are batting for British Rail rather than the passengers," was how one of them put it. In fact the question of who did what so far as the TUCCs were concerned could become academic by the time British Rail issued the statutory Section 56 closure notice as a result of Government plans to rejig the nationalised industry consumer councils. These included the merger of the Yorkshire and North Eastern TUCCs, which had some logic given the comparatively small network in the north east, and the adjustment of TUCC boundaries from the existing county or local authority borders to the dividing points between British Rail regions.

The projected changes could have far reaching consequences for the Settle–Carlisle closure proposal as the boundary between Eastern Region and the London Midland Region was at Snaygill, just south of Skipton. As a result, the Yorkshire TUCC – in its present form or as part of a merged TUCC for North East England – would lose all responsibility for the Settle–Carlisle line which would come entirely under the jurisdiction of the North Western TUCC.

I had argued very strongly against these proposals as I felt TUCC areas should be based on the interests and travel requirements of rail users rather than the management structure of British Rail. Whilst most people knew which county they lived in, few knew or even cared in which region of British Rail they resided. Moreover, all passenger services starting and terminating within the Skipton area which it was proposed to transfer to the North Western TUCC were managed by Eastern Region's Leeds division. In addition, the predominant traffic flows together with business and cultural interests were geared towards West Yorkshire.

Whilst there is never a right time to effect boundary changes, to have done so at a time when a closure proposal was imminent was tantamount to changing the boundary of a Parliamentary consti- tuency after the date of a General Election had been announced.

Meanwhile moves of greater importance were taking place elsewhere. The three major users groups – FOSCLA and the north western branches of Transport 2000 and the Railway Development Society – formed a joint umbrella organisation to co-ordinate the campaign against the closure under a single command structure known as the Settle–Carlisle Joint Action Committee. It was headed by Dr John Whitelegg of Lancaster University, a lucid advocate of the line with a background that included some time spent as transport and development officer for the Western Isles Council. Also from Lancaster was Peter Horton, an ebullient public transport campaigner with a flair for getting stories into the press – an undoubted asset for the high profile stance they planned. Completing the 'inner cabinet' was FOSCLA's Geoff Dickinson who would prepare evidence and brief a barrister for the Public Hearing.

Despite some initial tension, inevitable when three separate or- ganisations pool their resources, the Joint Action Committee quickly established itself as the main focal point for opposition to the closure of the Settle–Carlisle line. They were quick off the mark with a series of public meetings up and down the line backed by a stream of news releases, fact sheets and leaflets.

Individuals had a part to play, too. For example, an assistant National Park warden, Peter Davies of Brighouse, spent a week of his holiday undertaking a passenger survey on the trains on the line in October. Amongst those he interviewed was the chairman of the Yorkshire TUCC! FOSCLA were impressed with his efforts, their Newsletter No. 11 (December 1983) recording their thanks to Davies for his "extremely informative report" and asking for more volunteers to undertake similar work. However potential applicants were warned:

"Little trouble would be encountered in conducting the surveys but it would be advisable to watch out for management 'spies'. There is really nothing wrong in asking passengers questions and it is unlikely that any action would be taken to stop a survey but the best thing to do, as ever, is to use your discretion."

On 25th October, John Watson led a delegation from the Joint Action Committee to the Department of Transport in London where they were received by David Mitchell, the minister responsible for railways. As the FOSCLA newsletter recorded, in a style worthy of the BBC's diplomatic correspondent at his best, there was "a wide-ranging discussion lasting over 1½ hours" in which the case for the Settle–Carlisle line "received an encouraging response." The Minister and senior civil servants were said to be "impressed by the detailed economic arguments for the lines retention and for new investment and improved services." All good stuff which found its way into the press and added to the momentum of the campaign.

The media was playing a key role. Although most journalists, being pragmatic types, felt the line was a lost cause, they appreciated that it was providing them with plenty of good copy. It was also a natural for television, something the regional BBC and ITV newsrooms were quick to appreciate. Even the sight of a humble Class 31 diesel locomotive heading the four coach 15.37 ex Carlisle had a poignancy about it, especially if captured passing over Arten Gill Viaduct. Radio scored too; the sound of trains running on jointed track evoked mental pictures every bit as evocative as those shown on television.   Indeed, it was on Radio 2's 'You the Night and the Music' when, before turning in very late one night, I caught a piece from Michael Meech describing a journey he had recently made on the Settle–Carlisle line. His prose, delivery and the seemingly hopeless cause he was expounding almost brought tears to my eyes. Afterwards I wrote to him and he kindly let me have a copy of his text.

In a covering letter, he explained that his brief as a freelance broadcaster was a very broad one to provide radio essays. He added: "I'm perhaps more romantic than practical but it seems a shame that the line is almost certainly to close. It is too easy for purely monetary reasons to dispose of parts of our heritage when we fail to recognise that to replace them would cost even more."

October also saw the 'leak' of some fascinating operating costs for the line. Alan Whitehouse of the 'Yorkshire Post' was recipient of a single sheet of figures headed: 'Revenue Budget 1983, Service Group: Preston Local, Sector: Provincial, Profit Centre Description: Leeds–Carlisle (via Settle), Profit Centre No 1510'. Whilst hardly a title to set the world on fire, it nevertheless made very interesting reading.

Under the headline 'Doomed Line's Figures Fiddled', Whitehouse recorded that the costs of the four daily passenger trains on the line had increased between 250 per cent (train crews and diesel fuel) and 440 per cent (locomotive maintenance) in 1983 against 1982. Unable to believe his eyes, Whitehouse had dug a little deeper to discover from Shell UK Ltd that the price of diesel fuel had risen by about 12 per cent during the same period whilst the National Union of Railwaymen told him that their members had received a 4.5 per cent pay increase. British Rail declined to comment, leaving the field open to Dr John Whitelegg of the Joint Action Committee to denounce the figures as "a fiddle".

Less in the public eye but of greater significance was the progress being made by the joint steering committee of local authorities led by Cumbria County Council. Their meeting with British Rail in September had elicited a measure of co-operation. But even more important was the fact that their parent bodies had contributed over £30,000 to commission an independent report on the Settle–Carlisle line by PEIDA, the well known Edinburgh firm of planning and economic consultants. Their brief was to "advise on current cost and benefits of the line, other potential developments which could improve patronage, including tourism projects, and, in addition, to review the data which will be made available by British Rail on the condition of the Ribblehead Viaduct and other significant structures on the line."

The funding had come from the three county councils involved – Cumbria, Lancashire and West Yorkshire – plus numerous district councils including Leeds, Bradford, Calderdale, Craven, Pendle, Richmondshire, Eden and Carlisle. Settle town Council had put up £100 whilst other contributions had come from the Countryside Commission, the English Tourist Board, the Yorkshire Dales National Park and, to everyone's surprise, British Rail who provided £2,000. They felt it would be money well spent as the report would be bound to endorse the case for closure.

There was another move on the part of British Rail. They appointed a 'project manager' with the specific responsibility of closing the line. The apparently thankless task went to Ron Cotton, the divisional passenger manager at Liverpool. I didn't know him although I had heard of him by reputation. A marketing man, he had made a name for himself as innovator of the Saver fare. It seemed an odd posting, even though his remit allowed him to promote the line whilst closing it.

The appointment did not go unnoticed. Writing in 'Transport Review' (21st October 1983), Ian Williams observed:

"It's not often I have a soft spot for railway management. Even the good ones often seem forced into the mould of choppers and parers, running down the system on orders from above.

One of the outstanding exceptions to this rule was the former divisional passenger manager in Liverpool, Ron Cotton. I am glad he wasn't on the industrial relations side because he was a hard man to deal with, having sufficient self-confidence to push imaginative schemes but perhaps a trifle too much for an IR position.

His great virtue was that he believed in selling railways to the passengers rather than the road lobby, and this may have made him an object of 'suspicion' to a Board that gives £50,000 to their loony rivals to research turning rail into roads."

After chronicling Cotton's pioneering of the Saver ticket, which "filled the seats of the trains to overflowing" and became national policy "with the credit being taken by the very Board that had earlier tried to abort the scheme", Williams continued:

"Why am I rambling on like this about a BR manager who is not dead nor even retired? Because I heard on the grapevine, and saw confirmed in the press last week, that he has been moved to a new job. With a record like that, with proven skills in attracting traffic to the railway, it's obviously promotion to a higher position, isn't it?

Is it hell! This is British Rail. He has been deported to a new position as project manager for the closure of the Carlisle–Settle railway.

He could have the thing making a profit in a short time if he were given the job of developing it. But this is BR, the Board of which I would not entrust with my son's Hornby Dublo set."

I met Ron Cotton one afternoon in November for an informal chat over a coffee at the Queens Hotel, Leeds. A tall, big man with a broad jaw, he exuded a natural air of authority. Smartly turned out in a navy pin-stripe, he could easily have been mistaken for a merchant banker. I felt he would make a good impression with some of my lady members when it came to the Public Hearing. Our conversation was little more than mutual shadow boxing. However, I got the feeling that he looked upon his new job as, if not a piece of cake, then something that would not unduly tax him. Ensconced within the protective barrier of British Rail's management structure, I doubted if he was fully aware of the level of opposition he faced or, indeed, the complexities of the closure procedure.

Publication of the Section 54 advance warning notice on 17th

November was significant in two respects. First, 'The Times' (in which, along with 'The Daily Telegraph', the notice was published), carried a background feature facing the leader page by Alan Whitehouse of the 'Yorkshire Post'. He revealed to a geographically wider public that, behind the formal announcement of the proposal to close the Settle–Carlisle line, there was "an extraordinary story of leaked documents, contradictory letters of reassurance to MPs and others, and a secret closure plan which had been partly implemented even before its existence became known".

Stating that the arguments for closure fell into two categories, the condition of the Ribblehead Viaduct and whether the line was needed at all, on the former he wrote:

"BR says the viaduct is falling down and will become unsafe to use after 1986. A replacement, it says would cost between £4.5 million and £6 million. This claim is challenged by correspondents to the civil engineering press. The latest, Mr C L Wallis, writing in 'New Civil Engineer', described BR's statements on the viaduct as a red herring. All that is needed, he says, is to fill the hollow piers with concrete, add cross-bracing where necessary, treat external cracks with resin grout and lay a new waterproof decking on the top."

Whitehouse claimed that British Rail's estimate that Ribblehead Viaduct would be unsafe to use after 1986 fitted in "curiously well" with the closure timetable outlined in the 'Case Study' report:

"This predicts closure by the end of 1984, and seems at present to be running about 12 months behind schedule. It firmly links the condition of the viaduct to the wider issue of whether the line is really needed, despite BR's public assurances that the two matters were being considered separately."

After summarising assurances during late 1981 and 1982 by the then British Railways Board chairman, Sir Peter Parker, that there were no plans to close the line, Whitehouse asserted that at the time the assurances were made "a closure plan had been put together, and it has since been put into effect in all but the very last stage: the total withdrawal of passenger trains which today's announcement now proposes."

Sir Peter declined to comment on the matter. His secretary told Whitehouse that it was "a question of etiquette as he would not want to be seen commenting over the head of the present chairman." British Rail, too, were not prepared to comment, except to Whitehouse's reference to the leaked 'Revenue Budget' figures which had been dismissed by the Joint Action Committee's Dr Whitelegg as 'a fiddle'. This provoked the London Midland Region's new general manager Malcolm Southgate sufficiently to subsequently put pen to paper in a letter to 'The Times' (24th November).

"The figures quoted by Mr Whitehouse might prove more leaky than leaked. They are in fact the wrong ones to study when considering the criteria for closure of the line. They are figures produced for management information only and are not relevant, nor have they been used, to reach any decision about this line."

Not, I felt, an altogether convincing reply in that there was no explanation of such a wide disparity in the line's operating budget between 1982 and 1983.

The other significant occurrence on 17th November was a mishap on the main line near Garstang which caused all West Coast Main Line trains to be diverted over the Settle–Carlisle line from 3.00 a.m. until after midday. I doubted if even British Rail had budgeted for this!

Throughout the build-up to publication of the Section 56 notice – the 'they're off' so far as objections to the Settle–Carlisle closure proposal was concerned – the Yorkshire TUCC had been beset with other problems, not least that of British Rail's second attempt to close the Huddersfield–Sheffield line. When Norman Archer, our former secretary, retired in October 1982, he had offered to look in and lend a hand should we become overwhelmed with closures. Therefore, with Huddersfield–Denby Dale already on our plate and Settle–Carlisle in the offing, I had gladly accepted his offer.

He also proved invaluable in assisting the quest for a successor to our secretary who had returned to British Rail. This time we had a dozen or so applicants so there was no repeat of the situation where there had been a short list of one. In the event we whittled the field down and Norman, who was enjoying his return to the office, prepared a short written test for the two finalists. Therefore I was shattered to receive a telephone call just after 10.00 p.m. on Friday 4th November informing me he had collapsed at his bridge club in Scarborough earlier that evening and died shortly afterwards. I could hardly believe it for I had lunched with him in York a couple of days before and he had been in good form.

However, I have no doubt Norman would have approved of our new secretary, John Moorhouse. He had impressed at the first interview and sailed through Norman's test paper. He had another factor going for him as far as I was concerned; he was a Yorkshireman from Skipton, exiled in the Western Region as Area Passenger and Parcels Manager at Westbury. He wished to return north with his wife and young family. At 35 he had the flexibility to cast aside the mantle of British Rail's management mould, which was essential if he were to become an effective consumer representative, whilst he had the stamina to meet our heavy work load. A tall, slim chap with an engaging smile, he was an accomplished fell walker and something of a rail enthusiast or 'gricer' to boot. Just what we needed.

One of the points I had raised when I had met Ron Cotton, the project manager for Settle–Carlisle, was that the Section 56 notice should be published in the Bradford 'Telegraph and Argus' and a couple of national dailies – I had in mind 'The Guardian' and 'The Daily Telegraph' – in addition to the 'Yorkshire Post', the 'Carlisle Evening News' and two weeklies, the 'Craven Herald and Pioneer' and the 'Cumberland and Westmorland Herald'. He agreed to the 'Telegraph and Argus'. Indeed, he could hardly do otherwise as it was Settle's evening paper. However, the nationals were out as it was "a long established practice that Section 56 notices were only published in newspapers local to the line in question." A pity but I could not really argue with that.

So it was just a case of waiting to see what impact the Section 56 notice – backed by a reputed 800 posters on display at stations – would have. It was scheduled for publication in the 'Yorkshire Post' and the Bradford and Carlisle evening papers on Tuesday 13th December and in the local papers at the end of the week.

The battle was about to begin.

8

OBJECTIONS

"I wish to register my protest against the proposed closure of the Settle–Carlisle line as I consider British Rail have not seriously sought to publicise the line or increase its revenue. I have travelled on the line many times in recent years and have always marvelled at the beautiful scenery. It could so easily be a vital transport link if the redundant stations were re-opened. The opportunity to increase tourism, and thereby employment, must not be lost."

One of 1,536 objections.

I don't have my newspapers delivered, preferring to walk to the newsagent to collect them. It's a legacy from when we had a dog. If nothing else it ensures I get 10 minutes exercise each day. So it was on Tuesday 13th December 1983. As I walked back home, I flipped over the pages of the 'Yorkshire Post' seeking the Section 56 notice. But in the dim street lighting I couldn't find it. When I got back inside I had a closer look under the bright kitchen light. It wasn't there!

This was most odd. Surely British Rail had not slipped up on the publication date. Was the paper at fault? A quick call to the advertising department confirmed it was not. There was no booking from British Rail. The same was true at the Bradford 'Telegraph and Argus'. Could British Rail have had second thoughts and backed down at the last minute? I doubted it. Our secretary, John Moorhouse, got on to Ron Cotton, the project manager for the Settle–Carlisle line, who provided no explanations but said the notices would now be published in Cumbria on Thursday 15th December and in Yorkshire the following day. Obviously, someone had slipped up. What a shambles!

Nor was this the only reason for red faces at British Rail. Once again – as on the day of publication of the Section 54 advance warning notice – the appearance of the Section 56 notice in Cumbria coincided with another blockage on the West Coast Main Line. As before, trains were diverted over the Settle–Carlisle line. It was beginning to become a habit. A British Rail spokesman told the 'Yorkshire Evening Post' that so long as the line was there it would be used when it was required. He added: "Life is full of surprises."

However, there was no surprise at the excellent turnout for the specially chartered 'Cumbrian Mountain Express' on Saturday 17th December to open the campaign against closure. MPs and councillors of all parties, representing an electorate of several million in Yorkshire, Lancashire and Cumbria, joined over 350 enthusiasts on the steam-hauled train headed by former LMS Pacific No. 46229 'DUCHESS OF HAMILTON'.

The train made a special stop at Garsdale. Here, in the December mist, a news conference was held to launch the independent study by PEIDA into the future of the line and to publicise the opposition of the local authorities to its closure. The recently elected Penrith and Borders Conservative MP, David Maclean, was jubilant at the progress already made and felt there was a good chance of saving the line.

West Yorkshire's head of public transport, John Carr, questioned British Rail's estimate of £6m for restoring Ribblehead Viaduct; whilst the chairman of West Yorkshire's transport committee, County Councillor Wayne Jenkins, added with biting candour: "We don't like British Rail's methods and policies and we don't accept British Rail's arguments." The odd man out was Ron Cotton. He put on a brave face and smiled, saying that the reason for closure was one of simple economics. "It's purely a business decision," he added.

By the following Monday letters of objection had begun to arrive at our York office. The first was from John Watson. Another early objector was Colin Speakman. The procedure we adopted was this: John Moorhouse read all the letters to make sure they were valid objections. I read most of them too. It enabled me to get the 'feel' of users views on the closure proposal. Each letter of objection was given a number and acknowledged. With our letter of acknowledgement went a copy of British Rail's 'Heads of Information' which set out the reasons for the proposed closure and provided details of the alternative services, in this case a re-routed Leeds–Carlisle service via Carnforth plus a hotch–potch of buses. We distanced ourselves from this document which, despite its title, was sadly lacking in information and stressed that it had been "prepared and compiled by British Rail and gives details of the proposal as they interpret them."

The points of objection raised in each letter – some of them general, like those referring to the scenic attractions of the line, others more personal, as in the case of the child who travelled by train from Settle for music lessons as her family had no car – were summarised by John under a wide range of headings. When complete, they would be sent to British Rail and any other interested party, in this case Ribble Motor Services, for their comments. When these were received they would be incorporated in the final 'Summary of Written Objections' which would be sent to objectors prior to the Public Hearing.

Any remaining doubts regarding British Rail's integrity in its proposal to close the Settle–Carlisle line were shattered by an Alan Whitehouse 'exclusive' in the 'Yorkshire Post' of 12th January 1984. Headed: 'BR had secret plan to thwart closure critics', Whitehouse had unearthed a confidential document submitted to a meeting of the Railway Executive Group two years earlier in January 1982 by the then general manager of the London Midland Region, Mr J J O'Brien.

Although the document only ran to four pages, it was largely a precis of the bulky 'Case Study' of August 1981. This latest of a line of leaked papers stated that: "There is general agreement that closure of the line must be progressed." Then, in one telling sentence, O'Brien let the cat out of the bag:

"The view of the London Midland Region is that the proposal should remain confidential until through passenger services have been diverted in May 1982, as otherwise this diversion could be barred until the completion of statutory procedures."

As I read this over breakfast, it simply underlined and vindicated my lack of faith in the manner British Rail had handled the Settle–Carlisle issue to date. So much for Jim O'Brien's assurance to me in March 1982 that no decision had been taken to close the line and that the re-routing of the through Nottingham–Glasgow services would in no way prejudice its future. Then, quite apart from the assurances given to me, what of those given to a host of MPs? And what, too, of the letter dated 3rd June 1982 from the then chairman of the British Railways Board, Sir Peter Parker, who assured Mrs Barbara Castle MEP that there were no plans to close the line? It all struck me as being very shabby indeed.

The 'Yorkshire Post' piece caused quite a furore, not least

amongst objectors. The chairman of the Joint Action committee, Dr John Whitelegg, retorted: "It is disgraceful that British Rail have plotted so coldly and calculatedly to end the line." A few days later I received a letter from Colne solicitors Farnworth and Watson who had been retained by the Joint Action Committee. Referring to the 'Yorkshire Post' item, it pointed out the recommendation that the decision to close the line be kept secret until after the re-routing of the Nottingham–Glasgow service did not equate with the O'Brien assurance that the re-routing would not prejudice the future of the Settle–Carlisle line. It continued:

"We are not suggesting for one moment that British Rail have deliberately tried to circumvent the statutory closure procedure, but in view of the persistent rumours about 'closure by stealth', we feel it is a point which must be cleared up at the earliest opportunity so that some element of credibility and fairness might attach to these proceedings."

Throughout the objection period of seven weeks, the Joint Action Committee, FOSCLA and many individual users managed to keep the line in the public eye. The media responded, too. A BBC North television programme 'The Fight for the Settle–Carlisle', which had been shown locally the previous autumn, was networked. From the 'other side' actress Thelma Barlow – Mavis Riley in Granada's 'Coronation Street' – and FOSCLA president Russell Harty laid across the track at Settle in what the Bradford 'Telegraph & Argus' described as a "melodramatic silent protest against British Rail closure plans". Needless to say, they both emphasised that lying across railway tracks was not to be recommended. "It was," said Mr Harty, "a light hearted gesture with a serious motive and not something to be imitated."

More effective, I felt, was the spate of stories and letters which appeared in the regional and local press stressing the importance of users lodging their objections with the TUCCs. This was backed by the initiative of Settle Town Council which delivered a leaflet to every household explaining how objections should be made. Nor was media interest confined to the north. On 31st January, 'The Guardian' carried a letter from Mark Sullivan, the Leamington Spa based transport consultant, who argued that the Settle–Carlisle line was a 'Pennine Way' for the nation as a whole. He continued:

"If it closes few will be able to see the High Pennines, England's most magnificent landscape, especially in winter when it is at its finest and yet most inaccessible.

Of course, the present minimal train service is no lure. It could easily be doubled to four trains each way by efficient working and some stations now closed except to 'Dales Rail' charters properly opened. But alongside this the national need is surely a through London–Edinburgh tourist train via Leeds, Settle and Carlisle running in daylight all year. It would be easy to divert one InterCity 125 for this; with good marketing it could be very popular.

This would be to learn, as ever, from the French. In France one Paris–Marseille train, the 'Cevenol', eschews the new high-speed Paris–Lyon route and crosses the Massif Central on the Cevennes line, giving locals a train link with Paris and tourists a slow but superb through trip. If like France we had a Ministry of Tourism we would not be trying to close the Settle–Carlisle."

How very true!

Mark Sullivan's letter was taken up by the 'Telegraph & Argus' and formed the basis of an editorial which added:

"On this line we need a mix of fast trains for commuters and businessmen, and a more leisurely service for sight-seers. It does not take a marketing genius to make the line pay: just a commitment to its future development."

However, the immediate commitment was to rustle up as many objections as possible for it was, in many respects, a numbers game. They had been arriving at the TUCCs since Christmas at a steady but by no means spectacular rate. Although I had been asked on a number of occasions how many objections I thought there would be, my response had always been very guarded. But I had no doubt in my own mind that at least 3,000 were required to form a firm foundation for the Public Hearings that were to follow.

I had based this figure on the premise that the 1960s proposal to close the Hull–Scarborough line had generated well over 3,000 objections. More recently, the 1981 attempt to sever the Huddersfield–Sheffield link had led to 547 objections. Although direct comparisons between these earlier proposals and Settle–Carlisle were not wholly valid, as the former related to local services with a strong commuter content, neither had generated anything like the same level of regional, let alone national interest as the proposal to close 'England's greatest historical scenic route.'

Yet, notwithstanding the last minute influx when we were almost deluged with objections, the final number was disappointing. The overall total was 2,369, of which we received 1,536 (65 per cent) and our North Western colleagues 833. Of the 1,536 lodged with us, 12 were from MPs, 18 from local authorities and a further 102 from a wide variety of organisations of one kind and another, leaving 1,404 from individual users. I felt that, in educational terms, it represented a case of 'could have done better!'

However, any disappointment at the number of objections was more than offset by their quality. They were excellent. And what a wide variety of reading they provided, too. They ranged from the letter submitted by the Alfreton No. 1 Branch of the Old Age Pensioners Association to that sent by two young children who drew our attention to the herons, rabbits and hares one could see from the train. Many letters came from whole families. Others were from single people, like the lady from London who visited Settle each year and who wrote that her holiday would be incomplete without her "annual trip on the line." Aficionados of Dales Rail were particularly well represented.

There were long letters and short letters, typed letters, beautifully scripted letters and the occasional scrawled letter. Many indicated the role the line played in their lives, either for essential visits or recreational excursions. A 36 page screed full of intricate detail from a 'gricer' in Leicester was balanced by a single page plea from a chap in San Angelo, Texas, who wrote: "Surely you must realise that those of us who summer in England depend upon this line for transportation. What in the world will we do without it?". I could almost hear the 'JR' accent!

The Brownies of Settle rallied splendidly to the cause, sending 30 or so individual letters, many of them illustrated by sketches of trains – most of them passing over Ribblehead Viaduct. Even more poignant was the letter from Settle Parochical Church Council which drew attention to the death, through accident, of many of the workers who constructed the line, whilst a headstone in the churchyard also bore silent witness. It continued:

"We think we owe it to these people of the past, as well as to many living now, to add our voice to the widely-expressed concern of the proposed closure of the Settle–Carlisle line. This council, and our congregation as a whole, contains a cross section of people of varying ages and needs who would be adversely affected by the closure."

The most recurring theme in the letters of objection was that the Settle–Carlisle was no ordinary railway. It was – to quote British Rail, and many did – the "most spectacular main line in England built to take its trains over the hills at speed." Others had turned to one of the line's greatest devotees and quoted Eric Treacy, the former Bishop of Wakefield, who had equated the Settle–Carlisle line with York Minster and Hadrian's Wall as one of the three man made wonders of northern England.

Bishop Treacy had died in 1978 at Appleby Station where a commemorative plaque refers to him as 'Railway Photographer – Pastor to Railwaymen – Lover of Life and Railways'. How sad that a lack of love for railways appeared prevalent in the upper echelons of British Rail. How else does one explain their proposal to close the line in the first place? I once had the good fortune to meet Bishop Treacy on the 'Bradford Executive'. It was a heart warming experience and a marked contrast to the complacent as-tringency I had encountered in my meetings with British Railways Board chairman Sir Robert Reid.

Once the objection period was out of the way it did not mean that we could sit back and relax, certainly not so far as the Yorkshire TUCC were concerned. If I had been disappointed in the number of objections, the 1,536 we had received would keep us occupied for some time. Fortunately, Rene Phillippo volunteered to return from retirement to help us out with our closure proposals. This was just as well for, concurrent with Settle–Carlisle, we had another big one in Goole–Gilberdyke.

Here British Rail were faced, surprise, surprise, with repair costs stated to be £2 million for the Goole swing bridge over the River Ouse and proposed to re-route all services between Doncaster and Hull via Selby. They were presenting it as being something little short of the best thing to happen since sliced bread. There was even a glossy leaflet worthy of Smith Square or Walworth Road at their best. Headed 'Goole Bridge – From Dilemma to Decision', it proclaimed "When you weigh up the facts, it makes sense – the bridge has to go." It was pure Saatchi and Saatchi!

In fact, it was probably counter-productive and contributed to the grand total of 2,485 objections generated by the Goole–Gilber-dyke closure proposal. This topped the Settle–Carlisle total by 116 and, at first sight, made the Settle–Carlisle number all the more disappointing. But there were two major factors behind the un-doubted success of the Goole–Gilberdyke total. The first was that of geography. Whereas the Settle–Carlisle proposal covered 72 miles of railway, or 112 miles if you covered the area affected between Leeds and Carlisle; Goole–Gilberdyke was a mere 7 miles.

Moreover, with a population of about 20,000, Goole was far

larger than Settle (2,501) and Appleby (2,344) put together. This enabled the Goole and District Railway Action Group to concentrate its campaign on Goole which generated 70 per cent of the objections. By comparison, objections from places on the line between and including Leeds/Bradford and Carlisle only accounted for 47 per cent of objections received by the Yorkshire TUCC.

Second was the effectiveness of the campaign itself. Headed by Roddy Jardine, a former railwayman who was fully conversant with the foibles of British Rail management and therefore able to outwit them, and Bob Lewis, a sales executive who was active in the Liberal party and fully conversant with community politics; together they made a formidable team. Moreover, they were acutely aware and somewhat peeved that their closure proposal did not attract the same media attention as that for Settle–Carlisle. This added to their competitive and combative spirit.

However, the thing that really triggered it off for them was the pro-forma 'Passenger Survey' they devised which was widely distributed in the town and nearby villages. All an objector had to do was to complete the form by writing his or her name and address and ticking a number of boxes. These provided a mine of information which was easier to analyse than many letters of objection as it was possible to tell at a glance where the objectors travelled between; whether they took a bike, pram or wheelchair; and if they would use the replacement bus, switch to private transport or not travel at all.

At the bottom of the form there was a bold statement: 'I agree to this form being submitted to the Yorkshire TUCC as my objection to the proposed closure.' Then all that was needed was a signature and the date. The action committee even arranged collection and made bulk deliveries to our office in York.

Whilst I had some reservations about this type of objection as it lacked much of the individuality that came out so strongly in many letters we received, there was no doubt that the form was much easier to process. It also changed lodging an objection from a chore to something that could easily be accomplished in five minutes. Indeed, it could be said that the Goole and District Railway Action Committee had taken the procedure of lodging objections into the 1980s.

It was John Watson who first described the Settle–Carlisle line as being a very political railway. Certainly, there was no shortage of political interest following the objection period. Mike Thomas, a former Newcastle MP, made a brief fact finding trip on the line on behalf of the SDP on 10th February. He was followed a couple of weeks later by a rather more heavyweight team headed by the deputy leader of the Labour Party, Roy Hattersley, and including Norman Willis of the TUC and Jimmy Knapp, general secretary of the National Union of Railwaymen who had hired a special train.

The 'Hattersley Special' – a 2-car DMU – almost hit the buffers before it started. Initially British Rail refused to charter the train to the NUR, which prompted Labour transport spokesman Peter Snape, who also made the trip, to retort that this represented a "scandalous denial of the right to protest." In the event, British Rail had second thoughts – as well they should as the charter netted them £1,300 – and the journey proceeded smoothly to Carlisle, picking up Dr John Whitelegg and Peter Horton of the Joint Action Committee and others opposed to closure en-route. There was even a British Rail welcoming party to meet the train at Carlisle. However, the greeting proved perfunctory and was only to prevent Mr Hattersley and his party from holding a news conference on railway property!

Another active group of objectors, The Ramblers Association, threw their weight into the campaign. Their national secretary Alan Mattingley told a regional conference at Ilkley that the line offered "one of the most exciting scenic railway journeys in the country" and could be developed into a major tourist attraction with the support of the Tourist Boards, county and district councils, and the National Parks authority. "Substantial Government support – whether channelled through British Rail or otherwise – is also essential," he added.

But back to the politicians, this time in Parliament. On 12th March, David Maclean initiated a debate on the Settle–Carlisle line. He opened by quoting from British Rail's latest leaflet which described it as 'England's Greatest Historical Scenic Route' and 'the most spectacular main line in England.' Nor was this the extent of Mr Maclean's quotations for, backed by some diligent research by Kirkby Stephen photographer Peter Walton, the House of Commons was provided with chapter and verse from sources as varied as 'The Times' and 'Steam World'. He also drew extensively from the RDS pamphlet in emphasising the importance of the line for freight traffic.

Mr Maclean was particularly concerned that the overwhelming mass of evidence in favour of the line would not be presented at the Public Hearings as the TUCCs might be prepared only to hear evidence of hardship. This was very much the interpretation of the Act *a la* the North Western TUCC, so we would have to wait and see.

In a most perceptive contribution, John Watson questioned whether British Rail had followed the principle, spirit and practice of the closure procedure as set out in the Act. He suggested that four items led one to conclude they had not. First was the decision to re-route the Nottingham–Glasgow service which removed a large proportion of the passenger traffic which would have been a solid reason for the lines retention. Second was the paper presented to the Railway Executive Group on 6th January 1982, and thirdly, no real attempt had been made to promote the line's tourist traffic.

His fourth point, which he felt was "perhaps the most serious of all", was that he understood the eagerly awaited PEIDA report was likely to show that the line had been run down to such an extent that repairs to the value of £10 million would be required to ensure its survival in any form. If correct, this could mean that British Rail had effectively ensured that no one would be able to run a service over the line at any time in the future.

Considering the four factors together, John Watson concluded that the decision taken in August 1983 to propose closure of the line had been a mere formality; the consequence of earlier decisions had by then removed the economic value of the line so that arguments for its retention could be shown to be specious; that the true decision upon closure had been taken years earlier; and that the spirit and wishes of Parliament, so clearly reflected in the 1962 Act, had been frustrated accordingly.

I felt this to be the most damning indictment of British Rail yet. Nor was that all, for John then put to his fellow Parliamentarians a most subtle suggestion. He proposed that the TUCCs, in addition to reporting on hardship as defined in Section 56(9) of the Act, should have their terms of reference widened by the Minister in accordance with Section 56(10) under which he 'may require an Area Committee to make a further report'. Concluding his speech, he said that only by such a procedure could the charges of deliberate neglect, economic blackmail and closure by stealth be substantiated or repudiated for ever.

Michael Meadowcroft (Liberal, Leeds West) drew MPs attention to a report by Alan Whitehouse which had appeared in the 'Yorkshire Post' three days earlier. This stated British Rail were to stop using the Settle–Carlisle line for diversions other than in emergencies. It would mean passengers, whose trains were affected by weekend engineering work, would find themselves transferring to buses and then back to trains again. A British Rail spokesman had told Whitehouse that the decision had been taken to strengthen the case for closure of the line. Mr Meadowcroft claimed British Rail had a Philistine-like attitude towards the line and were guilty of great cynicism when what was needed was imagination and flair.

The prospect of West Coast Main Line passengers being bussed was too much for Sir Hector Monro (Conservative, Dumfries) who retorted that it would lead to "ruddy chaos!" Useful contributions from Mrs Elizabeth Peacock (Conservative, Batley and Spen), who spoke of the line's history and its place in the national heritage, and Ron Lewis (Labour, Carlisle) added to the substance of the debate. Peter Snape commended John Watson for raising important legal issues and dismissed the Cumbrian Coast line as an inadequate alternative for diverted services.

Apart from a brief outburst of oral fisticuffs between Mr Snape and the Under Secretary of State for Transport, David Mitchell, the debate maintained the all-party unanimity on the Settle–Carlisle line which had been one of the most rewarding features of the campaign since its inception. An understandably cautious Mr Mitchell, aware of his quasi-judicial position, replied that questions regarding the run down of the line, the re-routing of the Nottingham–Glasgow service and the inadequate promotion of tourist traffic were for British Rail rather than the Government.

Nevertheless, Mr Mitchell promised to consider John Watson's point regarding Section 56(10) of the Act and gave a firm assurance that the Secretary of State for Transport and himself would take all the relevant considerations into account in arriving at its decision, including the "invaluable contributions" made in the debate. Mind you, he could hardly have responded in any other way. My only regret was that the people who had the answers, British Railways Board chairman Sir Robert Reid and the joint managing director (railways) Mr J J O'Brien, got off scot-free.

Elsewhere, the Settle–Carlisle Joint Action Committee maintained the pressure. The objection period had been just one phase, albeit an important one, in a journey which would take them to the Public Hearings and beyond. Moreover, to the outside world if not to me, the figure of 2,369 objections – which seemed to have been rounded up to 2,500 in media reports – was regarded as a very respectable total indeed.

At the FOSCLA annual general meeting, David Burton – chairman since its inception – stood down in favour of Brian Sutcliffe, an executive with the GPO in Leeds. I felt this would lead to a more sophisticated approach, something that might provide an easier ride when it came to the Public Hearings. However, this did not detract from the splendid contribution David Burton had made to the campaign since the very beginning when it had been no more than two men and a dog – David, Graham Nuttall, and Graham's dog Ruswarp.

David Burton remained on the committee as vice-chairman and maintained control of the 'Sales Aid Campaign': a comprehensive selection of promotional products including ties, T-shirts, sweat shirts, pens, badges, postcards and a wide selection of books. The sales stall had become an established feature of FOSCLA and Joint Action Committee meetings whilst David and his loyal band of helpers frequently 'worked the train' en-route to such gatherings.

One of the most interesting items on the sales list was a replica of a Ford Model T parcels van in LMS livery in the Matchbox 'Models of Yesteryear' series. It was labelled 'Settle–Carlisle' and sold at £8 in a numbered limited edition of 1,000. I bought a couple and was recently told they had become collectors items.

9

BATTLE OF THE SMALL PRINT

"... any user of any service affected and any body representing such users may within the period specified in the notice lodge with the appropriate Area Committee an objection..."

Extract from Section 56(8) of the
Transport Act 1962.

Whilst the Joint Action Committee and its allies were busy seeking objections during the first five weeks of 1984, behind the scenes a battle of words had started between the Yorkshire TUCC and British Rail on a number of aspects of the Settle–Carlisle closure proposal. Although a relatively low key affair, it continued well after the final date for objections on 4th February and it wasn't until April that the outcome became known.

The special charter of the 'Cumbrian Mountain Express' the week before Christmas had been well covered by press, radio and television in the region. However, any elation as a result of this had been quickly overtaken by the more immediate priorities of the festive season itself. Either by accident or, as I suspected, design, the fact that British Rail had timed the statutory closure procedure to coincide with Christmas and the New Year effectively lopped off two of the seven weeks allowed for lodging objections.

When I had met London Midland Region officials at Euston the previous August, I had pressed them to avoid the Christmas and New Year period as I had little doubt that, if they didn't, someone would call 'foul'. I had also suggested that closure notices should be published in a couple of national newspapers – preferably the 'Daily Telegraph' and 'The Guardian'. Unfortunately my requests had fallen on deaf ears.

Therefore, I was not surprised to receive a copy of a letter from Richard Watts of the Railway Development Society to British Rail seeking an extension of the objection period due to the intrusion of the Christmas and New Year holiday and asking that the closure notice be published in national newspapers. Unfortunately the Transport Act 1962 makes no allowance for these situations, so I was not surprised British Rail turned down his request. However, I was pleased to note that in his reply to Mr Watts, Ron Cotton asked after his health and wished him a happy New Year. This was the most customer friendly sentiment to come from British Rail for some time.

British Rail's 'Heads of Information' document, which set out their case for closure, was a most paltry affair. I had never come across one so lacking in detail. It stated the line was "expensive to operate and maintain" and required "heavy expenditure on essential renewals to Ribblehead Viaduct and four other bridges." In addition "essential track renewals" were also required to "maintain the line to passenger standards." There were no financial details of the estimated savings that closure would bring.

Even worse was the paucity of data regarding train loadings – the number of people using the trains. It was standard practice to provide two sets of figures; one for a week in the summer, the other for a week in the winter. In this instance, although there were figures for two years, they were both incomplete. Those for 1982 only covered four out of six days during the week in August (there was no Sunday service) and three in November. The more recent figures for 1983 were even worse with three days for August and two for November. Even these were incomplete as there were no August '83 figures for the 16.00 Leeds–Carlisle train.

Even so, where it was possible to make a direct comparison, the figures suggested that 1983 train loadings were well up on the previous year – August by a massive 211 per cent and November by 63 per cent. The document coyly explained this by stating that "since media attention has been given to the possible closure of the route there has been an increase in patronage from those passengers wishing to have a nostalgic trip over the line," adding that the 1982 figures provided a "clearer indication of the basic loadings in normal conditions." As for Dales Rail trains and steam specials, they were dismissed as being "chartered by third parties but not forming part of British Rail's normal advertised passenger service."

As soon as Christmas and the New Year were out of the way, John Moorhouse wrote to Ron Cotton expressing our concern at the lack of detail in the 'Heads of Information' and outlined its numerous shortcomings. John also challenged the assertion on Dales Rail, pointing out that in 1983 these trains ran to a timetable advertised in a leaflet bearing British Rail's logo. In doing so he anticipated the response from objectors for it wasn't long before we started receiving complaints about the 'Heads of Information' itself.

Some, like FOSCLA's Philippa Simpson, lambasted British Rail for making no reference to the former use of the line by InterCity's Nottingham–Glasgow service prior to its re-routing in 1982 "much to the annoyance of many passengers." On the reference to media exposure, she astutely observed that it showed what better marketing of the line could achieve.

The Joint Action Committee's solicitors, Farnworth and Watson were also unhappy about the 'Heads of Information' which their clients felt to be of no value since the data provided was "sketchy and incomplete." They also felt their clients were entitled to know what evidence they needed to answer the points made, but felt unable to advise them properly "in the absence of any hard facts." After explaining that the law required government departments and statutory authorities like the TUCCs involved in judicial or quasi-judicial hearings to comply with the principles of natural justice, Farnworth and Watson asked us to put their points to British Rail and query if a revised 'Heads of Information' would be provided. This we did.

However, whilst all this was going on, John Moorhouse discovered something which, in legal terms, was of far greater significance. Amongst the hundreds of objections we had received, a very small number – no more than three or four – were from users who joined the 07.39 Settle–Leeds train at Long Preston, Hellifield or Gargrave. These stations were south of Settle Junction and therefore were not covered by the closure proposal as they would continue to be served by Leeds–Morecambe trains. John asked if I thought they were valid objectors.

I replied that I felt they were not valid as British Rail didn't propose to close those stations. As I understood it, one had to use the section of line proposed for closure – that is to say between Settle Junction and Carlisle Petterill Bridge Junction – to be a valid objector. At least, that was what I had been told and it had been the rule of thumb we had used in previous closure proposals.

John disagreed. He said that Section 56(8) of the Transport Act 1962 stated that "any user of any service affected" could lodge an objection. Therefore, those who joined the 07.39 Settle–Leeds train at Long Preston, Hellifield and Gargrave would undoubtedly be affected by the proposal to close the Settle–Carlisle line as this train would no longer serve those stations.

He was right and I was wrong. For what he'd discovered – and what everyone else involved in railway closure proposals for over twenty years, myself included, had overlooked – was that whilst British Rail's Section 56 closure notice stated that "any users of the rail service it is proposed to discontinue" could lodge an objection; the Act itself was more widely embracing when it stated "any user of any service affected" could lodge an objection. And there was no doubt at all that users of the 07.39 Settle–Leeds train were affected.

Moreover, this kind of situation was by no means unique to the Settle–Carlisle closure proposal. It was just as applicable to the others we had 'on the book'. For example, in the case of Goole–Gilberdyke, passengers who joined the 'Hull Executive' at Goole to travel to London were 'affected' by the proposal for, although Goole would retain a station it would lose its through service to King's Cross and passengers would have to change at Doncaster. This could undoubtedly cause inconvenience and, indeed, hardship for disabled travellers.

There was no doubt that John had unearthed a hot potato! But what should we do. First, I rang a solicitor I knew who was conversant with the law regarding railway legislation. I explained the situation and asked what he thought. He said he would ring me back. It only took him a couple of hours to arrive at an opinion. He said it was the wording of the Act rather than British Rail's interpretation of it which was paramount. Therefore, we should accept objections from those who joined the 07.39 at the intermediate stations between Settle and Skipton as valid.

This we did. On 23rd January, John wrote identical letters to London Midland and Eastern Regions referring to all the 'live' closure proposals we were handling at that time: Settle–Carlisle (London Midland), Huddersfield–Denby Dale, Goole–Gilberdyke, and Goose Hill–Wath Road (all Eastern). The letter simply stated:

"The wording of the notice of intent to withdraw railway passenger services states '... any users of the rail service which it is proposed to discontinue, and any body representing such users, may lodge an objection...'

The Transport Act 1962 Section 56(8) states: '... any user of any service affected and any body representing such users...' (may lodge an objection).

It has been put to us that the wording in the Section 56(7) notice is not compatible with the wording of Section 56(8) of the Act, and I would appreciate your comments on the matter and also your interpretation of the wording of Section 56(8)."

For the London Midland Region, Ron Cotton replied that the wording used in the Section 56 notice was that which was agreed between British Rail and the Ministry of Transport in 1963 and had been the accepted phraseology for the last 20 years. He added:

"It is our clear opinion that it accords with the requirements of the 1962 Transport Act in all respects."

Norman Blackstock – the Eastern Region's new chief passenger manager and the Yorkshire TUCC's new liaison officer (Ivor Warburton had moved on to become director of passenger marketing at the British Railways Board) – was a bit more explicit:

"My interpretation of the Section 56(8) of the 1962 Transport Act is that a legitimate objection requires that the objector actually uses the section of line proposed for the withdrawal of passenger train services."

Our response to Ron Cotton was to take up the matter of the 07.39 Settle–Leeds train in more detail. I put it to him that as British Rail were not proposing to withdraw all railway passenger services from Long Preston, Hellifield and Gargrave, the Section 56(7) notice implied that those who joined the train at those stations would not rank as valid objectors, whereas Section 56(8) of the Act '... any user of any service affected...' clearly indicated that they would. What had he to say to that?

Back came the reply:

"I confirm that these users have the right to complain about the proposed timetable alteration, but not under the terms of the Section 56(7) closure proposal. Any such representations would need to be submitted through the normal TUCC procedures, addressing their complaint to British Rail in the first instance, and only if not satisfied with our reply would they need to contact your Committee on the matter."

This was arrant nonsense and I politely told him so:

"You appear to assert that users who join this train at Long Preston, Hellifield and Gargrave do not enjoy the right to make representations to the committee under your closure proposal on the basis of Section 56(7) of the Transport Act 1962. However, this does not define who may or may not lodge an objection under the Act.

As your proposal to withdraw all passenger train services between Settle Junction and Carlisle (Petteril Bridge Junction) includes the withdrawal of the 07.39 Settle–Leeds train between Settle and Skipton, those who patronise this train at Long Preston,
Hellifield and Gargrave are users "of any service affected" in accordance with Section 56(8) and are therefore able to lodge an objection on the basis of the Act.

"Therefore it could be argued that your notice was in error as
it omitted to draw the attention of the public to this point."

A case of 'game set and match' to the Yorkshire TUCC, I felt;
although just what good it would do I didn't know.

Nevertheless, I thought the discrepancy between British Rail's
closure notice and the Act to be of considerable legal importance.
As it had come to light – thanks to John Moorhouse's perceptive
eye – during the period for lodging objections to two major closure
proposals (Goole–Gilberdyke was the other), I felt it only fair to
tip off the respective action groups of our discovery.

Therefore, it came as no surprise when, a week later, I received
a copy of a letter that solicitors Farnworth and Watson, advisors
to the Joint Action Committee, had written to the general manager
of the London Midland Region. It stated:

"We have studied your Notice of Proposed Closure carefully and
find to our concern that it is quite seriously defective and does not,
in our opinion, comply with the provisions of the Act.

We would draw your attention to the wording of Section 56(8)
which states that an objection in writing may be lodged by 'any
user of *any service affected*' by the proposed closure. Your Notice
states that 'any users of the rail service which it is proposed to
discontinue' may lodge an objection.

With respect, your Notice is misleading in that it gives the impression that only users of the present services which you actually
propose to withdraw may object, whereas on our interpretation of
the Act the class of potential objectors is considerably widened,
since other rail services on the Leeds/Skipton/Carnforth/Lancaster
route will be affected by the closure proposal. In our opinion the
users of those other services affected are entitled to object, but
your Notice gives the impression that they may not.

We have taken Counsel's opinion on this point, and we have
been advised that the Notice does not comply with the provisions
of the Transport Act 1962 and is therefore invalid.

We shall be pleased if you could confirm by return post that you will reissue the Notice in its correct form with due allowance for the statutory seven week objection period. If you are not willing to do this or we do not hear from you by return, we have been advised that a case exists for referring the matter to the High Court."

At the beginning of February, British Rail faced another broadside regarding the legality of their Section 56 closure notice. It came from Roger Smith, the Manchester businessman with a proven track record of opposition to railway closure proposals. In a letter to us he stated:

"Whilst British Rail have announced their proposal to discontinue all railway passenger services from Settle and Appleby, they have not done so for the other eight Dales Rail stations. These were reopened only after a considerable amount of money had been spent in restoring them to British Rail's and the Department of Transport's critical safety and operational standards. They were not reopened on any experimental or 'Speller' basis but for a regular, advertised, passenger train service which has been provided for several years now. I enclose a copy of the 1983 *public* timetable (ie, it is not a private charter service, unavailable to the public) which was clearly operated with British Rail's full cognisance and agreement. Therefore, the eight Dales Rail stations should be added to the list of stations proposed for closure and British Rail should state the alternative public transport facilities which will be available at each of them.

Because of these errors and omissions, I conclude that the present closure notice is invalid and should be withdrawn. When it has been correctly reissued, the period for objections should then recommence."

Once again this was a question for British Rail so we passed it on to Ron Cotton to add to those he had already received from the Joint Action Committee's solicitors, Farnworth and Watson, and a dozen or more other objectors who had raised points regarding the sparsity of detail provided in the 'Heads of Information' document.

Mr Cotton, no doubt acting on orders from on high ("I don't actually believe everything I write and send you," he was later to confide), responded in somewhat terse if not autocratic terms. To Roger Smith:

"Dales Rail services are not regular timetabled passenger trains, and the stations referred to by Mr Smith do not come within the scope of the closure proposal."

On Farnworth and Watson's request for a revised 'Heads of Information':

"Whilst I note reference to the Settle–Carlisle Joint Action Committee and have seen comments in the media regarding it, I am unsure of its status and constitution. The 'Heads of Information' was prepared in accordance with the agreed procedure, and in the circumstances I must decline the request to issue a revised document.

The case for the TUCCs to hear concerns hardship for the people affected by the proposal. Diversion of the Nottingham–Glasgow service has no bearing on the case under consideration, so it would not be helpful to comment on BR business decisions."

Nor, I guess, on all the assurances given by Sir Peter Parker, J J O'Brien and others which had proved so false.

To Graham Nuttall, who had complained to me that no figures were given for through travel between Leeds and Carlisle or the Dales Rail stations, and claimed it was unfair to detract peoples attention from the improved loadings for 1983 by claiming that 1982 gave a better picture, as the service was only introduced in 1982 and needed time to 'bed down', Mr Cotton replied:

"So far as Mr Nuttall's comments are concerned, only Settle and Appleby passenger figures are needed to consider the matter. Dales Rail services are not regular services in the accepted sense, and therefore are not eligible for consideration in this case."

On the final point, Mr Cotton conceded that Mr Nuttall was "entitled to his opinion" and added:

"It is a fact of life that the threat of closure has stimulated additional short term interest, though I acknowledge that more intensive marketing will create additional patronage but this would be marginal in relation to the magnitude of the financial problems on the line."

However, I feel that Graham should have the last word. He had concluded his letter to me thus:

"I remain convinced that BR stands for Blooming Rogues!"

I must confess I felt inclined to agree with him.

If there were those who considered British Rail as rogues, there were others who looked upon the Yorkshire TUCC, and its chairman in particular, as vagabonds! For whilst British Rail were beset with legal problems, we had our own 'little local difficulties' with our colleagues over the Pennines, the North Western TUCC based in Manchester. They were, of course, as much involved in the Settle–Carlisle closure proposal as we were, although they had shown precious little interest in the line during recent years.

In his excellent book 'To Kill a Railway' (Leading Edge Press and Publishing), Stan Abbott provides an absorbing study of both TUCCs with which I would not argue. Certainly at this time they were poles apart. There were, I felt, two main reasons for this. First, the North Western committee was larger and included a hard core of members who dated back to the early and mid-Sixties. Their views on closures were based on experience gained during the Beeching era. By contrast, Yorkshire members were all post-1970 appointees whose recent closure experience had been gained in a more consumer orientated climate.

The second and possibly more significant difference was that whereas it was the chairman and committee of the Yorkshire TUCC, rather than the secretariat, who decided policy and how to implement it, our North Western colleagues relied heavily on the contribution of their secretary, Frank Haywood. A seconded railwayman of many years standing, he was a benign, Pickwickian character who held great sway over both his chairman and the committee. As a consequence the North Western TUCC were sometimes seen as little more than a rubber stamp for British Rail – as in the case when they supported withdrawal of the Manchester–Euston sleeping car service only to find that, following pressure from users and MPs, British Rail decided to retain it!

The Yorkshire TUCC members – who were strongly consumer orientated – and myself had felt it prudent to distance ourselves from the views of our North Western colleagues. Our differences were of policies rather than personalities and centred largely on different interpretations of the role of TUCCs under the Act. Nevertheless, we had to get together to discuss just how we were going to handle Settle–Carlisle and a meeting was fixed for 17th February in Manchester.

When a closure proposal involves a line which runs through two (or more) TUCC areas, as in the case of Settle–Carlisle, the Act states that the committees involved should either report jointly or agree that the responsibilities be delegated to the committee which appeared to be principally concerned. In this case Yorkshire members had no doubt that they were the committee principally concerned. Patronage on the line was largely of Yorkshire based folk

travelling north and back, the only local service was the 07.39 from
Settle to Leeds and, from the beginning, it had been the Yorkshire
TUCC which had taken up the cudgels of those opposed to the
re-routing of the Nottingham–Glasgow service. Moreover, to cap
it all, we had received almost twice as many objections as the North
Western TUCC.

The day before our negotiating team – deputy chairman Barbara
Ashwin, Councillor David Heseldin, an exceptionally good
member from Selby, John Moorhouse and myself – set forth to
meet our North Western counterparts, we received firm instructions from our own committee:

"That the sub-committee appointed to meet representatives of
the North Western TUCC be mandated to reiterate that the Yorkshire committee handle the proposal in its entirety. If this is unacceptable to the North Western TUCC the Yorkshire Committee
would be willing to co-opt two or three members of the North
Western TUCC solely for the purpose of this closure proposal.
Failing this, each committee should deal with the proposal separately and each submit a report to the Minister of Transport."

Whilst the Act did not actually cover separate reports for the
same proposal, there had been a precedent during the Beeching
era in the case of the Hope Valley line when both the Yorkshire
and North Western TUCCs submitted separate reports. Anyway,
it was worth a try and something to fall back on.

I viewed the meeting with some trepidation as I felt the basic
differences in the interpretation of the Act were all but irreconcil-
able. For example, under Section 56(9) it states that the committee
"... shall consider the objection and any representation made by
the Board concerned (British Rail) and report to the Minister as
soon as possible on the hardship, if any, which they consider will
be caused by the proposed closure..." The North Western TUCC
felt they could only consider hardship, even though the word 'only'
did not appear in that section of the Act. Thus, in their letter of
acknowledgement to objectors, they stated:

"Under the terms of the Transport Act 1962 the Committee is
restricted to the consideration of hardship..."
and advised objectors to send all their other observations and points
of objection regarding the proposal direct to the Secretary of State
for Transport! As if he didn't have enough on his plate. Moreover,
there was nothing to this effect on the closure notices nor, more
importantly, in the Act.

For our part, we adopted a more flexible approach; one that had been devised many years ago by Norman Archer. After explaining to objectors that we had to report on hardship, we qualified this by adding:

"Issues other than those relating to hardship have been raised regarding this closure proposal. The statutory duty of the committee to report on hardship will not preclude us from conveying to the Minister any strength of public feeling expressed on these issues."

There was another contentious issue at stake. The North Western TUCC were very anxious that both committees reached an agreement on the interpretation of 'hardship' *before* they had considered the objections, both in writing and at the Public Hearings. I had received a letter from their chairman, Olive Clarke, to this effect. Referring again to something Norman Archer had once drafted, and in an attempt to nip this in the bud, I replied:

"As there is no strict ruling on what constitutes hardship, our policy is to consider the effects the proposal would have on all categories of passengers using the service British Rail wish to discontinue. Whether inconvenience or hardship would be caused is a matter on which each member will make their own assessments.

In recent closure proposals we've handled, a consensus view on the interpretation of hardship only emerged during the committee's deliberations after consideration of all the objections and, where applicable, the evidence submitted at the Public Hearing. To endeavour to agree an interpretation prior to this might be considered as pre-judging the issue."

It appeared they accepted our stance on this for we heard nothing further about it.

The meeting turned out to be as difficult as I had anticipated. The North Western TUCC indicated that they were prepared to handle the whole proposal themselves, which they must have known was a non-starter; just as our suggestion that we take it on as we felt – with every justification – that we were the committee principally concerned was a non-starter with them. We looked to be heading for a stalemate.

Prospects of an agreement were not helped when North Western secretary Frank Haywood explained that his committee considered its role as consumer representatives to be "quite separate" from its statutory duties in railway closure proposals. In handling closures they had to be "impartial and neutral" between objectors

and British Rail. This was antipathy so far as the Yorkshire delegation was concerned. Moreover, there was nothing in the Act to
substantiate Haywood's case. John Moorhouse remarked that
TUCCs had a responsibility to report on behalf of the objectors.
In response to North Western assertions that we were too biased
in favour of the Settle–Carlisle line to conduct a Public Hearing,
David Heseldin retorted that anyone who took the trouble to read
the Yorkshire TUCC's reports on the Humber Ferry and Huddersfield–Sheffield closure proposals would find them most objective.

The North Western committee said they were prepared to participate in joint Public Hearings. I was not keen, given the wide
gulf between the committees. Nor was it covered by our mandate
– and Yorkshire members had left me in no doubt the previous
day that they were not looking for a 'sell out' to the North Western
TUCC. It was the War of the Roses all over again!

The stalemate was broken by Councillor Harold Taylor of Ac-
crington, who had been taking a somewhat detached stance from
his North Western colleagues. He suggested that each committee
should hold its own public hearings, with members from the other
committee in attendance as observers. I quickly latched on to this
which led to the following agreement which was subsequently
ratified by both TUCCs:

1) The North Western TUCC would stage a Public Hearing in
Cumbria for the benefit of those who have lodged valid objections
with their committee; and the Yorkshire TUCC would stage a
Public Hearing in Yorkshire for the benefit of those who have
lodged valid objections with their committee.
2) Each committee to draw solely from their own members to
formally attend the Public Hearing to be staged within its own
area. Representatives of the other committee would be invited
to attend as observers.
3) After each committee had considered all the written and oral
objections, a joint report would be prepared in accordance with
Section 56(9) of the Transport Act 1962. The report would incorporate any divergence of views between the committees should
they occur.

Travelling back to Yorkshire on a North Trans-Pennine train,
we reflected on the sheer incredibility of so much of what we had
heard from our North Western colleagues. I'd heard of

backwoodsmen but this was ridiculous. In particular I recalled Frank Haywood's patently sincere yet totally outrageous charge that the TUCCs were in danger of being engulfed by "politically motivated fringe groups involved in an environmental crusade!" A case of 'Greens under the bed'?

He was referring to the Joint Action Committee's high profile leaders, John Whitelegg and Peter Horton. Politically I understood them to be in the mainstream, Dr Whitelegg being a Labour supporter while Mr Horton had been active in the Liberal Party. Moreover, their campaigning on behalf of the Settle–Carlisle line was on a non-party or all-party basis and was fully supported by Conservative MPs John Watson and David Maclean. That was good enough for me.

Mind you, as I sat back and considered the day's events, it did strike me as perhaps a little unfortunate that Messrs Whitelegg and Horton both had beards. Who knows, perhaps they wore sandals as well!

10

OBJECTIONS ENCORE

"The Board had been giving further consideration to the wording of the Section 56 notice following your letters and have now decided that it would be appropriate to re-issue the notices, it being recognised that certain users may have been discouraged by the wording of the present notices."

Extract from British Rail letter to Yorkshire TUCC dated 11th April 1984.

When the significance of the 'any user of any service affected' clause of the Act was fully appreciated, the Yorkshire TUCC adopted a low key approach to the issue. We had, of course, accepted letters from users of Dales Rail, steam specials and diverted services as valid objectors because we were sufficiently confident that our interpretation of the Act was correct. This was more than proved by the case of users who joined the 07.39 Settle–Leeds train at Long Preston, Hellifield and Gargrave. We felt we owed it to users to interpret the Act to their best advantage rather than to the advantage of British Rail who held most of the aces anyway.

Therefore we continued to press British Rail for answers to queries relating to the Act, in particular with regard to users of the 07.39 Settle–Leeds train and, in the case of the Goole–Gilberdyke proposal, those using stations between Goole and Doncaster where there was a similar although more pronounced situation as the trains involved included the InterCity 'Hull Executive' to and from London.

Both the London Midland Region (Settle–Carlisle) and Eastern Region (Goole–Gilberdyke and a handful of other proposals) continued to insist their interpretation of the Act was correct and that the closure notices were valid. This was further endorsed when I received a letter from Norman Blackstock, our British Rail liaison officer. Dated 20th February, it stated:

"The opinion of the Board's chief solicitor and legal adviser is that for an objection to be sustainable the objector must use the service between the points mentioned in the closure proposal."

My initial reaction was that this was simply what the Board's chief solicitor and legal advisor would say. But it didn't necessarily mean that he was right. A more considered reflection suggested that, on the basis of the Act, his interpretation lacked substance. There was nothing in the Act which stated that an objector had to travel between points A and B. Indeed, the only qualification required to be an objector was to be a user of 'any service affected'. Moreover, as my personal legal adviser maintained, it was the Act itself rather than any interpretation which was paramount.

Therefore the issue was something for British Rail and the respective action committees to battle out amongst themselves. It was not our role to initiate legal action. We had played our part by bringing the matter to light and informing those principally concerned. Nevertheless, if British Rail held most of the aces, it appeared that we held the joker in the form of the Act itself!

During March there was something of a lull in the battle of words on both the Settle–Carlisle and Goole–Gilberdyke fronts. We were preoccupied with processing objections and beginning to think about the time scale for the Public Hearings. However, intelligence reports from within British Rail suggested that, behind the confident exterior, all was not well. I was told the letter from Farnworth and Watson, the Joint Action Committee's solicitors, had stirred up a hornets nest. There was disquiet, too, about the strength of feeling expressed by MPs in the House of Commons debate.

Putting a brave face on things, Ron Cotton told us that "unfortunately there will be some delay before I can reply in detail" to the dozen or more outstanding letters from John Moorhouse and myself. He also conceded there was concern about certain legal issues. These were being examined as British Rail wished to be "absolutely fair." John Whitelegg confided that Mr Cotton had asked if the Joint Action Committee were proposing to take legal action, to which Dr Whitelegg had replied that they were committed to it on principle because they would almost certainly win. They had also been advised that action in the Courts would put them back £2,500 – money they simply did not have.

On 10th April, John Moorhouse and myself, together with our opposite numbers on the North Western TUCC, Frank Haywood and Olive Clarke, met Ron Cotton at his request in Manchester. For one moment I thought he was going to give us a dressing down.

He opened by saying that British Rail were very concerned at the bitter criticism of them due to the events of the past three years which had led to allegations of "closure by stealth" and suggestions that they had "twisted things." I wasn't prepared to stand for this, so I told him that they had only themselves to blame.

Dismissing my intervention with a look of pained resignation, Mr Cotton continued that, in order to be "absolutely fair", British Rail had decided to revise and re-issue the Settle–Carlisle closure proposal, and that for Goole–Gilberdyke. The revised proposal and Section 56(7) closure notice would differ from the original on three major points:

1) 'Any user of the rail service which it is proposed to discontinue...' would be replaced by 'Objections to the proposed closure may be lodged by any user of any service affected...'
2) The notice would include all the Dales Rail stations.
3) The Blackburn–Hellifield line together with Clitheroe station, which although formally closed in 1962 was used by Dales Rail, would be included in the proposal. This line was also used by trains diverted over the Settle–Carlisle line.

What a turn-up for the book! Indeed, I could hardly believe my ears as Ron Cotton, with all the solemnity of an undertaker in a funeral parlour, spelt out the details. Frank Haywood was not impressed. He felt it was all unnecessary and a waste of time. But John and myself could hardly contain our delight as the decision represented an unprecedented 'about-turn' by British Rail; both with regard to acceptance of 'any user of any service affected' and recognition that Dales Rail was a service within the Act. Indeed, British Rail's special note for information, which would be incorporated in the new closure notices, would state they had been revised to "broaden the scope for making objections."   All that was required was for the TUCCs to agree that all existing objections would remain valid. This would present no problems as it would have been most unfair to expect each objector to re-submit his or her letter of objection, especially as some had written at great length and incorporated much detail in their submissions. Another consequence of British Rail's change of heart was that the Public Hearings would be deferred. Ours, provisionally set for the autumn, would have to be put back until the spring of 1985. If nothing else, this guaranteed an extra six months life for the line.

The following day the news broke in the media. In the 'Yorkshire

Post' it made the front page. Under the headline 'Rail Closure Setback', it opened: "Plans to axe the scenic Settle to Carlisle railway received a setback yesterday as anti-closure campaigners won their first major victory." The same evening the Bradford 'Telegraph and Argus' reported Joint Action Committee secretary Peter Horton as having said: "British Rail's decision to re-publish reflects the immense pressure that has been put on them to act in a proper manner on this issue."

By coincidence the Yorkshire TUCC had a routine meeting the same day as the news broke. Members were in an almost festive mood as John and myself reported on the previous day's meeting with Ron Cotton. Now we also had it in black and white as that morning I had received a letter from Norman Blackstock, our British Rail liaison officer, which stated:

"The Board has been giving further consideration to the wording of the Section 56 notice for the Settle–Carlisle and Goole–Gilberdyke closure proposals following your letters and have now decided that it would be appropriate to re-issue the notices for the closure proposals in a revised form, it being recognised that certain users may have been discouraged by the wording of the present notices."

Members warmly welcomed British Rail's change of policy, but agreed with me that it should also apply to the other closure proposals being handled by the committee, Huddersfield–Denby Dale and Goose Hill–Wath Road. We put this to our liaison officer only to be told that these proposals did not have the same characteristics as Settle–Carlisle and Goole–Gilberdyke. I replied that this was beside the point. No two closure proposals were the same, the only common factor was the Act itself. Therefore the revised policy should be applicable to all proposals and not just the two which had attracted most media attention. Blackstock – whose role was little more than that of a messenger – said he would seek advice and come back to us.

British Rail's revised Section 56 closure notices for Settle–Carlisle were published on 17th May (those for Goole–Gilberdyke had come out a week earlier) and the closing date for objections was 7th July. We had issued a news release emphasising that the objections we had already received would remain valid. In it John Moorhouse explained how the re-issued notice would broaden the scope for making objections whilst I welcomed the 'about turn' by railway management:

"Up to a couple of months ago they were adamant that their

original notices were correct. Now they accept our interpretation of the Act. This undoubtedly ranks as something of a victory for rail users and the consumer movement as a whole."

Thursday 17th May was also the day chosen by David Mitchell, the Parliamentary Under Secretary of State for Transport with responsibility for railways, to make an official journey on the line. In a press notice from the Department of Transport, the Minister explained:

"My visit will be a fact-finding one. I want to look at the line and understand the issues involved. I will not myself be entering into a public debate on the merits of BR's proposals. That would be quite wrong because of my ministerial role in considering the case. But I will be looking carefully at the condition of the line and the Ribblehead Viaduct, and at the countryside through which it passes."

The Minister travelled on the timetabled 10.40 Carlisle–Leeds train to Appleby where he was met by a party of civic dignitaries before being whisked off to address a public meeting in the town. An hour later he was on his way by special train to Settle for a repeat performance, after stopping en-route to inspect the Ribblehead Viaduct from a hydraulic inspection platform which was swung over the edge so he could get a closer view of the suspect structure. Afterwards, he told Stanley Goldsmith of the 'Daily Telegraph' that he was "taken aback" at the poor state of the viaduct which, it was announced during his visit, would shortly have its double track replaced by a single, centrally aligned track to alleviate strain on the structure.

Visits by ministers, even relatively junior ones, are rare events in Settle so it was a packed Victoria Hall that welcomed Mr Mitchell when he stepped on to the stage. He explained that he was there to listen and learn as "one cannot sit at a desk in Whitehall and understand what is involved."

Colin Speakman opened the batting for the users. An eloquent and persuasive speaker, he said that the Settle–Carlisle line was unique as it represented the high water mark of Victorian engineering. Highlighting the success of Dales Rail and the lines contribution to the leisure business, he called for a commitment to the development of the line for tourism and recreation. Mrs Clare Brookes, a former Liberal Parliamentary candidate, questioned British Rail's accounting procedures whilst Councillor Cooke of Giggleswick said the line had been deliberately run down.

Councillor Beth Graham said Settle was dependent on tourism. David Burton of FOSCLA called for financial support from the EEC, a point also made by Margaret Billing, another former Parliamentary candidate and Labour party activist. A Mr Beaumont dismissed Giggleswick station as an alternative to Settle. "Why, why, why, when we have got railways, are we running them down?", he asked.

Perhaps the most telling contribution came from Bernard Houghton, proprietor of the Golden Lion Hotel. Pessimistically, he anticipated the Minister would eventually, and with regret, consent to the line's closure. Turning to Mr Mitchell, the licensee exclaimed: "I am a Conservative and if this is the Conservative Party, for God's sake start to conserve! Money is not everything."

The meeting had proved to be something of a rehearsal for the Public Hearing which would probably take place in the same hall. Therefore I was astonished when the Minister said the North Western TUCC would probably hold its Public Hearing in July whilst our's would be in September – and he was referring to 1984! Who wrote his script? Hadn't anyone told him that British Rail had re-issued the closure notice that very day and the final date for objections wasn't until 7th July? Whilst one cannot expect a Minister to know everything, one is surely entitled to expect him to have been adequately briefed by his civil servants. So, afterwards, I had to do their work for them and tell him that, so far as the Yorkshire TUCC was concerned, there would be no Public Hearing before the spring of 1985.

Nevertheless, it had been an interesting day and there was no doubt that, aside from the *faux pas* regarding the dates of the Public Hearing, the Minister had created a generally good impression. One point that didn't escape my attention was the excellent job the Area Manager at Carlisle had done to ensure that the Mark 1 coaches on the morning Carlisle–Leeds train were in as near pristine condition as their age would allow. There was a distinct whiff of carbolic in the corridors whilst the windows were spotless. But most noticeable of all were the white headrests which had been placed on the back of each seat throughout the train, not just in the first class.

Shortly afterwards I met David Mitchell at a Central Transport Consultative Committee meeting and drew his attention to the special treatment given to his train which was far from representative of those on a line where complaints about dirty trains were rife. He seemed quite put out that the standard he had encountered was not par for the course. Perhaps even Ministers, like the chairman of the British Railways Board, should occasionally don a heavy disguise and travel incognito to see how the rest of us fare.

Indeed, the poor condition of much of the rolling stock assigned to the Settle–Carlisle line, especially that on the two most popular workings – the 09.03 from Leeds and the 16.35 return from Carlisle, was a constant cause of complaints. The situation had got worse since May when the morning train from Leeds started at Hull. Whilst I welcomed this move, as it provided Humberside with a through service to Carlisle (although the change had been introduced for 'operating reasons' as it saved a set on the Hull–Leeds route during the morning peak), the external washing facilities at Hull Botanic Gardens appeared to be non-existent judging by the condition of the stock. Frequently the coaches were so filthy that people could hardly see out of the windows.

It was beyond my comprehension that management had the effrontery to deploy stock in such a deplorable condition on any route on a regular basis, let alone one they were promoting for its scenic attractions. It just highlighted their own incompetence. The situation was so bad that, at Leeds, I frequently witnessed passengers endeavouring to clean the windows themselves. What a pity Mr Mitchell was not there to see it for himself.

Yet, notwithstanding such shortcomings, business on the line was booming. So much so that we were also receiving complaints about overcrowding. Yet no one at British Rail appeared interested. At our April meeting, and in a sense of frustration, I put it to Norman Blackstock that he should provide a relief service on Saturday mornings for the Leeds–Carlisle service and its afternoon return, and pressed for the provision of seat reservation facilities and a buffet or refreshment trolley. Therefore, I was pleasantly surprised when, at the beginning of June, he told me that "provision of some additional train working was under close study". A case of 'we're getting there' at last, perhaps.

Meanwhile a dark cloud that could significantly affect the closure proposal loomed over the Yorkshire TUCC. At the Central Transport Consultative Committee meeting on 20th June, secretary Len Dumelow announced that it had been agreed that the revised TUCC structure would take effect from 1st September 1984. There was uproar! Who had agreed it? Certainly not the TUCC chairmen whose committees were affected, most of whom were unaware the change was so imminent.

It appeared the 'deal' had been struck between the Central Transport Consultative Committee secretariat and civil servants at the Consumer Affairs Division at the Department of Trade and Industry. And what of British Rail? Did they have any input to the proposed changes?

Frankly, I was prepared to believe anything. For the changes could, almost at a stroke, alter the whole tenor of TUCC 'watchdog' representation throughout Yorkshire and Humberside. On the basis of numbers, our merger with the North Eastern TUCC to form a new TUCC for North East England would leave the Yorkshire TUCC outnumbered by 15 to 12. Then who would be chairman? My opposite number in the North East, James Currer Briggs struck me as the firm favourite. He had been active in the Conservative Party and, like other Government supporters in Olive Clarke and Colonel Bill Dalziel, the Scottish TUCC chairman, was a firm believer that 'the men from British Rail know best'. This contrasted with the more consumer orientated approach of the 'Gang of Three' – Barry Flaxman (East Anglia), Jim Ward (East Midlands) and myself.

However, it was the implications for the Settle–Carlisle closure proposal that worried me most. For the reorganisation as planned would mean that, from 1st September, virtually all the line would come within the North Western TUCC area as they would take over the Craven District of North Yorkshire. Moreover, the new TUCC for North East England might decide that 'consideration of the objections and representations relating to the closure and the making of the report to the Minister' be delegated to the North Western TUCC who, certainly in geographic terms, would be the committee principally concerned. Indeed, I understood that Gerald Newton – the existing secretary of the North Eastern TUCC who had been seconded from British Rail for longer than John Moorhouse and was therefore senior – had suggested just that. For anyone who believed in the 'conspiracy theory', all the ingredients were there.

Be that as it may, and those were only thoughts that passed through my mind at the time, it was Jim Ward who summarised the views and feelings of most TUCC chairmen. He acidly remarked that whereas his secretary had been informed of the changes, he hadn't. Moreover, although the principle of reorganisation had been accepted, albeit with many reservations, the boundary changes had been presented as a *fait accompli*. Above all, the time scale for such radical changes was totally unrealistic, especially where the merger of two committees was involved.

Barry Flaxman agreed, and so did I; for Jim had summed up the position admirably. Prior to his retirement, Jim Ward had been an accountant with much experience in industry. He had been chairman of the Dobson Park Group and the Nottingham Chamber of Commerce. He combined his TUCC work with that of chairman of Nottinghamshire County Cricket Club. Whilst he worked closely with Barry Flaxman and myself, his commitment to the railway was less pronounced so his views probably carried more weight with the 'wets' on the Central Committee.

It was left to James Briggs to present the minority view. He was staggered that his fellow TUCC chairmen were so unprepared for the changes. He had known of them for six months and had been in direct contact with the Department of Trade and Industry on the matter. He said his major responsibility was to the TUCC staff and his secretary Gerald Newton had already made arrangements to move to York. This was the first I'd heard about this, so I retorted that surely the major responsibility of TUCC chairmen was to look after the interests of rail users.

Mrs Alison Munro, the Central Committee chairman had a problem on her hands. Not that this posed any difficulties for she had the right background for dealing with such matters. Following a distinguished career in the civil service, culminating as an under secretary at the Ministry of Aviation, she had become High Mistress at St Paul's Girls School. In addition to her railway watchdog role, she was also chairman of Chichester Health Authority. As befits someone who knew her way about Westminster and Whitehall, she said she would take up the matter with Consumer Affairs minister, Alex Fletcher, as the 1st September deadline was quite impractical.

The following day I had to report to my own committee. To say that they were shattered would be an understatement. Indeed, their indignation verged on anger, not least with regard to how the changes might affect the Yorkshire TUCC role in the Settle–Carlisle closure. Anticipating this, I had drafted a short resolution which was passed unanimously. It simply said:

'The projected TUCC for North East England shall honour all agreements and assurances made by the Yorkshire TUCC with regard to railway closure proposals initiated under Section 56 of the Transport Act 1962.'

This covered the agreement with the North Western TUCC regarding the Public Hearings and subsequent report, plus the assurances given to objectors to this and other proposals that the committee's reports would convey any strength of feeling on issues other than hardship to the Minister – a policy not adopted by either the North Western or North Eastern TUCCs at the time. Whilst I doubted whether the resolution carried any legal clout, it represented a clear indication of our commitment to rail users. It also took a little heat out of the situation and enabled me to persuade members not to make direct representations to the Minister, something I wished to avoid as I had every confidence in Mrs Munro.

I also alerted John Watson – himself a solicitor – and had a word with my own legal adviser. I put it to them that, although there was nothing in the Act to prevent a merger between two TUCCs, so far as existing closure proposals were concerned, the committee which received the objections had to consider them and report to the Minister. So far as Settle–Carlisle was concerned, we had received far more objections than the North Western TUCC and, as the second period for objections was drawing to a close, they were coming in by the bundle every day.

The Joint Action Committee had followed the lead of the Goole and District Railway Action Group and come up with a printed pro-forma based on that so effectively deployed in the Goole–Gilberdyke proposal. In fact they had gone one stage further by actually 'working the trains'. That is to say, volunteers from the committee handed out leaflets on the trains for passengers to complete. They were then collected and forwarded to the North Western TUCC or ourselves in bulk. If nothing else, this ensured that there was no doubt about the validity of the objections as the passengers were using a service affected by the proposal and completing their objection at the same time.

By the time the statutory period was over on 7th July, we had received a further 5,931 objections – making our overall total 7,467. The North Western TUCC had received another 2,800 or so, making their total about 3,650. Thus objections to British Rail's proposal to close the Settle–Carlisle line had topped the 11,000 mark. The Yorkshire TUCC total alone was over 4,000 more than the 3,444 objections received in 1968 to the proposal to axe the Hull–Scarborough line. I felt this most important in what had, in many respects, become a numbers game.

Not that there was much time to gauge the significance of the numbers for, whilst the Settle–Carlisle objections had been coming in, we had been involved in another dispute with British Rail, that relating to Goose Hill–Wath Road. It had blown up into quite a row. Eastern Region, no doubt under instruction from the Board in London, had steadfastly refused to revise and re-issue the notice for this closure proposal and that for Huddersfield–Denby Dale. Although Goose Hill–Wath Road had only generated 15 objections – a far cry from 11,000 plus! – most were of considerable substance and included those from the Metropolitan Counties of West and South Yorkshire, the City of Sheffield, Barnsley Borough Council and one or two 'regulars' like Dr Hugh Porteous of the Sheffield Passengers Association and Roger Smith.

In view of the decision to re-issue notices for Settle–Carlisle and Goole–Gilberdyke, I felt British Rail's stance to be completely irrational. Moreover, we had discovered a further factor that compounded doubts regarding the validity of the closure notice. They had omitted any reference to the 12.46 Fridays only Portsmouth Harbour–Leeds train. Such are the sophistications of the closure procedure.

Although we decided to go ahead with the Public Hearing, relations with British Rail became even more soured when they refused to respond to the 'Summary of Written Objections' because they claimed none of the points were valid. This was utter nonsense as there were no restrictions on the grounds of objection under the Act. Indeed, there were doubts whether they would turn up at the Public Hearing although, come the day, they were there; albeit their contribution was hardly sparkling.

Nevertheless, it was a good Public Hearing. Afterwards we decided to take a leaf out of British Rail's book and dig our heels in. We sent a memorandum to the Department of Trade and Industry explaining the situation that had arisen regarding the validity of the closure notice and stating that, until such time as we received a reply from them, we intended to defer consideration of the proposal. After all, if the Yorkshire TUCC was to be abolished on 1st September, we might as well go down fighting. And what better epitaph than: 'They died on the battlefield of Goose Hill–Wath Road'!

However, it was not to be; for on 12th July I received a letter from the chairman of the Central Committee, Alison Munro. Like the Settle–Carlisle line, the Yorkshire TUCC was to be guaranteed a further six months life as introduction of the new TUCC structure was to be deferred until 1st April 1985. This was good news and we had everything to play for. Yet, I could not help smiling at the date – 'all fools day!'

11

'WANTON NEGLECT', GHOST TRAINS AND STILL MORE OBJECTIONS!

"Of course, the biggest asset the campaigners have is British Rail itself."
Editorial in the 'Craven Herald', 7th
September 1984

Whilst the Yorkshire TUCC were preoccupied with the fracas of Goose Hill–Wath Road, rumour was rife regarding the conclusions of the PEIDA report on the Settle–Carlisle line sponsored by the consortium of local authorities and other bodies, including British Rail who had chipped in with £2,000 towards the £34,000 it cost. When formally made public on 26th July 1984, the reading was by no means all doom and gloom. True, estimates that £21.2 million would have to be spent on the track and structures during the next 20 years had a daunting ring to them. I agreed, too, with Dr John Whitelegg of the Joint Action Committee that a cost-benefit analysis and an evaluation of different ways of marketing the line would have been useful additions.

Overall, though, there seemed more in the report to please objectors than British Rail, and that was what mattered most at the time. Not least was PEIDA's damning indictment of British Rail's "wanton neglect" – a phrase which the report said had been carefully chosen – at the way the line had been deliberately run down. Although PEIDA accepted retention of the line would involve considerable expenditure, it emphasised this would have been far less if adequate levels of investment and maintenance had been undertaken in recent years. The report continued:

"The consequence of this is that a decision to retain the line would require higher capital expenditure than would have been necessary had reasonable renewal and maintenance been undertaken. This policy could be described as one of wanton neglect. The action British Rail has taken has made it more likely the line will close."

The PEIDA report was likely to form the foundation of the objectors evidence presented at the Public Hearings, especially that by the local authorities headed by Cumbria, Lancashire and West Yorkshire County Councils. For their part, the Joint Action Committee had fought a most effective, albeit unexpected, 'second innings' when it came to the actual work required to score the highest possible number of objections. In addition to having 'worked the trains', which generated the vast majority of the additional 8,700 plus additional objections, they had backed their efforts with a series of regular, punchy newsletters titled 'Settle–Carlisle Campaign Special' complete with cartoons.

With the Public Hearings very much in mind, the Joint Action Committee formed themselves into a limited company with John Whitelegg as chairman and Peter Horton as secretary, roles they were already playing. Other directors included Brian Sutcliffe and Philippa Simpson of FOSCLA and Richard Watts of the RDS. Although their reported budget of £55,000 to fund the campaign for the next 12 months struck me as a trifle optimistic, they did have financial backing from the railway unions and a number of other bodies. Moreover, there are always times when it pays to think big and this was undoubtedly one.

Meanwhile business on the line remained brisk. To my astonishment, our request for a relief train on Saturday mornings to augment the Leeds–Carlisle train and its afternoon return was not only met, but extended throughout the week (including Sundays) between 14th July and 9th September. It was almost beyond belief. Whilst the Monday to Friday relief workings were by DMUs which started from and worked back to York, the Saturday and Sunday trains were loco-hauled and usually comprised Mark 2 stock. What luxury! Moreover, they were timetabled with a degree of imagination. For whereas the Monday to Friday DMU service left York at 08.59 and Leeds at 09.31, arriving in Carlisle at 12.02 and returning at 12.45; the Saturday and Sunday service left York at 11.00 and Leeds at 11.31, arriving in Carlisle just after 14.00. This allowed almost one-and-a-half hours before the return at 15.30. It meant that on Saturdays people from London, the Midlands and other parts of the country could arrive in York or Leeds in time to catch the mid-morning train and, with a bit of luck, still return home by midnight. What might be termed as a good day out!

Rather less of a surprise was the promotion of the additional services. It was pathetic. So much so that I christened it 'The Ghost Train' for when the new Saturday service made its debut hardly anyone within British Rail knew anything about it, let alone the public. Indeed, my suspicious mind wondered whether it was a deliberate ploy to up the line's operating costs and curb additional revenue in an attempt to strengthen the case for closure! Either it was that or else sheer incompetence. Not a happy choice whichever way one looked at it.

The first I learnt about the extra trains was when, on 3rd July, a member of the public – albeit a FOSCLA activist – told me. At first I could hardly believe my ears. But such was the extent of the detail relating to departure and arrival times that it had an un-doubted stamp of authenticity. So I rang the Leeds travel centre to check. They knew nothing about it. So I asked John Moorhouse to ring Ron Cotton who proved more forthcoming. Yes, there would be extra trains commencing on 14th July; but it was all very confidential so he would rather we didn't say anything about it! What a way to run a railway!

By Friday 13th July, the news that there was an additional train from Leeds to Carlisle had penetrated the Leeds travel centre. On the strength of this my wife and myself decided to try it the following day. Although shown on the VDU screens, no one knew what time the return working left Carlisle. Nevertheless, we felt it was worth risking. The train duly arrived from York and comprised of clean Mark 2 stock, a welcome change from the filthy, clapped-out Mark 1 coaches designated to the 09.00 Leeds–Carlisle. The only thing that appeared to be missing were the customers – and this was hardly surprising.

Although we left Leeds with 46 passengers, most were en-route to the Keighley and Worth Valley Railway and by the time we left Skipton we were down to 21. At Settle they seemed more *au-fait* with the situation and a further 21 passengers joined the train. Appleby, too, were on the ball. So much so that they put railway management to shame. The enterprising railman, Paul Holden, had even placed an advertisement in the local paper which he had paid for out of his own pocket!

At Carlisle there was at least a crudely written notice by the barrier indicating the departure time of the new Carlisle–York ser-vice, subsequently described by the station tannoy as a 'special'. However, in the adjacent Travel Centre they had no knowledge of the service at all! By contrast the Tourist Office in the city centre was awash with leaflets for it; due, I later learnt, to the initiative of Appleby railman Paul Holden and a local FOSCLA member. On returning to the station, I left a leaflet with the Travel Centre. The look of incredulity on the clerk's face is something I will not forget. It was as if I had handed him a £50 note!

Relishing my new role of detective in quest of 'the case of the missing ghost train', I called in at the Travel Centre at Leeds on our return and asked if there was a through train to Carlisle the following day (Sunday). "No, sir," was the response, "you'll have to change at Lancaster." Later that evening I rang train enquiries at York and asked for the first service to Carlisle on Sunday. "12.30 change at Newcastle, arriving in Carlisle at 15.55," was the authoritative reply. But wasn't there a through train leaving York at 11.00 which arrived in Carlisle at 14.18, I ventured to suggest. "No, sir," was the reply.

I took the matter up with our liaison officer, Norman Blackstock, and asked what had gone wrong with the marketing and promotion of the new York–Carlisle service, suggesting that perhaps the cynic on the train was right when he remarked: "They don't want any passengers on this train in order to strengthen the case for closing the line." On 18th July, Blackstock replied:

"I accept we have not yet done an adequate job in publicising the additional services. Please be assured that we are not attempting to demonstrate any lack of patronage; the new service has been put on in the face of demand (not least from your committee) and we have every hope of making money from the exercise."

Recalling the debut of the 'Ghost Train' in some detail clearly demonstrates how an undoubted commercially good idea initially came unstuck due to the inability – which must surely rank as incompetence – of management to see it through properly. By the time British Rail eventually got their act together, a quarter of the eight week season the trains ran was over. In the event the business picked up, as can be seen from the train loadings. For example, whereas total patronage of the first York–Carlisle train on 14th July was a mere 74, and the number on the train when it left Settle 42; by 4th August the figures had risen to 163 and 102 respectively. On the 18th August the figures peaked at 312 and 229 whilst on the final Saturday (8th September) they were a respectable 273 and 195. Although the additional trains probably turned out to be a 'nice little earner' overall (especially as they attracted people from all over the country), revenue would have been considerably more if only the public had been aware of the service when it was introduced.

These train loading figures were taken from the comprehensive joining and alighting details I had been taking whenever I used the Settle–Carlisle, although these Saturday journeys had been essentially 'off duty' jaunts. I certainly didn't claim any expenses, which was probably just as well as we endeavoured to do ourselves well. Ever since I had persuaded my wife, Muriel, much against her better judgement to make the return Leeds–Carlisle journey on a Nottingham–Glasgow train in March 1982 so that she could see what all the fuss was about, she had become a devotee of the Settle–Carlisle line and was, of course, an objector to the closure proposal. Therefore, we both found the 'Ghost Train' provided a most enjoyable day out.

It enabled us to get our weekend shopping done in good time to catch the connection from our 'local', New Pudsey, into Leeds to join the 11.31 Carlisle train. Immediately on our arrival in Carlisle, we dashed along to Marks and Spencer's in the hope that the good folk of Cumbria had not completely emptied the food shelves. Then, after a quick look at some of the other shops or a wander through the excellent market, it was back to the station and off home to Leeds in a style worthy of the 'Thames–Clyde Express': Terrine of Trout with Salad, followed by Raspberry Royale, and all washed down with a nice M & S house dry white. I am sure George Pullman would have approved.

Although the Yorkshire TUCC had won a reprieve until 31st March 1985, there was considerable concern regarding the possible effect of its demise. Dr John Whitelegg of the Joint Action Committee expressed anxiety at the transfer of the Craven District – which, of course, included the southern section of the Settle–Carlisle line – to the North Western TUCC who, he claimed, were "less pro-rail" than us.

In the House of Commons on 30th July, John Watson tactfully asked the Minister with responsibility for railways:

"When is the public enquiry into the Settle–Carlisle line likely to start, and will my Hon. Friend confirm that the enquiry will be held under the auspices of the Yorkshire TUCC?"

Mr David Mitchell replied:

"There will be two enquiries, one under each TUCC. I understand that one is likely to start early in the autumn and the other as soon as can be arranged. At present there is talk about the early spring, but I hope that it will be before then."

Afterwards, John Watson explained the position to the 'Craven Herald'. There would be two Public Hearings because the line passed through two TUCC areas. He continued:

"Each will report its findings to the Minister. I think it is quite possible that one hearing could recommend that the line should be retained whilst the other will be prepared to acknowledge the need for closure. In those circumstances the degree of public pressure brought upon the Minister could well be crucial to the outcome."

John had, with characteristic perception, summarised more or less how I felt things might work out. Yet I remained at a complete loss to understand why David Mitchell – or, more probably, his civil servants – were still under the impression that the North Western TUCC would hold its Public Hearing early in the autumn. Given that the last day for receipt of objections had been 7th July, it was an impossibility. Before the Public Hearings could proceed, each TUCC had to submit a summary of the written objections to British Rail for their comments. These would then be incorporated in a composite document which would be sent to each objector. There was no way all this could be completed by the autumn. Indeed, the Yorkshire TUCC would be very hard pressed to get the work completed in time for a spring 1985 Public Hearing. There was no knowing, too, how long it would take British Rail to meet their part of the equation.

So what was David Mitchell up to? I knew that he was reputed to be a bit of a 'gricer', so did he want to go down in history as the chap who saved the Settle–Carlisle before he was moved elsewhere in a Government reshuffle? Or did he wish to seal his political future by displaying a firm hand on behalf of the taxpayer by consenting to the closure of the line? I felt most uneasy about it all.

But before I had time to do little more than ponder, the whole Settle–Carlisle saga took yet another bizarre turn which, if nothing else, put paid to any Public Hearing in 1984 and made ours planned for the spring of 1985 a most doubtful starter, too. This was all because British Rail had been rather lax at their geography.

When, in August 1983, British Rail finally announced that it planned to close the Settle–Carlisle line in accordance with the procedures set out in Section 56 of the Transport Act 1962, we

made a special point of making quite sure which part of the line
came within the Yorkshire TUCC's area. In doing so we made a
rather interesting discovery.

Following the reorganisation of local government in 1974, a substantial slice of the western part of the West Riding of Yorkshire
was transferred to the new county of Cumbria. So, whereas prior
to reorganisation our section of line extended to just north of
Garsdale station, afterwards the boundary between the Craven
District of North Yorkshire and Cumbria, and between the Yorkshire TUCC and the North Western TUCC, was bang in the middle
of Blea Moor Tunnel. As a consequence, the former Yorkshire
TUCC stations of Dent and Garsdale had come under the North
Western TUCC.

Both John Moorhouse and myself went to great lengths to check
this, digging out all the maps we could find, both old and new. We
also took the precaution of checking with Craven District Council
that our findings were correct. It was whilst we were doing this
that we discovered a small section of the line between Garsdale
Head and just to the north of Aisgill Summit of about 2½ miles
was not in Cumbria but in the Richmondshire District of North
Yorkshire. This came under the jurisdiction of the North Eastern
TUCC!

Anticipating – correctly as it turned out – that we would run into
a number of little local difficulties with the North Western TUCC,
the last thing we needed was a situation where these were dupli-
cated and we were outnumbered. Therefore, John and myself decided to do nothing. We didn't even tell our committee. Not that
there was any reason why we should. It was nothing to do with us
as our boundaries were not affected. It was a matter for the North
Western and North Eastern TUCCs. Nevertheless, it was another
possible joker that remained at the back of my mind.

On Thursday 26th July I was putting in a morning at the Yorkshire TUCC office in York as John Moorhouse was on leave. Quite
apart from the 7,000 plus Settle–Carlisle objections, not to mention
the 2,570 for Goole–Gilberdyke (the second objection period only
generated an additional 85 objections), I was anxious that the
routine complaints we received regarding British Rail services –
which were at an all-time high as the cuts began to bite – were
promptly attended to. Indeed, I was delving into a tricky claim for
a refund relating to travel between Leeds and Inverness, when the
telephone rang. It was Peter Horton of the Joint Action Commit-

tee. After the exchange of pleasantries, he came straight to the point. Did I know that a short stretch of the line north of Garsdale was in the North Eastern TUCC's area? I replied that I did, but that it wasn't really our problem as our boundary was not involved.

He then suggested that, as there had been no reference to the North Eastern TUCC in the December 1983 and May 1984 British Rail closure notices, they were invalid. I replied that this was something he should take up with the Joint Action Committee's legal advisers, although I added he was probably correct.

I immediately saw what he was getting at and, quite frankly, wasn't particularly enthusiastic for another re-run of the objection period. Although I seldom take more than a couple of weeks holiday a year, I had already given up a week I had planned in order to help clear the mountain of objections we had received. More seriously, I felt there was a danger of overkill and that the objectors might find it more prudent to bank their latest discovery of a British Rail oversight as an insurance policy for use at a later date. For example, if the Minister were ultimately to consent to closure, they could point out that the proposal was invalid and the whole process would have to start again.

Horton took my point, although he didn't seem too enthusiastic about it. Not that I blamed him, for I was conscious that my thinking was coloured by the fact that we had more than enough objections to be going on with. So when I put down the phone I felt I had not heard the last of it. The following afternoon, whilst working in my office at home, I received a telephone call from the typist at York to say that Mr Cotton had left a message to say that the closure notice was going to be re-issued. She could not believe it! I, too, was surprised; but only because British Rail appeared to have capitulated so swiftly to the Joint Action Committee.

So there we were, if not back at square one, then certainly back at square two. Indeed, the whole Settle–Carlisle closure proposal was developing into a farce – a case of 'Carry On Objecting!' British Rail's Ron Cotton put a brave face on the latest turn of events. He dismissed suggestions that another round of objections represented a further setback. As he told the 'Yorkshire Post':

"The only fact as I see it, is that it gives six more weeks for people to get objections in. We decided to re-advertise in the North East to make sure that there is absolutely no cause for criticism and to block all possible loopholes."

The chairman of the North Eastern TUCC, James Currer Briggs, was not particularly amused. He was quoted as being "amazed" that British Rail had "given way" on the issue and felt there was no need for the proposal to be referred to his committee as no stations were involved in their section of the line. For my part I simply referred to it as an "extraordinary and bizarre situation" and added that I had been about sufficiently long not to be surprised at anything involving British Rail. As for the Joint Action Committee, they were positively crowing – and who could blame them? Secretary Peter Horton told the Bradford 'Telegraph and Argus':

"If this reflects the calibre of railway management, no wonder that nobody takes them seriously any more. It's time the Minister put an end to this farce and told British Rail to get on their bikes!"

As if to endorse Mr Horton's derision and my scepticism, when British Rail's third attempt to get the closure notice right made its debut in the 'Northern Echo' on 9th August, it still did not fully comply with the Act! Whereas the two earlier notices had omitted, due to an oversight, reference to the North Eastern TUCC, the latest effort made no reference at all to the North Western and Yorkshire TUCCs. This was clearly wrong, for the Act stated that, where a notice has been published, any user of any service affected could lodge an objection with the appropriate area committee. This was the committee or committees for the area in which the station or the line, or any part of the line, affected by the proposed closure was situated.

Therefore, as the proposal was to close the line between Settle Junction and Carlisle Petteril Bridge Junction, not just the 2½ miles between Garsdale Head and Aisgill Summit, all three committees were involved and should have been listed; a fact we spelt out in a letter to Mr Peter Hodge, the Shire Counties Liaison Officer for Provincial Services at the British Railways Board, who appeared to have been brought in to reinforce the hapless Mr Cotton.

As it happened, Hodge appeared no more aware of the provisions of the Act than Cotton. In his reply – commendably by return – Mr Hodge claimed the latest closure notice was not a re-advertisement of the earlier notices, but a new one "relating solely to the area which the North Eastern TUCC is responsible." His punchline, no doubt inserted in the hope we would immediately touch our forelocks, was that Leading Counsel had confirmed that this was the position.

Needless to say this didn't have the desired effect for, quite frankly, what Hodge stated was arrant nonsense. Therefore I responded, more in sorrow than in anger, setting out the position as it related to the Act. I pointed out that, in order to correct the earlier mistake of excluding the North Eastern TUCC, British Rail had compounded that error by leaving out the North Western and Yorkshire TUCCs from the latest notice. In doing so they had, no doubt unwittingly, flouted the provisions of the Act. I concluded:

"The view of the writer is that this is a classic case of two wrongs *not* making a right! As there is nothing in the enactments which permits you to deliberately exclude an appropriate area committee – and in this case two! – from fulfilling their obligations under the Act, the explanation of your interpretation of the Act appears spurious to say the least. Moreover, as your notice published on 9th August covers the same closure proposal as that published on 17th May, it relates to the area for which this committee, as an appropriate area committee, is responsible."

That, I hoped, would put paid to Mr Hodge. Indeed, we heard nothing further from him for almost a month and when he did come back he had nothing new to say. More serious, though, was the fact that on 15th August Ron Cotton bounced back with a letter which really raised my hackles. Addressed to John Moorhouse, our secretary, Cotton wrote:

"I am writing to you to clarify certain aspects of this closure proposal.

The current closure notice allowing objections to be submitted up to 29th September to the North Eastern TUCC are, so far as British Rail are concerned, related strictly to the North Eastern committee.

Any objections made under this notice which we are prepared to accept must have been made direct to the North Eastern committee. We would regard as invalid any objection submitted to your committee after 7th July, even if they were sent forward to the North Eastern committee. I feel it only fair to make our position quite clear on this issue.

When you forward me your Summary of Objections would you also let me have copies of all the actual individual objections."

This time Cotton – or his scriptwriter – had overstepped the mark and I was not prepared to go along with it at all. Resisting the initial temptation to respond straight away by telling Mr Cotton and British Rail to go and take a running jump, I felt that because of the important principles involved, not least those of our independence, a more considered reply endorsed by the whole committee would be appropriate. So once again I got in a huddle with my solicitor – who was thoroughly enjoying his excursions into the Transport Act 1962 as a break from the monotony of conveyancing – and together we came up with a draft which was considered and unanimously approved by the Yorkshire TUCC at its meeting on 20th September. It said:

"The committee has now considered the points raised in your letter of 15th August and have asked me to respond as follows:

It has already been pointed out to the British Railways Board that its interpretation of the Transport Act 1962 is open to question and is at variance with that of the committee which remains convinced that the Section 56(7) notice of 9th August, in its attempt to rectify the Board's earlier unfortunate errors, should have made it clear that objections could be sent not only to the North Eastern TUCC, but also to the North Western TUCC and ourselves. The committee is determined to act fairly in accordance with the Transport Act 1962 and will therefore continue to accept objections received on or before 29th September from any user of any service affected by your proposal.

Furthermore, if you read the Transport Act 1962 carefully, you will see that it is 'the appropriate area committee' who are obliged to receive and consider objections and not the British Railways Board. Your remarks regarding the validity of objections are therefore irrelevant. The committee is not obliged nor prepared to let you have copies of all the individual objections but will, in accordance with normal practice, forward you a Summary of Objections in due course for you to comment on (should you so wish) for the benefit of objectors and to assist the committee in its consideration of your proposal.

The committee have also asked me to convey to you its deep concern at the content and tone of your letter which they feel is an attempt to interfere in the committee's business of meeting its obligations under the Act.

Finally, the committee feels that your letter demonstrates a basic misunderstanding of the relevant provisions of the Transport Act 1962, and therefore fails in its objects of trying 'to clarify certain aspects of this closure proposal.'"

I felt relatively happy with our response and nothing further was heard from British Rail – for the time being at any rate. As we were battling with words, the Joint Action Committee and their constituent organisations, who had barely time to charge their batteries from the exertions of the second objection period, were again mobilised and placed on 'objection duties' working the trains on the line. Moreover, with the additional summer service in full swing, they had extra trains to work and, most importantly, more passengers to lobby.

The high spot of their campaign was a rally in Settle on 15th September. Organised by the Ramblers Association in conjunction with the Joint Action Committee and the Yorkshire Dales Society, it attracted over 500 people, including 200 who had arrived by special train from London and the Midlands. They gathered on the playing fields of Settle High School which were alive to the sound of music from the splendid Giggleswick and Settle Brass Band. There to greet them was the president of the Ramblers Association, Mike Harding the entertainer.

Adopting a more serious stance to that associated with 'The Rochdale Cowboy', he introduced a formidable team of speakers headed by Lord Melchett, a leading conservationist and Labour spokesman on environmental matters in the House of Lords, and John Watson, the local MP who had played a major role both in Parliament and behind the scenes in fostering the case for retention of the Settle–Carlisle line. Other speakers included County Councillor Beth Graham, Colin Speakman, Peter Horton, Richard Harvey, the Yorkshire Dales National Park officer and 91-year-old Tom Stephenson, the founder of the Pennine Way.

If the contributors had little to say that was new, and this was only to be expected for the campaign was, in showbiz terms, now in its 'Third Great Year!', there was a growing confidence that they were in with a chance of saving the line. The event was previewed by the 'Craven Herald' in a most perceptive editorial which opened:

"It promises to be a rally with all the razzmatazz we are currently seeing in connection with the American Presidential election. It is the Dales Rally, aimed at drumming up even more support for the campaign to prevent closure of the Settle–Carlisle line.

Of course, the biggest asset the campaigners have is British Rail itself. One would have imagined that, knowing how emotive line closures are – and especially this one for a variety of reasons – they would have got their procedural plans accurate. But no, they make a complete fist of it, and have to start the whole thing again. In terms of staff time and advertising, it is likely that that in itself would go half way to repairing the allegedly ailing Ribblehead Viaduct. The amazing thing is that British Rail appointed a man whose only purpose in life was to work himself out of a job. His brief – to mastermind the closure of the line. Could it be that he is, secretly, himself a Settle–Carlisle lover?"

After a comprehensive summary listing the attributes of some of those involved in the rally, the editorial continued:

"It all adds up to a pretty impressive show of strength. Just one niggling thought remains. How many of those who attend on September 15th will travel over the route regularly if and when the battle is won? It is all very well for the steam enthusiasts and preservationists to pack the steam-hauled trains which are so much in vogue these days. If the line is to be saved, however, ways and means have to be found of making it a more viable proposition than is the case at present.

Although they have remained pretty silent, there are plenty of people who really can't see an economic future for the line. They argue, albeit privately, that the motor car has superseded the train, and that nothing will change that situation.

In battling, quite rightly, for the line to be retained, those who wish to see it continue ought to be applying their fertile minds to the problem of increasing usage. It can be done. The line is magnificent. Even British Rail have themselves pointed the way with their own publicity about its unsurpassed scenery and engineering excellence.

Having won the first battle – to save the line – we hope that those who imaginatively directed that contest will not sit on their laurels, but ensure an increasing future usage. That will be to the benefit of Craven as a whole, and not just the Settle–Carlisle line."

To me, this summed up the position admirably.

Round three of the statutory period for receipt of objections ended on 28th September, although it was several days before we were able to tot up the final total. Once again the Joint Action Committee and their supporters had excelled themselves. We received a further 7,430 objections, making the Yorkshire TUCC's overall total for the three objection periods 14,897. About 3,500 new objections were lodged with the North Western TUCC and just 69 with the North Eastern TUCC in Newcastle. So much for British Rail's edict that the objections related "strictly to the North Eastern TUCC." In fact the 69 objections were quickly delegated to the North Western TUCC to consider, a sensible decision in view of the section of line involved. Thus, the final overall total for the North Western TUCC was 7,253 which, added to our 14,897 made an overall grand total of 22,150. It really was a remarkable achievement.

12

AN UNEXPECTED ALLY

"TUCCs are Transport Users Consultative Committees and their role is
to represent the views of rail users."

Treasury Solicitor at the Department
of Transport. October 1984.

Whilst the third period for objections to the Settle–Carlisle closure
proposal was in full swing during August and September, the Joint
Action Committee had also spotted the flaw in the latest closure
notice and their solicitors had taken up the matter with the Chief
Solicitor and Legal Adviser of the British Railways Board. The
case put was basically the same as ours, simply that British Rail
had no power to exclude an appropriate TUCC or TUCCs from
the Section 56 closure notice. However, the solicitors, Farnworth
and Watson, received no more joy from the Board than we had
done from the Provincial Services sector.

Meanwhile another battle with considerable legal implications
which had been simmering on the Goose Hill–Wath Road front
suddenly came to the boil. Following doubts regarding the validity
of the notice for this closure proposal, the Yorkshire TUCC had,
if not actually gone on strike, then certainly 'blacked' the proposal
pending a response to a report we had submitted to our sponsoring
ministry, the Department of Trade and Industry. Mind you, I don't
think they were very pleased with us for, in my limited dealings
with them, they struck me as liking the quiet life. Nevertheless,
they had replied at the end of July and the news wasn't all bad.

First they said that it was not for us to decide on the validity of
the closure notice. This would be a matter for the Secretary of
State for Transport to consider when deciding whether or not to
consent to British Rail's proposal to close the line. I read this as
very much a case of 'slapped wrists' for the Yorkshire TUCC.

However, Trade and Industry were more helpful when they
stated we could receive objections and representations relating to

the validity of the notice and suggested that we should give objectors and British Rail an opportunity to comment accordingly. This, the department said, would give British Rail "a chance to reconsider their position." However, if they stood firm, we would have to refer any legal points to the Secretary of State for Transport in our final report. This struck John Moorhouse and myself as worth a try so, on August 10th, we wrote to all the objectors and British Rail with a request that they should let us have any comments on the legality of the notice by the middle of September.

It seemed we had called British Rail's bluff for, within a week, they informed us that they intended to re-issue the Section 56 notices for the Goose Hill–Wath Road and Huddersfield–Denby Dale proposals in order to broaden the scope for making objections by incorporating the "any user of any service affected" clause used in both re-issued notices for Settle–Carlisle. In view of the long rearguard action British Rail had fought to avoid this, together with the bitterness it had caused between them and the committee, this ranked as an unprecedented climb down and a famous, if somewhat obscure, victory for the consumer and the Yorkshire TUCC. Needless to say we were very pleased.

However, with 14,897 Settle–Carlisle objections on our plate, we didn't have time to let the success go to our heads. Nor did I feel it was worth pressing British Rail further for yet another re-issued closure notice for, even if one were forthcoming, on past record they were bound to get something wrong. Moreover, I had a feeling that both the Joint Action Committee and the TUCCs had had enough of objections and felt it was time to move forward to the Public Hearings.

I was conscious, too, that time was no longer on the side of the Yorkshire TUCC and myself. When, in July, we learnt the date for the merger of the Yorkshire and North Eastern TUCCs had been deferred for six months to 1st April 1985, we felt we were in with a chance to hold the Public Hearing in March under the Yorkshire TUCC banner. As for the report to the Secretary of State, we would worry about that when the time came; but it was inconceivable that those who had conducted the Public Hearing would not be responsible for the report as well.

However, following the third round of objections we were in a new ball game. For a start the number of objections lodged with the Yorkshire TUCC had virtually doubled. This would put the whole closure timetable back by at least six months, probably more.

Therefore a Public Hearing before the autumn of 1985 was out of the question. By that time the Yorkshire TUCC would have been swallowed up in the new TUCC for North East England. This might adopt a stance more akin to that of North Western TUCC. Certainly I felt it was very doubtful I would be asked to chair the new committee, whilst we already knew that, because of British Rail's grading and seniority rules, John Moorhouse – who had done such a splendid job on behalf of rail users during his short time with the Yorkshire TUCC – would, at best, be left playing second fiddle to the present North Eastern secretary Gerald Newton, or else working his passage back to British Rail. Moreover, Gerald Newton appeared to be a disciple of the North Western TUCC's Frank Haywood when it came to closure proposals and was on record as having said the Yorkshire TUCC should delegate the whole Settle–Carlisle issue to the North Western committee.

Therefore, notwithstanding the success of our skirmish on the field at Goose Hill–Wath Road, so far as the big one was concerned – the battle for Settle–Carlisle – we were being driven into a siege position. It was all very complex and I didn't like the look of it at all.

Nor, too, did the Joint Action Committee. For whilst they probably viewed us with some caution, understandable given the precariousness of our position, they knew who their friends were and they were certainly not the North Western TUCC at that time. In 'To Kill A Railway' (Leading Edge Press and Publishing), Stan Abbott provides a graphic and amusing account of when the Joint Action Committee's chairman, Dr John Whitelegg, was invited to meet North Western members for what he hoped would be a useful exchange of views. He found, to his astonishment, that he was carpeted for opinions he had expressed to the media. Needless to say, the good doctor was not amused.

By contrast, ever since my first contacts with FOSCLA, we had built up a good working relationship with the principal objectors, just as we endeavoured to keep on a similar footing with British Rail, although that was often far from easy. Indeed, we were sandwiched between the two. Therefore we required the co-operation of both sides. Otherwise, we would never get through the Public Hearing.

I knew the Joint Action Committee were worried about our future so I wasn't surprised when, on 20th September, we received a letter from Peter Horton, the secretary, expressing concern at the "rumoured reorganisation of the TUCC structure." He posed the following questions:

- Is the Craven District of Yorkshire to be incorporated into the area of the North Western TUCC?
- Are the Yorkshire and North Eastern TUCCs to be amalgamated under the chairmanship of the present chairman of the North Eastern TUCC?
- Are these changes due to take effect as from 1st April 1985?
- Will these changes in any way affect the current closure proposal for the Settle–Carlisle line?

They were very good questions, so I replied: Yes, the Craven District would be incorporated in the North Western TUCC's area; the chairmanship of the 'amalgamated' committee was still under consideration by the Department of Trade and Industry; and that the changes would take effect from 1st April 1985. As for how all this would affect the Settle–Carlisle closure proposal, I replied that all British Rail closure proposals currently before the committee including that for Settle–Carlisle, would be handled in accordance with Section 56 of the Transport Act 1962. I could, I suppose, have left it at that. But I felt it prudent to expand my answers thus:

"With regard to the first item, the Yorkshire TUCC argued against and regrets the proposal to transfer the Craven District of North Yorkshire to the North Western TUCC on the grounds that:

- it would be the only part of Yorkshire not within the projected TUCC for North East England;
- all rail services starting and terminating within the Craven District are Eastern Region trains which are managed by the Leeds Area of British Rail;
- the business, employment, cultural and leisure interests of those resident in the Craven District are predominantly directed towards West Yorkshire.

Referring to your final point, the Committee are of the opinion that, as the Yorkshire TUCC is a committee with whom objections have been lodged, it is under an obligation to consider the objections and report to the Minister in accordance with the Transport Act 1962.

Whilst I have endeavoured to answer your points on the basis of the information at my disposal, I would suggest that you may wish to seek clarification from the Consumer Affairs Division of the Department of Trade and Industry at Millbank Tower,

Millbank, London SW1P 4QU who have overall responsibility for the TUCCs."

Peter Horton put my response to good use. On 10th October he wrote to Alex Fletcher MP, the Parliamentary Under Secretary of State for Trade and Industry with responsibility for consumer affairs expressing the Joint Action Committee's concern at the proposed reorganisation of the TUCCs. His letter continued:

"You will be aware that the North Eastern, North Western and Yorkshire TUCCs are currently involved in the consultative process for the proposed closure of the Settle–Carlisle railway line. We are particularly concerned at the proposed shift of the Craven District of Yorkshire from the Yorkshire TUCC's realm into that of the North Western TUCC. Not only is it at an inappropriate time for such a reorganisation, but it is also one that demands further explanation on the following grounds:"

Horton then listed, virtually word for word the three points I had made to him in my letter regarding the foolishness of the decision as it related to the Craven District. He then concluded:

"You are, Sir, no doubt aware of the contentious nature of the proposed closure of the Settle–Carlisle line and also that some 21,000 people have registered objections to the proposal – 15,000 of them with the Yorkshire TUCC, many of them from the Craven District. I am sure, therefore, that you will understand why your department's reorganisation may be viewed as central government manipulation of a consultative procedure that is supposedly independent."

It was all good stuff and grist to the mill. It might just even have helped convince the Department of Trade and Industry that the Settle–Carlisle closure procedure was heading for an almighty row. Peter Horton, seldom backward in coming forward, circulated copies of this letter to the media. As he told the 'Craven Herald' (19th October):

"The sneaky intervention of Ministers behind the scenes and tampering with procedure has all the hallmarks of people trying to avoid one banana skin by treading on an even larger one!"

I liked that. With off the cuff remarks of this kind it was little wonder the Joint Action Committee were getting such a good press. However, what fascinated me most of all was whether the juggling with the Craven District was part of the plan to bring TUCC boundaries into line with those of British Rail's regions – a fruitless exercise given the reorganisation that was taking place as a result of the new Sector management structure – or whether it was part of a plot to hand the Craven District and all our 14,897 objections over to the more 'reasonable' North Western TUCC in order to facilitate the closure of the Settle–Carlisle line.

Whichever it was, and perhaps it was a bit of both, the fact that it was handled in such a hamfisted way reflected little credit on those involved. In this case I suspected the responsibility lay more with the civil servants than the politicians.

It was probably just coincidence, but the phrase 'banana skin' – albeit in the plural – cropped up later in the month when the North Western TUCC chairman, Olive Clarke, and myself were summoned by the Department of Trade and Industry to a meeting in London on 24th October. It was ostensibly held so we might "discuss any matters" we wished to raise on the "administrative implications of the forthcoming Settle–Carlisle hearings." That could mean anything. The chairman of the Central Transport Consultative Committee, Mrs Alison Munro, had also been invited and a representative from the Department of Transport would be present. Frankly, I didn't like the sound of it. It wasn't as if there was anything I really wanted to discuss. Then why were the Central Committee trying to get into the act? Individual closure proposals were nothing to do with them.

However, one is never too old to learn so I went along prepared to listen and determined to give nothing away. In the event the meeting proved somewhat larger and more formal than I had anticipated. Miss Joyce Blow, an Under Secretary at the Department of Trade and Industry was there with an underling. The Department of Transport were represented by a Mr R A Allan, who I believed to be quite important, and Mr G Beetham who I discovered was very important as he was the Treasury Solicitor. Mrs Munro was supported by Central Committee secretary Len Dumelow and an assistant secretary Mike Patterson, while Mrs Clarke had brought Frank Haywood along. I felt rather outnumbered.

Miss Blow "took charge" – she was that kind of person. She had no doubt regarding the "substance" of the closure proposal but was concerned about the "mechanics" relating to Settle–Carlisle because of the public interest and organised opposition. The Minister was beginning to get interested and it had all the elements of a "banana skins" situation.

Mrs Clark and myself were asked to set the scene. She said the

North Western TUCC had received about 7,200 objections and made a number of other points. Miss Blow's interventions suggested her knowledge of the proposal and Section 56 of the Transport Act 1962 was limited. Indeed, I doubted if she knew where the line actually was. But there was no doubting her concern at the possible cost of the Public Hearings.

Therefore, I took it upon myself to summarise the position back from the spring of 1981, covering the re-routing of the Nottingham–Glasgow service, British Rail's lack of candour to MPs and others, the first round of objections, the "any user of any service affected" clause leading to round two and British Rail's geographic gaffe which led to an unprecedented third objection period. As for the question of costs, they were bound to be higher than they would have been if British Rail had got it right at the start.

Miss Blow then asked for a definition of hardship. Here I repeated the Norman Archer hypothesis that hardship was something that each member of the committee would evaluate after they had read and heard all the evidence. I was pleased to note that Mr Beetham, the Treasury Solicitor agreed. Mrs Clarke and Frank Haywood then launched into a tirade against Dr Whitelegg and the Joint Action Committee and implied they were "fanatics!" I was asked for my view. I replied that they were undoubtedly enthusiasts – and what was wrong with that? – but I would not describe them as fanatics. Mr Haywood said that the Joint Action Committee had threatened the North Western TUCC with legal action, to which I remarked that we had not had any problems of that kind.

Mr Beetham warned that objectors might deploy the disruptive methods adopted at some motorway enquiries and would seek the right to cross examine British Rail. Objectors could also seek an adjournment of the Public Hearings to test in the High Court the ability of the TUCCs to handle the issue. They might even present an injunction to prevent the Public Hearing from continuing.

When asked by Mr Allen of the Department of Transport about the length and venue of the Yorkshire TUCC's Public Hearing, I replied that it would certainly run to six days, probably more. It would be split between Settle, Skipton and Leeds. Mrs Clarke said the North Western TUCC hearing would take place in Appleby, Carlisle, Preston and Manchester. Miss Blow was strongly against holding the hearing in Manchester.

eg. (It is interesting to record that the North Western TUCC received 457 objections from Greater Manchester against 280 from

Appleby and 315 from Carlisle). It should be held 'on the line' irrespective of any inconvenience to those wishing to attend to give evidence. But what of Preston, I wondered. Perhaps she thought it was on the line!

The question of reporting on issues other than hardship was raised. Here I got in quickly and quoted the Norman Archer clause that the statutory duty to report on hardship would not preclude us from conveying to the Minister any strength of public feeling expressed on 'non-hardship' issues. Once again Mr Beethem agreed. Mrs Clarke and Mr Haywood preferred to confine consideration to hardship. Indeed, Haywood confided that he had a girl in the office who was busy "extracting all the hardship items from the objections."

I pointed out that the Act didn't limit the grounds for objection by "any user of any service affected" and that the TUCCs had to consider the objections, irrespective of their content. Mr Beetham agreed. "The scope for objection is wide open," he said. He went on: "TUCCs are Transport *Users* Consultative Committees and their role is to represent the views of rail users." This was an unexpected bonus. Poor old Frank Haywood could hardly believe his ears.

Mr Beetham said that, in addition to reporting on hardship, TUCCs had a role in reporting on other issues to the Minister, but "without comment." He added that whilst the 1962 Central Committee guidelines were 'pure form' for handling closure proposals at that time, public participation had developed a great deal since then. Unknowingly, he had encapsulated the crux of the difference in style and approach between the Yorkshire and North Western TUCCs. Whereas we had handled a number of recent key closure proposals and had come to terms with the 1980s, they had not and were still living in the 1960s and the Beeching era.

In reply to the question as to when the Public Hearings would be held, Frank Haywood said January, February and March were out because of the weather. I said it would largely depend on how long it took British Rail to respond to the 'Summary of Written Objections', but there was no way the Yorkshire TUCC would be able to complete its work by 1st April 1985.

I then referred to the merger with the North Eastern TUCC and repeated the view of our legal member, John Lambert, that as we were a committee with whom objections had been lodged, we had to see them through and report to the Minister. This could mean

that the Yorkshire TUCC would have to remain in business for a
period after 1st April – in parallel with the new TUCC for North
East England – solely to clear our outstanding closure proposals,
of which Settle–Carlisle was but one, albeit by far the largest. I
had put this view to the Central Committee as long ago as July but
had received no response.

Miss Blow and her colleague from the Department of Trade and
Industry were aghast at this, no doubt at the thought of the cost
and what it would do to their budget. Suddenly it seemed that the
merger was of far greater importance than the reason for the meeting – Settle–Carlisle, unless, of course, the two were interrelated.

Referring to his copy of the Act, Mr Beetham expressed the
view that the new TUCC for North East England would take over
the responsibilities of the Yorkshire TUCC. As the North Eastern
TUCC had handed their 69 objections over to the North Western
TUCC for consideration in accordance with Section 56(9) of the
Act, and as the Craven District would come within the North Western TUCC area from 1st April, then the whole issue could be
handled by the North Western committee. At this Mrs Munro
remarked that she "thought it would be handed over to the North
Western TUCC with the transfer of Craven."

I quickly intervened to say that this was not how we saw things.
Moreover, it would be a very contentious move which would be
subject to strong opposition by many objectors. I didn't add that,
so far as I was concerned – and felt that was true of the whole
Yorkshire committee – we simply would not be prepared to go
along with it. However, Miss Blow got the message. She said the
Department of Trade and Industry had received a number of
queries regarding the merger and the transfer of Craven. She asked
Mr Beetham to study the matter and give those concerned his
considered opinion in due course. This was agreed.

With that the meeting closed. It had been quite an afternoon.
The storm cloud on the horizon was that of our position vis-a-vis
the Craven District and it looked very much as if we were fast
approaching a 'Custer's last stand' position. Yet all was not doom
and gloom. I had been particularly encouraged by the stance taken
by Mr Beetham, the Treasury Solicitor, who had backed the Yorkshire TUCC's interpretation of the Act on all the other issues. In
particular I warmed to his definition of TUCCs as being there to
represent the views of rail users. This put a fresh complexion on
much that had happened during the past three years. Far from

being mavericks, it was the Yorkshire TUCC who had been upholding the Act.

By a happy coincidence, it had been arranged for Yorkshire members to travel over the Settle–Carlisle line the next day. This enabled me to report fully on the previous day's discussions. Members were horrified on learning of the moves which appeared designed to squeeze the Yorkshire TUCC out of the Settle–Carlisle closure proposal and utterly opposed any thought of the entire responsibility being placed in the hands of the North Western TUCC. The committee were determined that their Public Hearing would be held prior to the transfer of the Craven District to the North Western TUCC and the merger of the Yorkshire and North Eastern TUCCs on 1st April 1985. In other words, John Moorhouse and myself were told to get on with it!

Whilst such a rushed Public Hearing would be far from satisfactory, it represented a better bet than throwing in the towel and opting out of Settle–Carlisle altogether. Indeed, that was an option I would not have been prepared to accept. Above all we had the full support of the committee which was an essential requisite. The problem, of course, would be getting out the report by the end of March. But we would worry about that when the time came. One way would be to present a preliminary report.

By the end of October, John Moorhouse had provisionally booked the Victoria Hall in Settle for the first two days of our Public Hearing on 4th and 5th March 1985 and had venues lined up in Skipton (6th and 7th March) and Leeds (9th, 11th and 12th March). This would allow just over two weeks to reach our conclusions and submit some sort of report. Phew!

Another, more immediate problem had been drawn to my attention by Cumbria County Council. They complained that, from the end of October, a number of Sunday trains would no longer be diverted over the Settle–Carlisle line during the winter. Instead they would be replaced by buses between Carlisle and Preston whilst a Liverpool–Glasgow service would be diverted via York and Edinburgh! Cumbria were also peeved that the North Western TUCC had rubber stamped the decision.

Whilst avoiding the temptation to chide our colleagues across the Pennines – other than to remark that I assumed they were aware of the inconvenience this would cause to those with young children, heavy luggage and bikes, and that the journey time from Liverpool to Glasgow would increase from 6 hours 26 minutes to

7 hours 45 minutes – I said this raised a couple of interesting legal points.

Firstly, it was most irregular to withdraw a service from a line during the actual closure procedure, although the Act did not preclude this in so many words. The second and more important point was that the closure notice had been at fault – again! – for not referring to these services as, when British Rail propose to close a line, they were obliged to give 'particulars of any alternative services which it appears to the Board may be available.' Therefore details of the alternative bus service between Carlisle and Preston and the diverted rail service via York should have been included in the Settle–Carlisle closure notices.

I referred the matter to British Rail's Peter Hodge, now operating under the title of Planning Officer, Provincial Services; not that I expected it would lead to anything. It didn't. Six weeks later he came up with the old chestnut that diverted services did "not form passenger services within the meaning of Section 56(7) of the Transport Act 1962." As the Act refers to *all* railway passenger services and makes no reference to diverted services, I didn't think this stood up at all. However, as the last thing we wanted was yet another round of objections, we decided to let the matter rest.

I had let John Watson know of the latest developments, if only as a means of alerting him on the possible date for the opening of the Public Hearing for, as the local MP and objector No 1, I had promised him the first slot. I also told him that I understood the Department of Trade and Industry had deferred responding to a number of queries regarding the future of the Yorkshire TUCC and the position relating to Craven District, including one from an MP, pending receipt of legal advice from the Department of Transport.

John replied that he had, indeed, been waiting for such a reply and when he eventually received one from Lord Lucas of Chilworth, who had taken over responsibility for Consumer Affairs from Alex Fletcher, John had felt it necessary to ring Lord Lucas's office to ask what it meant. John continued:

"They said, with refreshing candour, that it was just a holding reply because they hadn't really made up their mind. I pointed out the political explosions which would result if the Public Enquiry were to be moved from the Yorkshire TUCC at this stage. The risk was acknowledged. I suspect that they will go on fudging the issue until it is too late to move the Enquiry away from your own sphere of responsibility."

As the year had progressed, I'd become increasingly fed up at the way this aspect of the Settle–Carlisle issue had been handled. For over a year – ever since October 1983 – we had continually stressed to the Department of Trade and Industry, Department of Transport, and the Central Transport Consultative Committee the adverse implications of transferring the Craven District to the North Western TUCC and the difficulties surrounding the merger of the Yorkshire and North Eastern TUCCs as they related to the Settle–Carlisle closure proposal. Yet nobody appeared the least bit interested.

Now, a month had passed since the 'summit conference' in London under the auspices of Miss Joyce Blow of the Department of Trade and Industry and we were still none the wiser. The situation had all the ingredients of a 'Yes Minister' episode, but for the fact it was not much fun being on the receiving end of the aggro generated by what I could only assume to be a combination of Ministerial indecision and departmental ineptitude – or was it the other way round? I neither knew nor cared. Therefore, I wasn't altogether amused when some mandarin at the Department of Trade and Industry suggested that it "might be helpful" if we could submit a paper to them on our closure proposals and the TUCC reorganisation. A case of better late than never, I supposed.

This we duly did. With attachments it ran to twelve pages for, in addition to Settle–Carlisle, we had Huddersfield–Denby Dale, Goole–Gilberdyke, Goose Hill–Wath Road, and the faintly erotic sounding Five Curves – a number of short lines in the Halifax, Huddersfield and Wakefield area used largely by freight, summer Saturdays only and diverted services. It wasn't until just before Christmas that John Moorhouse received a telephone call from one of the mandarins at the Department of Trade and Industry who "intimated" – funny how they can never actually tell you – that we would be remaining in business after 31st March 1985 to complete our closure proposals. But in what form we had no idea. On the strength of this we cancelled tentative arrangements for a March Public Hearing and decided to aim for May.

Even so, we had pulled out all the stops. John did a splendid job in compiling the 'Summary of Written Objections' which was sent to British Rail on 19th December. Of the 14,897 objections we received, 12,873 had been completed on the printed forms provided by the Joint Action Committee and were largely completed by passengers as they travelled on trains over the Settle–Carlisle line. The remaining 2,024 objections were in letter form. John extracted all the points of objections and placed them in the relevant section of his summary. This was broken down into seven main headings:

1) Use of Services Affected by the Proposal
2) General Use
3) Alternative Travel
4) Policy
5) Social and Economic Consequences of Closure
6) Freight Traffic
7) Other Issues

Each section was divided into a number of sub-sections which, in turn, comprised of specific points of objection of which there was an overall total of 369. For example, under (1) Use of Services Affected by the Proposal, there were 15 sub-sections ranging from (A) 'Settle' to (O) 'Long Distance Travel'. Under Settle there were 40 of the 369 points of objection ranging from the most popular:
"Objectors travel from Settle to Scotland, Leeds and beyond, the Midlands, Southern England and other parts of the country to visit friends and relatives, for holiday and other leisure trips at intervals of one month or more."
which was raised 78 times to that of the single point made by:
"A daily commuter from Langcliffe who uses the 07.39 train to reach her job in Bradford would have this journey to work made impossible. She had a young child to get ready before leaving home and so the early bus is out of the question. Again the extra walk to Giggleswick would be extremely inconvenient."
When they eventually responded, British Rail declined to answer the first point. To the second, and other queries regarding the 07.39 Settle–Leeds train, they replied:
"The problems faced by passengers currently travelling by the 07.39 from Settle to Leeds are appreciated, British Rail have therefore amended their proposal for this train to start from Giggleswick at 07.38 and to call at Long Preston, Hellifield and Gargrave in the same timings as now."
which might have satisfied some people but would be of little joy to the lady from Langcliffe, given that Giggleswick station was one mile from Settle station and there was no bus service.
Under Section (2) General Use, (B) Dales Rail, some 1,455

objectors made the general point that:

"Users of the Dales Rail services from both Lancashire and West Yorkshire will suffer considerably from this closure proposal. Most of these people use Dales Rail and the Dales Rail stations as access points for walking and other outdoor activities in the Yorkshire Dales and Eden Valley. The Dales Rail service is the only reasonable access to these areas because of the sparsity of other public transport and poor roads."

To this, British Rail replied:

"It is accepted that journeys to or from the areas served by Dales Rail stations would become difficult without private transport. By definition the expression Dales Rail stations relates to those stations served solely by Dales Rail trains and not to the British Rail stations at Appleby and Settle where alternative services will be available as already listed in this (Heads of Information) document."

Under Section (3), Alternative Travel, Giggleswick station came in for a great deal of criticism. Quite apart from the fact that 124 objectors said it was not well located to serve either Giggleswick or Settle communities, there was no bus service and that the road to it was unlit and dangerous for pedestrians; the station was dismissed by 55 objectors as not having the same facilities as Settle station. At Giggleswick there was no telephone, no toilet, an inadequate dilapidated shelter, whilst the Lancaster platform could only be reached by crossing the line. British Rail accepted much of this criticism, pointing out that Giggleswick was no different from many other unmanned stations throughout the country. They promised to "ask" British Telecom to provide a public telephone in event of consent to closure of the Settle–Carlisle line being authorised. Big deal!

The re-routing of the Nottingham–Glasgow service had not been overlooked. 342 objectors complained that:

"The diversion of the Nottingham–Glasgow service and the substitution of an inferior Leeds to Carlisle service in 1982 had been the biggest element in the run down of the line. Many objectors refer to the process as being 'Closure by Stealth'."

There was a particularly positive sub-section on Future Policy and Promotion. Among the many worthwhile suggestions 255 people pressed for the re-opening of the Dales Rail stations on a regular basis. On General Leisure use I was pleased to see that no fewer than 117 folk had asserted that:

"Railway enthusiasts enjoy travelling on the line especially with 'Class 40' or other interesting diesel motive power. Closure would deprive them of this pleasure completely."

To which British Rail responded that these comments had been "carefully noted."

So, too, was the point that was raised by the largest number of objectors – 2802 in all:

"The Settle–Carlisle railway line is a unique, outstandingly scenic, line both with regard to its engineering and construction and with regard to the countryside through which it passes. It is a magnificent and beautiful line, many say the 'best scenic route in England'. Travellers using the line derive great pleasure from their journey because of this. By and large they consider this to be the finest way of viewing the countryside through which it passes. Closure would deprive these people of this pleasure which is an important part of their lives."

In other words, as the British Rail leaflet put it, the Settle–Carlisle line is 'England's Greatest Historical Scenic Route.'

Whilst John had been engaged on his marathon task of preparing the 'Summary of Written Objections', I lent a hand extracting some of the statistics from the 12,873 objection forms. On alternative services, 15% would use the rail service via Carnforth, 10% would go by bus or coach, 32% would use private transport and, most significant of all, 43% would not make the journey at all.

A breakdown of the reasons for travel on services affected by the closure proposal indicated:

Work/Business	4%
Education	5%
Leisure	60%
Medical	1%
Shopping	9%
Visiting	21%

There was no doubt that the document represented a mine of information. Indeed, it provided a veritable kaleidoscope of almost every aspect of the Settle–Carlisle line and British Rail's proposal to close it.

The other task I undertook to relieve the pressure on the office, and one that I rather enjoyed, was preparing the geographical analysis of the addresses of those lodging objections. Whilst the cities and towns served by the Leeds–Carlisle service generated almost half (47%) of objections during the first round, the combined figure for the second and third rounds was 29% and the overall total came to 30%. During the first round of objections, Settle generated 200 objections representing 13%, more than Leeds which was just behind with 181 (12%). However, in the second and third rounds the position was reversed for whilst Settle amassed a further 253 objections it only represented 2% of those lodged, whereas Leeds with 1,438 was 11% of the total in the second and third rounds.

In the final countdown covering all three objection rounds, the area covered by the Yorkshire TUCC generated 7,622 objections (51%), Cumbria and the North Western TUCC Area 2,516 (17%), the North Eastern TUCC area 644 (4%) and the Rest of the United Kingdom 3,840 (26%). London and the Home Counties accounted for 900 objections (6%) and Scotland 673 (5%). the 275 objections from overseas represented 2% of the overall total. Of this figure, 34% were from the United States, 15% from Australia, 13% from Canada and 8% from West Germany. There was one objection from Libya. Colonel Gadaffi, perhaps?

13

AN UNACCEPTABLE REQUEST

"In these circumstances I would ask you to please let me have a copy of every individual objection. I am sure you must agree that it is every bit as essential that we understand the full nature of the objectors case as it is for them to understand ours."

Letter from British Rail to Yorkshire
TUCC dated 10th January 1985

During 1984, two important factors had emerged during the course of the seemingly endless Settle–Carlisle line closure proposal. That they had come to light owed much to the dogged determination of the Yorkshire TUCC. First was British Rail's acceptance of the 'any user of any service affected' clause in Section 56(8) of the Transport Act 1962 which had broadened the scope for objections to railway closures. The second related to the overall role of the TUCCs themselves. As the Treasury Solicitor at the Department of Transport had so succinctly said, it was to represent the views of rail users.

The latter point was of particular significance as it offered TUCCs an opportunity of a renaissance in the interpretation of their duties which could lead to them becoming consumer champions rather than the toothless watchdogs many claimed them to be. I recall that when I first joined the Yorkshire TUCC in 1973, my initial impression was that the committee was part of British Rail! True the misunderstanding was partly because the meeting was held at a British Rail hotel and in the presence of British Rail management. By contrast we had no formal contact with rail users.

When I became chairman in 1979, I endeavoured to correct this, but only had limited success. Whereas I got to know many users via their local action groups – usually formed to fight closure proposals or mount campaigns against cuts in services – and was occasionally invited to speak at their meetings, it was a one way traffic. Other than at Public Hearings, they seldom participated in ours, yet railway management was in attendance at virtually all our meetings.

Indeed, I recall one occasion when I invited a well known (to railway management) user to a meeting so that we could benefit from his specialist knowledge on a couple of the agenda items. As soon as British Rail got wind of this, there was uproar and they tried to get me to rescind the invitation. The reason they gave was the need to maintain confidentiality – an argument which simply didn't wash in this instance, given the integrity of the person involved. Moreover, British Rail leaked like a sieve anyway. I suspect the real reason for this particular fit of pique was because they were afraid of being upstaged by one of their customers.

If British Rail had a tendency to look upon the TUCCs as an extension of their public relations department, all too often TUCCs went along with it. For members, the get-togethers with British Rail were enjoyable occasions which provided an agreeable break, none more so than the annual trip in the general manager's saloon. Indeed, I suspect there were some members for whom this was the nearest they got to rail travel for I winced at the number who used their cars to attend committee meetings rather than sampling the train.

However TUCCs saw their role, it certainly wasn't one of primarily representing the views of rail users. Rather it was that of a quasi-judicial body that took a strictly neutral stance between British Rail and its customers, especially when it came to closure proposals. Yet one was bound to question how neutral that stance really was. For whilst TUCCs were staffed by British Rail personnel and were in close contact with railway management – often on a first name basis – contact with the actual users tended to be far more limited when, of course, it could be argued that it should have been the other way round.

My own views had not been all that different. If I was more consumer orientated it was largely because I felt I had a responsibility and duty to get to know the product and I could only do that by regularly using it – much to the chagrin of one senior British Rail manager who told me I travelled on too many trains! The same chap, when appointed liaison officer to the Yorkshire TUCC, asked me whether I was interested in Shakespeare or cricket and was a bit taken aback when I replied I was more interested in trains!

But I digress. When I chaired my first Public Hearing I had interpreted my role as being similar to that of a referee in charge of the game: British Rail v Objectors. It wasn't really until Settle–Carlisle when, in sporting terms, I felt British Rail had started to play dirty that my approach changed. It was because of this I felt we owed some sort of moral support to the users and objectors. It wasn't as if I could send Ron Cotton and Jim O'Brien off the field!

Our change of approach did not occur overnight. Nor was it generated solely by British Rail's handling of the Settle–Carlisle issue, although it undoubtedly was a major factor. Others included Eastern Region's handling of the Goose Hill–Wath Road and Huddersfield–Denby Dale proposals whilst the seemingly endless round of cuts to services from 1981 had drawn the Yorkshire TUCC's views closer to those of the users. Therefore, to discover that our role was to represent the views of rail users provided a considerable boost to our morale.

By no means all TUCCs took the same view. The London Regional Passengers Committee, for instance, had fallen foul of the Greater London Council for overlooking the 'any user of any service affected' clause by seeking to report to the Minister "on the hardship which they consider might be caused to the present users by the closure of Broad Street station." The Greater London Council pointed out, quite rightly, that the words "to the present users" were not in the Act; therefore the word 'hardship' should not be qualified in this restrictive manner.

Nor did the Central Transport Consultative Committee altogether help when it came out with a paper offering guidance to objectors giving evidence at Public Hearings. This, which I strongly questioned, sought to be equally restrictive. It stated that it was not the function of TUCCs "to consider and report on any other aspects of the proposal" (other than hardship) when, of course, under the Act TUCCs were obliged to "consider the objection" and the grounds for objection were wide open. More ludicrous, certainly so far as Settle–Carlisle was concerned, was the claim that "committee members have been supplied with copies of all the objections." All 14,897 of them? Not likely. Members relied on the 'Summary of Written Objections', copies of which were made available to British Rail and objectors so that everyone was on an equal footing.Therefore, the Yorkshire TUCC decided to take no notice of the Central Committee edict. After all, it wasn't in the Act.

Such was my faith in the Act, that I coined the phrase 'Trust the Act'. Yet of all who sat on the Central Committee, only Barry

Flaxman – the East Anglian chairman – appreciated just how nuances within the Act could be used for the benefit of rail users if only TUCCs were prepared to grasp them. True, this would mean that they would have to discard their cloak of neutrality, but this was largely worthless, certainly so far as closure proposals were concerned, as it was the Secretary of State for Transport and not the TUCC who decided whether a line remained open or not.

Time for reflection on the finer points of the railway closure procedure and role of TUCCs proved short-lived. For 1985 was not two weeks old before we were once again engaged in a battle of words with British Rail. On the basis of the assurance from the Department of Trade and Industry that the Yorkshire TUCC would continue its responsibility for Settle–Carlisle after 31st March, secretary John Moorhouse had put back the provisional bookings for a March Public Hearing a couple of months to May. In order to get all our documentation out to objectors in good time, we required British Rail's response to our 'Summary of Written Objections' no later than 8th March.

On 11th January, John received a letter from Ron Cotton, the Settle–Carlisle project manager, which "acknowledged receipt" of the summary which would be studied in detail in conjunction with the summary to be submitted by the North Western TUCC which was not expected for "some little time." The letter continued:

"We had correspondence some months ago over my request for copies of individual objections to be sent to myself. We have considered the matter again in light of your reply and feel that it is essential that we have copies of individual objections. The summary is insufficient for us to fully understand the detail of objections and to be properly briefed for the Public Hearing.

In these circumstances I would ask you to please let me have a copy of every individual objection. I am sure you must agree that it is every bit as essential that we understand the full nature of the objectors case as it is for them to understand ours."

I was very cross indeed. Quite apart from the fact that I thought the matter had been settled last September, I felt Cotton – who in terms of British Rail seniority was several grades higher than John Moorhouse – was trying to 'pull rank' in order to overrule a decision made by the committee and which had been confirmed in correspondence by myself. As for stating that John's summary was "insufficient"; well, that was rich coming from one who had provided such a scant 'Heads of Information' document that it was virtually worthless. Moreover, if British Rail were not already aware of the objectors case against closure, they were even bigger fools than I took them to be.

So we drafted a reply in which John reiterated the points in my letter of 20th September that it was the committee and not British Rail who were required to consider the objections. He also stressed that the 'Summary of Written Objections' was representative of all those objections lodged and added that, so far as the Public Hearing was concerned, there was no knowing what objectors might say on the day.

Back came the reply dated 24th January:

"I have duly noted your letter of 16th January and am at a loss to understand your refusal to let me have copies of the individual objections when your colleague at the North Western TUCC has so readily agreed to supply me with details of all objections submitted to the North Western committee.

This closure proposal is the most important and contentious closure case for many, many years, and the relevant parties concerned should be in possession of all the relevant facts to enable them to make a meaningful contribution to the proceedings."

Mr Cotton also declined to give an assurance that he would provide a response to the summary by 8th March. He made the point – which had some substance – that British Rail were considering the matter in an overall concept, notwithstanding that two TUCCs were involved, therefore I could understand his wish to withhold his response until he had received the North Western TUCC's 'Summary of Written Objections.'

I realised that we had something of a problem on our hands, as we were required to report to the Minister of Transport as "quickly as possible" on the proposal and I was acutely aware that David Mitchell, the Minister responsible for railways who would have a big say in the final decision, was anxious to have our report as quickly as possible. Therefore I asked the general manager of the London Midland Region, Malcolm Southgate, whether he was in a position to provide an assurance that we would have British Rail's response to the summary by 8th March, and if not by then, when would it be ready.

Mr Southgate replied on 12th February to the effect that he could give no such assurance:

"As you will know, we have serious reservations about the form of your summary. To enable us to be in a position to respond fully at the Public Hearings, we need to have a clearer view of the detailed background to a significant number of the individual objections mentioned in the summary.

I fully understand the sheer volume of work involved in this case and would certainly not want unnecessarily to delay the procedure in any way but in the circumstances I feel I have no alternative other than to wait until we have had a chance to study the details to be provided by the North Western TUCC.

So far as the proposed dates of the hearing are concerned, I should perhaps advise you that we will probably be represented by Leading Counsel in this case. It would therefore be appropriate for the hearing dates to be agreed between ourselves and both TUCCs before any firm arrangements are made."

The Yorkshire TUCC met on 20th February and considered the Cotton/Southgate correspondence. Members deplored British Rail's arbitary approach and the way they had attempted to exert pressure on John Moorhouse to reverse a decision of the committee. As we had no idea when British Rail's response to the 'Summary of Written Objections' would be ready, it was agreed that the provisional bookings for the Public Hearing in May be cancelled and consideration of alternative dates be deferred until after a response had been received.

Members did not take kindly to Mr Southgate's inference that, as British Rail would probably be represented by Leading Counsel, the dates for the Public Hearing had to be agreed with British Rail – and, no doubt, Leading Counsel's chambers – before any arrangements were made. I remarked that whether British Rail were represented by Leading Counsel or the Queen of Sheba, the dates for the Public hearing were a matter for the committee; in this case in consultation with the North Western TUCC as it had been agreed there would be no clash of hearings. I was asked to respond to Mr Southgate accordingly, which I duly did, save that I made no reference to the Queen of Sheba!

Just as the Yorkshire TUCC steadfastly refused to let British Rail have copies of the individual objections, so, too, it rejected the Joint Action Committee's request for a list of objectors. The North Western TUCC also refused the request on the basis that letters of objection were treated as confidential between the writer, the committee and the Secretary of State for Transport. Whether he would actually find time to read them was unclear, whilst the North Western committee appeared to have overlooked that copies of all their objections had been sent to British Rail!

The Joint Action Committee also asked both TUCCs not to proceed with the Public Hearings until results of a judicial review on the Marylebone closure procedure were known. This was an extension of the 'little local difficulty' which had occurred during the Broad Street proposal and had been sought by the Greater London Council on a decision by the London Regional Passengers Committee not to allow objectors to the Marylebone proposal to be represented by counsel for the purpose of cross-examination of British Rail and making final submissions.

We had no difficulty in agreeing to the request because British Rail's delay in responding to the 'Summary of Written Objections' would mean the judicial review should be completed well before our Settle–Carlisle Public Hearing which I didn't envisage taking place before the autumn at the earliest. Mind you, I had little enthusiasm for the involvement of counsel in Public Hearings, either appearing for the objectors or representing British Rail. They would only take up much valuable time with long winded legal niceties. Moreover, we had managed quite well without them in the past.

However, I was concerned that the consequences of the judicial review, rather than leading to a greater flexibility in the interpretation of the Act, could end up with some learned judge stating that, to all intents and purposes, the Act meant TUCCs could 'only' consider hardship, even if it didn't say so in so many words. Such judgement would be exploited for all its worth by British Rail (and, perhaps, by the North Western and other TUCCs) and would undermine all the efforts of the Yorkshire TUCC and myself to gain acceptance of our more liberal interpretation of the Act.

I was concerned, too, that the judicial review could add to doubts which were already being expressed regarding the ability of the TUCCs to handle the complexities of the closure procedure. This would weaken what credibility we had which, in turn, would make the task of staging the Public Hearing all the harder. The Association of Metropolitan County Councils and the Joint Action Committee were amongst those who had pressed for the Settle–Carlisle line proposal to be passed to a Public Enquiry so issues other than those related to hardship would be given fair vent and British Rail subjected to cross examination. I felt it was not the time for such a move. We had lived with the case for almost four years and should be allowed to complete our task. If, after consideration of our report, the Minister consented to closure of the line, that would be the time for a Public Enquiry.

Nor, too, were my problems eased when we learnt that the Joint Action Committee were blandly seeking at least seven days to present their evidence at the Public Hearing. On this basis there would be only two days left for the local authorities and the hundreds of individual objectors who wished to speak. It simply wasn't on. Moreover, I was aware such requests could ultimately alienate my committee who, largely due to British Rail's continual bungling of the issue, were generally sympathetic towards the objectors. To expect lay members to sit for more than nine days was, I felt, unreasonable.

I was concerned that, by making such demands, the Joint Action Committee could be playing into British Rail's court. If British Rail's representations at the Public Hearing were adroitly presented and delivered with charm, tact and good humour by a QC well versed in such techniques, they might run rings round hour upon hour of evidence from an assortment of hikers, bikers, gricers and local government officials.

Nearer home a more immediate problem was finally resolved. On 24th January I had been asked to meet Lord Lucas, the minister responsible for consumer affairs. He sought my views on the impending merger of the Yorkshire and North Eastern TUCCs. I told him that whilst the committee and myself had argued against it because both the size of the committee and the area could prove unwieldly, I was confident that a structure could be evolved to make it work.

Briefly, what I had in mind was this: the new TUCC for North East England or, for the sake of brevity, North East TUCC, would consider major policy and general issues applicable throughout the region; whilst three sub-committees covering the traditional North East, North Yorkshire and Humberside, and West and South Yorkshire would consider specific items relating to their respective areas.

I also used the opportunity to stress to Lord Lucas the absence of logic in excluding the Craven District from the area covered by the new committee and added that, as the Yorkshire TUCC would be unable to fulfil their commitments to all the 5 current closure proposals, we felt we would be obliged to complete our work after 31st March. That didn't go down too well. I also suggested a decision should be made as to who was going to be chairman of the new committee as time was running out.

Yet it wasn't until almost a month later on 21st February that I was told I was to chair North East TUCC from 1st April and that the new committee's area would include the Craven District for the time being. So after months of fudging the issue the Department of Trade and Industry had finally made up its mind. Whether the delay was due to the politicians or civil servants, or a combination of the two, it struck me as a most unbusinesslike way of handling things.

I suspected my continued involvement in the Settle–Carlisle saga owed more to events than any wish on the part of those responsible for my appointment. Therefore, it looked as if John Watson had been right when he said they would continue to fudge the issue until it was too late to move the Public Hearing away from my responsibility. Even Peter Horton of the Joint Action Committee was pleased. "We think this is good news. Common sense has prevailed at last," he told 'The Craven Herald'.

Deliberations regarding my future coincided with a remarkable boost to business on the line.For if I had been critical of Ron Cotton's failure to understand the closure procedure, I had nothing but admiration for his track record as a marketing man. His first year as project manager for the Settle–Carlisle line had seen a big increase in patronage. During 1984 the line had taken 80% more revenue than in 1982, the year the Nottingham–Glasgow service was re-routed away from the line.

Not that all this was due to Ron Cotton. The very fact that British Rail wished to close the Settle–Carlisle line had made it a brand named product on the strength of media coverage alone. Then FOSCLA and, more recently, the Joint Action Committee had generated much interest and had been promoting the line, both on their own and in co-operation with British Rail. Indeed, pontifica-tions by my humble self since 1981 were said by at least two senior railway managers to have been contributory factors to the revival of the line's fortunes!

But few would deny that Ron Cotton, often up against insuper-able odds (particularly from 'colleagues' in Eastern Region), played the major role in exploiting the unique attractions of the line from 1984. In doing so, he must have posed senior British Rail management with a problem of schizophrenic proportions. It did not help the case for closure when revenue had almost doubled within two years, yet the hard earned cash was sorely needed by

THE AUTHOR The Author about to board a diesel multiple unit at Doncaster.

Yorkshire Post

A MAN ALONE. British Rail's Settle–Carlisle project manager, Ron Cotton. Sent to close the line, he decided to promote it and usage more than doubled.

Barry Wilkinson

THE COMMITTEE. The Yorkshire TUCC about to board a Sheffied-bound DMU at Huddersfield *circa* 1981.

Huddersfield Examiner

STAR SUPPORT. Actor Bill Owen – 'Compo' of BBC TV's 'Last of the Summer Wine' leaving Leeds for Carlisle on 20th March 1985. *Yorkshire Post*

RED STAR PARCELS. Settle also does a good parcels business. *K & J Jelley*

Councillor Michael Simmons – Chairman of the West Yorkshire Passenger
Transport Authority.   *Jack Hickes*

John Watson, MP for Skipton
and Ripon until June 1987.

POLITICIANS WHO HELPED THE FIGHT.

Councillor Bill Cameron – Chairman of Cumbria County Council's Highways and
Transportation Committee.

DALES RALLY VIPs. Pictured at the Dales Rally on 15th September 1984 (left to right) are John Watson MP, Coun. Tommy Cardus, Mike Harding, Peter Horton (Settle & Carlisle Joint Action Committee) and Coun. Beth Graham. *K & J Jelley*

YOUNG CAMPAIGNERS. Schoolchildren show their support for the line at Hellifield Station. *K & J Jelley*

'ENGLAND'S GREATEST HISTORICAL SCENIC ROUTE'. County Councillor Beth Graham, pictured alongside Ribblehead Viaduct.

The Independent

SEEING THINGS FOR HIMSELF. Junior Transport Minister David Mitchell MP (on the right) taking a close look at the Ribblehead Viaduct on 17th May 1984.

Yorkshire Post

LANDSLIP AT MALLERSTANG. Thousands of tons of ballast were required to strengthen the embankment following a landslip on 5th January 1988.   *Peter Walton*

THE THAMES–CLYDE EXPRESS. The 'Thames–Clyde' from London St. Pancras to Glasgow was the most famous of the Settle & Carlisle Line's trains. It combined the activities of a St. Pancras to Sheffield service with those of a service from the East Midlands to Glasgow. Patronage was good and relief services had to be provided at busy times. This photograph shows Rebuilt Royal Scot 4–6–0 No. 46145 'THE DUKE OF WELLINGTON'S REGIMENT (WEST RIDING)' on the northbound service on 3rd October 1959. The train is composed of BR Mark I stock, except for the first class kitchen-diner which is of LMS period II vintage.   *Gavin Morrison*

NOTTINGHAM–GLASGOW. The through services from St. Pancras were withdrawn in 1976 requiring passengers from Leicester and Kettering (which generally included a large number of 'Corby Scots') to change at Nottingham. This was the first nail in the coffin of the line. The morning Glasgow–Nottingham service is seen at Ais Gill on 15th April 1981 with Class 45 No. 45056 heading a rake of Commonwealth-bogied Mark I coaches.

Les Nixon

STEAM FREIGHT. Class 9F 2–10–0 No. 92233 of Carlisle Kingmoor depot approaches Blea Moor on 31st August 1967 with the Long Meg–Widnes block anhydrite train.

Mike Goodfield

DIESEL FREIGHT. Class 25 No. 25125 seen at Ais Gill on 15th April with a southbound train of 4-wheeled vans. *Les Nixon*

PLANNED DIVERSION. Class 47/4 'Generator' No. 47410 seen at Stainforth at the head of a southbound express comprising Mark III stock diverted from the West Coast main line. The train would then use the Hellifield–Blackburn route to regain the West Coast Route near Preston. *Les Nixon*

UNPLANNED DIVERSION. On 20th June 1984, Class 47/0 No. 47269 is seen piloting Class 87/0 No. 87018 'Lord Nelson' at Gallensay near Crosby Garrett with the 16.31 Carlisle–Euston. The train was diverted due to the wires being down on the WCML. *Peter Walton*

DALES RAIL. Two two-car Class 108 DMUs are seen at Horton-in-Ribblesdale with a Dales Rail special for Appleby on 3rd December 1983. *Les Nixon*

LOCAL SERVICE. The Nottingham–Glasgow services were re-routed leaving the Settle & Carlisle line with a Class 31-hauled local service. 31313 is seen at Helwith Bridge with a motley collection of BR Mark I-bogied Mark I stock forming a Carlisle–Leeds train on 24th July 1982. *Les Nixon*

▲**PEACE.** The only sign of life in this snow scene at Garsdale on 4th January 1984 is the wisp of smoke emanating from the station building on the right.
Les Nixon

▼**BUSTLE.** A busy scene at Appleby as passengers disgorge from a down steam-heated train.
Pete Walton

RECORD BREAKER. 1988 was the Centenary of Class A4 Pacific No. 4468 'MAL-LARD's unbeaten world speed record for a steam locomotive. This was celebrated by a series of railtours, including this one on the Settle & Carlisle line on 27th August. No. 4468 is seen approaching Ais Gill Summit having restarted from a stall at Birkett.

A J Woof

FREIGHT POWER. In complete contrast to the above, Class 8F 2–8–0 No. 48151, a type of locomotive designed for heavy freight haulage, is seen at Blea Moor on 25th June 1988.

John Checkley

RELIABLE RAIL. The railway often keeps going when roads are affected by snow. Class 45/1 No. 45101 heads the 09.07 Leeds–Carlisle out of Blea Moor Tunnel on 4th January 1984. *L A Nixon*

INNOVATION. In order to attract modern-image railway enthusiasts to the trains at times of low demand, one return trip between Leeds and Carlisle was piloted by locomotives normally only used on freight services on Saturdays during November 1989. The experiment was a great success, passenger loadings as high as 1000 being recorded! Class 20s 20061 and 20093 are seen piloting Class 47/4 No 47444 (required for train heating) at Ribblehead on 25th November 1989. The experiment has been repeated in 1990 with similar success. *Les Nixon*

a British Railways Board committed to reducing the Public Service Obligation (government subsidy) by 25% in three years. If only InterCity had performed half as well!

The official British Rail and, indeed, Ron Cotton's answer to all this was that it was policy to market the line whilst it was still there and that the increased patronage was due to a mix of enthusiasts making a last run over the line together with an influx of leisure travellers who had heard of its scenic attractions and wished to see them before it closed. Both markets had a relatively short life.

I wasn't so sure. I had a gut feeling that the potential of the Settle–Carlisle line was more sustainable, given its unique attractions and the wide variety of the market segments which used it. Therefore, I had little doubt that the market existed. What it required was effective promotion. It was here Ron Cotton was in his element. He belonged to the railway equivalent of Tesco's late Sir Jack Cohen's "pile 'em high and sell 'em cheap" school of marketing.

Ron Cotton put this philosophy to the test during the traditional quiet months of February and March with a 'Fantastic Offer!' pitched at £5 (£3 for children and railcard holders) for day return travel between any two stations between Leeds and Carlisle inclusive. Backed by nothing more than a simple hand bill which exclaimed "If you haven't travelled the Settle–Carlisle in winter – you ain't seen nothing yet", it was just a case of waiting to see how the public would respond. They didn't let him down because they knew a good offer when they saw one and against £11.60 for the normal fare, this was a bargain.

Within a couple of weeks the normal weekday train of 5 coaches had to be doubled in length – it had already been strengthened to 10 coaches on Saturdays. There were such acute overcrowding problems on Saturdays that relief trains were provided on 23rd February and 9th, 16th, 23rd, and 30th March. Business became almost an embarrassment on weekdays, too. From counts I made at Leeds station, the 09.00 to Carlisle left with 304 passengers on Wednesday 20th March. A week later it was full and standing with over twice that number – I made it about 630. The following day business fell back by a couple of hundred to a still very respectable 425, so there was just about a seat for everyone who joined at Leeds. Yet exactly a year before on Thursday 29th March 1984, the same train had left Leeds with only 86 passengers. Cotton had hit the jack pot!

On the final Saturday of the offer some 500 joined the 09.00 comprising 2 Class 31 locomotives hauling 10 Mark 1 coaches. It was followed 12 minutes later by a Class 47 locomotive hauling 8 Mark 2 coaches with 410 on board whilst a second relief comprising 1 x 4 Car DMU and 1 x 2 Car DMU, due out at 09.28, eventually got away at 10.04 with 176 stragglers, the delay being due to a late running connection from Doncaster – a Class 141 DMU had failed and arrived over an hour late hauled by a Class 47 locomotive.

On that March Saturday morning, almost 1,100 passengers had left Leeds station for a journey over 'England's Greatest Historical Scenic Route.' Indeed, after including those who joined the trains at Keighley, Skipton and Settle, Philippa Simpson of FOSCLA recorded an overall total of 1,466. It was a remarkable achievement.

It struck me as a particularly happy coincidence that it should occur on the penultimate day of the Yorkshire TUCC. If nothing else, our resistance to British Rail's bovver boy approach to the closure proposal could be said to have made a modest contribution to that day's success. Whether it marked the dawn of the line's renaissance or just its final fling remained to be seen.

14

A SOLICITOR'S LETTER

"I have been asked by the Chairman to write to you because he is greatly concerned that your committee has declined to supply copies of individual objections..."

Extract from a letter from the Chief solicitor and Legal Advisor, British Railways Board, dated 17th April 1985.

With the merger of the Yorkshire and North Eastern TUCCs on 1st April 1985 into the new North East TUCC – complete with the Craven District, for the time being – I felt rather like a captain who had taken charge of a larger ship with a mixed crew, half of it of unknown quality. It wasn't something I particularly relished and, but for the fact that I felt I still had a positive input to make in an endeavour to save the Settle–Carlisle line, I would not have been too sorry had I been stood down. But fate, or Lord Lucas, had decided otherwise.

Whilst I knew the direction in which I wished to steer the new committee, I was by no means confident I would be able to persuade those members of the crew who were unknown to me that I was piloting the vessel in the right direction. Therefore, I felt the best strategy would be to adopt a 'business as usual' approach in the hope that both 'sides' of the committee would gell together reasonably quickly and smoothly. That they did, but for the odd doubts relating more to style than policy, reflected credit on all concerned and within six months any 'us and them' syndrome had been cured.

But during those first six months of new North East TUCC I had a number of tricky channels to negotiate, not least those relating to the Settle–Carlisle closure proposal. Of all the unfinished business from the former committees, it was by far and away the most formidable. With regard to the other closure proposals, that for the Five Curves had been wrapped up by the old Yorkshire

TUCC in March. Goole–Gilberdyke, which had been in limbo for some time pending a deal between Humberside County Council and British Rail, was reprieved when the county council coughed up £800,000 towards the cost of repairing the swing bridge at Goole. As good a case of extortion as I'd come across!

That only left Goose Hill–Wath Road, the report for which was in the final draft stage, and Huddersfield–Denby Dale, the Public Hearing for which was scheduled for the autumn. Neither had attracted much interest from the former North Eastern members. It was Settle–Carlisle that they were attracted to, quite understandably, as it was the 'big one' and they were anxious to participate in the action.

I did not blame them. Had I been in the same position I would have felt exactly the same. Yet I was wary. Unlike the former Yorkshire members who I knew well and had worked with for several years, the North Easterners I'd inherited were a largely unknown quantity. What little I knew of their track record suggested they might be more acquiescent towards British Rail; like the North Western committee.

So when Settle–Carlisle came up at the first meeting of the new North East TUCC on 16th April and former members' of the old North Eastern Committee expressed a wish to participate in the Public Hearing, I endeavoured to steer over the issue by explaining that, as the old Yorkshire TUCC had received the objections, it should be the former Yorkshire members who should, as far as possible, complete the procedure and report to the Minister. As there was no indication when British Rail would be ready for the Public Hearing, it was agreed consideration of the matter be deferred.

The next hurdle I faced was a meeting with members of the North Western TUCC to consider arrangements for the Settle–Carlisle Public Hearings, although British Rail could give no indication when they would be ready. It was a 'return date' for the meeting held in February 1984 which had generated a good deal of rancour as our North Western colleagues had all but carpeted us for being too pro-user. Since then much had happened and we entered the second round of discussions in a far stronger position.

It was as a result of our initiative that British Rail had revised and re-issued its closure notices to broaden the scope for objections. Then the pronouncement by the Treasury Solicitor at the Department of Transport that TUCCs were there to represent the views of rail users had legitimised our stance. Also, I suppose that, much to many people's surprise, I had been appointed chairman of the new North East TUCC ranked as a plus point. We were also acting as host and I was on home ground as the meeting took place in a private room at the Queen's Hotel in Leeds on 22nd April.

From the outset it was evident that there was a new mood of conciliation in the air, not that we allowed it to lead to any concessions. I opened by referring to the two factors which could significantly affect the Public Hearings and about which there was little we could do. First was British Rail's decision to be represented by leading counsel. As a result I expected the county councils and Joint Action Committee to follow suit. This could result in the Public Hearing becoming a stage for some long winded legal diatribes and extend the time required for the Public Hearings, something none of us wanted.

Second, the impending judicial review regarding the rights of objectors to cross-examine British Rail at the Marylebone Public Hearing would not only affect that case, but could have an impact on all future Public Hearings, especially those for the Settle–Carlisle line which had attracted so much public interest.

Olive Clarke, the North Western chairman agreed. She felt it important that both TUCCs should present a united front. Nevertheless, she appreciated the many pitfalls that could lie ahead and agreed that she and I, as the respective chairmen, would require as much freedom of discretion as possible to meet any eventualities on the day. After consideration of a number of minor points, it was agreed that the Public Hearings would be conducted in accordance with the Transport Act 1962, and that was that. It had been a very happy meeting.

I'd have enjoyed it more but for one thing. It was the letter I had received that morning from the Chief Solicitor and Legal Adviser to the British Railways Board. To say it was burning a hole in my pocket was an understatement. Nevertheless, I decided it would be prudent to keep it under wraps, for the time being at any rate, because I did not like the look of it at all. It stated:

"I have been asked by the Chairman to write to you because he is greatly concerned that your Committee has declined to supply copies of the individual objections, notwithstanding paragraph 40 of the 'Handbook on Transport Users Consultative Committees'.

That paragraph says in part –

'Copies of the objections will be circulated by the Secretary of the Committee to the Board concerned, and an opportunity will be given to the Board concerned, prior to the consideration of the case by the Committee, to reply in writing to the grounds of objections, and if so, this will be sent to the objectors.'

The Summary which has been supplied does not meet the requirements of that paragraph and, without copies of the individual objections, the Board can neither understand fully nor reply adequately to the points which have been canvassed.

I hope therefore that your Committee will reconsider its position on this issue. If there is concern that certain objections may have been sent by members of the Board's staff, the Board will be happy to receive copies with the names and addresses deleted.

I have been asked also to request that the Committee modifies the Summary by cross-referencing each point of objection to the reference numbers for the individual objections. In view of the sheer volume of objections, I am sure you will agree some system of cross-referencing will be desirable for the purpose of the hearings. The Committee for the North Western Area has done this and it has greatly facilitated our Project Manager's consideration of the analysis and individual objections copies of which that Committee has given us.

Finally, may I touch on your comments to Mr Southgate about dates for the hearings and your view that the fixing of dates is a matter solely for the Committee. Whilst I would agree that the final responsibility for fixing dates rests with your Committee and the Committee for the North Western Area, we do believe, given the complexities of this case and the likely length of the hearings, that it is reasonable and in the interests of all persons for there to be agreement on the dates and for them to be fixed as far in advance as possible. Perhaps you will be kind enough to let me know what dates the two Committees have in mind."

I was not amused. In fact, I was very angry. For a start, I had met the British Railways Board chairman, Sir Robert Reid, on a number of occasions when we had passed the time of day on various issues – although not Settle–Carlisle. Therefore, the least he might have done was to write to me personally, rather than fire the first shot across our bows under cover of a solicitors letter.

Perhaps I'd led a sheltered life, but I had never been involved in litigation – or as near as dammit – before. Until my involvement in the Settle–Carlisle case, my dealings with the legal profession had been most amicable. In business I had engaged solicitors, largely to draw up or check agreements. I had also used their services for conveyancing property. Indeed, a highlight of my year was attending the Bradford Law Society dinner as a guest. So whilst I was acquainted and conversant with the law, I was not used to being on the receiving end of letters phrased in 'pay up or else' terms. Moreover, I had already gone to great pains to explain to Ron Cotton why we could not meet his request for copies of the objections.

Nor, at the back of my mind, was I quite sure how my new committee would respond. That the North Western TUCC had so readily agreed to provide British Rail with copies of the objections might make the stance adopted by the former Yorkshire members appear unreasonable in the eyes of the ex-North Eastern faction on the committee. Yet, at the end of the day, it was a matter of principle on which I felt we could not afford to budge. Therefore, I was in no hurry to respond. Taking a lead from British Rail's chief solicitor, I asked John Moorhouse to acknowledge the letter thus:

"I have been asked by the Chairman to thank you for your letter of 17th April. He will be replying to you in due course."

I then set forth to consult my 'railway' solicitor.

By now, George – that's not his real name by the way – had got to know the ins and outs of the Transport Act 1962 quite well. He was a bit of a gricer, too, which helped. In this instance there were two things which particularly bothered me. First was the reference in the letter to the 'Handbook of Transport Users Consultative Committees'. It had been out of print for years. Indeed, I'd never heard of it until three or four years after I'd become a TUCC chairman so it had never been standard issue for chairmen or committee members. Whilst I had considerable difficulty in acquiring a copy, British Rail quoted from it as if it were the law.

The other matter that concerned me was that the letter had come from the Chief Solicitor and Legal Adviser himself. It was one thing taking issue on legal matters with Ron Cotton or, even, the general manager of the London Midland Region. But chief solicitors and legal advisers were a completely different ball game. I felt out of my depth and didn't like it at all.

George was reassuring. "You never know, it could be a try on," he said. Moreover, he doubted whether the TUCC handbook had any real clout. So we sat down and came up with the following draft:

"The Committee is handling the Settle–Carlisle closure proposal in accordance with the provisions of the Transport Act 1962. Section 56(9) of that Act clearly states that it is the Committee, not the British Railways Board, who are obliged to receive and consider objections; a point that was made abundantly clear in the statutory notices published by the Board under Section 56(7) of the Act.

The practice of providing a Summary, to which the Board subsequently respond, was established prior to my appointment as Chairman in 1979. It has been employed in every closure proposal held under my jurisdiction and, until now, both the Board and objectors have found the procedure satisfactory. Therefore I am surprised that the Board can neither understand fully nor reply adequately to the points raised in this instance.

I am aware of the terms of paragraph 40 of the Handbook on Transport Users Consultative Committees. This handbook has, of course, no statutory authority and is intended merely to provide guidelines for interpreting the Act. Furthermore, the latest edition of the handbook was published over 20 years ago and since then the practice and procedure involved in a closure proposal has been modified and developed into the form mentioned in the previous paragraph. The only constant factor is the Act itself and in particular Section 56(9) which the Committee is determined to follow.

For these reasons I am unable to recommend that the Committee should reconsider its position and concur to your request that the Board should be provided with copies of the objections.

Whilst noting your request that we modify the Summary by incorporating a cross-referencing system, and that where copies of the objections have been given to the Board, this has greatly facilitated your Project Manager's consideration of the Summary and the individual objections; I can only refer again to Section 56(9) of the Act and repeat that it is the Committee, not the Board, who are obliged to receive and consider objections.

I agree that dates for the Public Hearing should be fixed as far in advance as possible and that, where possible, these should be agreed with those involved although this is difficult in a case where over 300 objectors have intimated a wish to speak. The Committee will consider the question of dates when it receives your response to the Summary or, failing that, confirmation that you do not wish to respond to the Summary.

Finally, I would add that the Committee are most concerned at the possible length of the Public Hearing. That this is likely to be even more extended due, in part, to the manner in which the Board have handled the whole Settle–Carlisle issue since 1981, is a matter of regret."

I was happy with the draft, especially at the way George had got round the question of the handbook. I had asked Len Dumelow, secretary of the Central Transport Consultative Committee about the handbook as they were given as the publishers. He had replied that he'd "thrown it out of the window!" years ago. That was encouraging. If only we could persuade the Chief Solicitor and Legal Adviser to do likewise.

As British Rail frequently took six weeks or more to respond to relatively simple letters, I didn't reply immediately after George and myself had agreed the draft as I wished to seek the views of some of my members. A meeting of the North East TUCC's West and South Yorkshire sub-committee on 13th May proved an ideal opportunity to explain the situation to them. They unanimously endorsed my letter which I posted immediately after the meeting. As one member, Mrs Anita Woolman said, it was as if British Rail were asking for all the evidence before going to court. I particularly appreciated her analogy as she was a JP.

Legal issues continued to dominate the scene as, on the same day, Mr Justice Kennedy was giving judgment in the High Court on the Greater London Council's application for a judicial review on the procedural arrangements for the London Regional Passengers Committee's Public Hearing into the Marylebone station closure proposal. It was a complex case and the judgment ran to many pages. However, the crux of it was to uphold the committee's right to decide how they conducted their Public Hearings and their decision not to allow cross-examination of British Rail.

Whilst the judgment came down on the side of the committee rather than the objectors, the Joint Action Committee found at least one crumb of comfort. They wrote to Ron Cotton seeking a "clear exposition" of British Rail's case for proposing closure of the Settle–Carlisle line. In his letter, secretary Peter Horton claimed that in broadcasts, public and private interviews, railway officials had given a variety of reasons including the cost of repairing the Ribblehead Viaduct, that the line was a 'sore thumb' and no longer required, and that it was a 'political' decision. He continued:

"In giving his decision, Mr Justice Kennedy said that everybody involved had a right to know the case they had to meet. At the present time we feel this is not the situation as regards the Settle–

Carlisle proposals and that the closure process should not proceed until such a statement is forthcoming from British Rail."

Horton had sent a copy of his letter to us and asked for our comments. As we had yet to read the official court transcript and understood there was to be an appeal, there was little we could say. So I just replied that we were handling the Settle–Carlisle closure proposal in accordance with the Transport Act 1962 and left it at that.

I felt court action of this kind wasn't particularly helpful. It was a pity the London Regional Passengers Committee had been man-oeuvered into a position where users – or, in this case, representatives of users – had so little faith in the committee that was meant to 'represent the views of rail users' that they took the issue to court. It had also given the judge an opportunity to emphasise that TUCCs do not decide any issue other than hardship. This did not help us with regard to Settle–Carlisle, although Mr Justice Kennedy did add a qualification that, whilst TUCCs must be distinguished from bodies which have rights of decision in relation to an individual's livelihood or his property, the distinction must not be carried too far because many individuals may be seriously affected if there is a railway closure and the effect may extend to their means of livelihood. That could be helpful.

But overall, I felt the case had not encouraged those like myself who had, on a softly, softly basis, been extending our remit by taking account of issues other than hardship and referring to them in our reports. We had just done that in the report on Goose Hill–Wath Road. This had concluded that whilst there would be no hardship to users of the two summer services involved, rail services between Leeds and Sheffield had been run down to an inadequate level. We even took up the suggestion of objectors that reinstatement of the Sandal curve would benefit an improved Leeds–Sheffield service which would serve Wakefield and retain the option for provision of a park and ride InterCity station at Cudworth, a project which had once been seriously mooted.

These struck me as valid, constructive observations and certainly worthy of inclusion in our report. Whether they would be appreciated by the Minister and the Department of Transport civil servants was their problem rather than ours. Even so, I was rather surprised and just a little sad to find our initiative rebuked by 'Modern Railways' (August 1985) who referred to our "remarkable interpretation of the role of TUCCs" in closure proposals. However, honour was restored a couple of months later when they published a letter from Dr Roger Bullivant of Sheffield who said:

"The TUCC was surely right to relate the closure proposal not just to the atrocious service actually run over the line, which no doubt few people will miss, but to the reasonable service which should – and anywhere else in the country would – have run between two large cities."

The widespread criticism of British Rail's handling of the Settle–Carlisle closure proposal, for so long the prerogative of activists seeking to retain the line, began to surface elsewhere. An editorial in the 'Yorkshire Post' (24th April) noting the presentation at the House of Commons of a 35,000 signature petition collected by Skipton and Ripon Constituency Labour Party – in which the splendid Skipton guards had played a prominent part by checking tickets and collecting signatures at the same time! – questioned the "lengthy trauma" users were being subjected to.

A determined effort at closure would, said the 'Yorkshire Post', have had some logic, as would a decision to retain the line. But British Rail took neither route and by stimulating new traffic they were questioning their earlier closure decision. The editorial continued:

"It is easy to see why many objectors have dark suspicions that British Rail has been playing a cat-and-mouse game over the line's fate all along. If the British Rail planners have indulged in such tactics, however, their footwork seems to have been sadly misplaced."

The piece said it was ironic that the demise of Dr Beeching had coincided with the growth of railway preservation which went far beyond the amateurish days of the 'Titfield Thunderbolt' and concluded:

"The Settle to Carlisle route commands respect from the engineer, enjoyment from the traveller and an affection bordering on intensity from many Yorkshire people. The Government will not be able to avoid taking a final decision for much longer, if the choice between amenity and profitability is to be suitably resolved."

I felt that summed up the position admirably.

Following the example of the Skipton and Ripon Labour Party, the Joint Action Committee took their campaign to London on 5th June. At a news conference presided over by Des Wilson, chairman of the Campaign for Freedom of Information, Peter Horton accused British Rail of a "long catalogue of deceit" over the future of the Settle–Carlisle line and claimed objectors no longer had confidence in the existing TUCC consultative procedures. The Joint Action Committee, by no means discouraged at the outcome of the judgment in the High Court regarding the Marylebone proposal, referred to leaked reports which suggested British Rail had told lies and called for a judicial review to be followed by a public enquiry.

Joint Action Committee chairman Dr John Whitelegg also revealed he was investigating reports that the North Western TUCC photocopied all the objections and passed them on to British Rail. "TUCCs are supposed to be independent," retorted Dr Whitelegg who claimed TUCCs were "completely impotent" and failed to protect the interests of rail users.

So much for all my efforts in resisting British Rail's demands for copies of the 14,897 objections lodged with us. And what of 'any user of any service affected'? There were times when I wished Messrs Whitelegg and Horton would realise who their friends really were. Mind you, they had every reason to be aggrieved about the photocopying business. It was really quite disgraceful. I was surprised they didn't make more of it. I gather they took it up with the Central Transport Consultative Committee and that Len Dumelow had told them the normal procedure was to summarise the objections, as we had.

Following the ultimate success of the 1984 'ghost trains' which had run between York, Leeds and Carlisle from 14th July to 9th September, British Rail had brought forward the 1985 service to start on 18th May and run until the end of September. It was in the timetable, too. But this did not absolve sensible promotion and once again Eastern Region flopped when it came to selling the extra trains in York, Leeds and West Yorkshire where the principal market was. It made one wonder if British Rail were serious in their claim of wishing to "maximise revenue potential" on the line.

Whilst Regional Headquarters at York shared my concern that they were "missing important business building opportunities", there was no shortage of excuses. "The initiative for marketing the line and print production is undertaken by the London Midland Region, even though the service originates in this region." The issue was also taken up by FOSCLA's indefatigable Philippa Simpson in a letter to the 'Yorkshire Post' in which she astutely observed: "British Rail keep reminding us that they are required to operate on a commercial basis but if they do not distribute their

Carlisle trains to make anything but a loss?" A good question.

Once again my wife and myself made good use of the Saturday 'ghost train' and were able to see how business built up. Checks on the outward or down journeys showed:

Date	Total Loading	Number on Train Leaving Settle	Number Alighting in Carlisle
18th May	91	37	29
1st June	121	70	50
15th June	192	142	105
29th June	206	123	83
13th July	174	115	95
27th July	219	143	118
10th Aug	241	518	109
24th Aug	255	172	127
7th Sept	236	171	145
21st Sept	251	196	154
28th Sept	348	277	248

The trains developed an almost 'club car' atmosphere about them and built up a considerable regular clientele as well as attracting patronage from all over the country. Needless to say, Marks and Spencer's and other retail and licenced establishments in Carlisle benefited considerably from the extra trains – if our own spending patterns were anything to go by.

By the middle of August, three months had elapsed since my reply to the Chief Solicitor and Legal Adviser in which I had told him, politely I hoped, what he could do with his request for copies of all the objections. Apart from an immediate acknowledgement recording receipt of my letter, I had heard nothing. Therefore, I was beginning to hope that was the end of the matter.

Confirmation that this might be so arrived in our office at York in the form of a letter from Ron Cotton to John Moorhouse. In view of the various changes to local bus services since the last 'Heads of Information' had been issued in June 1984, British Rail were arranging for a revised edition to be published. It would include all known information as at 1st August 1985 and would be a "properly printed document" and should be available in bulk by October. In addition a reply to our 'Summary of Written Objections' should be ready by then.

This was good news. First it looked as if we had seen off the Chief Solicitor and Legal Advisor. At least, there was no reference at all to the request for copies of the objections in Cotton's letter. More importantly, we could begin to plan for the Public Hearing. The whole Settle–Carlisle case had been dragging on for far too long. Moreover, I rather liked the thought of Settle in the spring.

15

CLEARING THE DECKS

"I must emphasise how important the TUCC hearings are to this association. We must make our presence felt. If this association cannot produce a high percentage of its members at the hearings we will have failed and through the media the public will be told we have failed. Please don't let this happen."

Brian Sutcliffe, chairman of FOSCLA, November 1985.

August 1985 – two years and 14,897 objections on (or 22,150 including those lodged with the North Western TUCC) since British Rail publicly announced it wished to close the Settle–Carlisle line – and it looked as if the end of the tunnel for this part of the journey would soon be in sight. Having lived with the saga since plans to re-route the Nottingham–Glasgow service came to light in May 1981, I couldn't say I was sorry.

Now, with British Rail's assurance that their revised 'Heads of Information', a copy of which would be sent to each objector, and the long awaited response to our 'Summary of Written Objections' would both be ready by October, we could start planning for the Public Hearing. We already knew that, in addition to the local authorities and the Joint Action Committee, some 250 individual objectors wished to speak. It would be an almost impossible task to fit everyone in during the 9 days we had allowed.

It was agreed that the North Western TUCC would hold their Public Hearing during March 1986, three days in Appleby and three days in Carlisle; whilst we would open on 14th April in Settle for three days, followed by three days in Skipton and three days in Leeds; the latter would include a Saturday for the benefit of those travelling from other parts of the country.

Quite apart from Settle–Carlisle, the late summer and autumn were a busy time for the new North East TUCC. Both the members and secretariat had quickly adapted to the many changes following the merger in April and the new structure, based on the three area sub-committees, was working well. It had been introduced with the enthusiastic support of Eastern Region general manager Frank Paterson.

I had a high regard for the 'GM', an affable yet exceptionally canny Scot. Therefore I was sorry to learn that he had decided to opt for early retirement in December at a youthful 56. I felt he still had much to offer. He would have made an admirable addition and considerably strengthened the British Railways Board, had they the imagination to co-opt him. However, it was said he had reservations regarding Sector management and was no longer 'flavour of the month' with those who mattered most in London.

There were other changes which more directly affected us. Dame Alison Munro had retired from the chair of the Central Transport Consultative Committee at the end of July. A doughty champion of the consumer, she stood no nonsense, least of all from British Rail. Pending the appointment of a successor, Barry Flaxman took charge. He was, of course, the ideal candidate to follow Dame Alison and a number of members, including Jim Ward and myself, wrote to Lord Lucas recommending this.

There was nobody else on the Central Committee who could match his grasp and knowledge of railway issues. As managing director of an important Philips subsidiary, he had a wide business experience and was used to negotiating at high level, something that would put him in good stead to provide the lead the committee needed in its dealings with Ministers, civil servants and, above all, British Rail. In the event, the opportunity was missed and by September the committee had a new chairman in Major General Lennox Napier.

However, the most interesting change and one that could undoubtedly affect the Settle–Carlisle closure proposal was even nearer to home. North Western TUCC secretary Frank Haywood, who had not enjoyed the best of health for several years, also plumped for early retirement. The obvious solution was that John Moorhouse should step into his shoes. Since former North Eastern TUCC secretary Gerald Newton had taken charge of the office, John had acted as 'closure secretary'.

I viewed the move with mixed feelings. John had been a tower of strength and become something of an expert when it came to closures since his discovery of the significance of the 'any user of any service affected' clause. We would undoubtedly miss him. But it would be an enormous advantage if the North Western committee had the services of someone with recent experience of closure proposals and Public Hearings. Whilst I did not see his new role as that of a Trojan horse, I felt he might be able to chivvy the North Western TUCC from their Beeching era outlook into the more consumer orientated Eighties. Mind you, he had a formidable task ahead of him.

Before John departed to pastures new on the other side of the Pennines, we had the Public Hearing for Huddersfield–Denby Dale to get through. The background to this, the second attempt to sever the Huddersfield–Sheffield rail link, was so complex and bizarre that it is worthy of a book in its own right. Suffice to say on this occasion that there were three issues which had some bearing on the Settle–Carlisle proposal.

First was that both Kirklees Metropolitan District Council and the Huddersfield–Penistone–Sheffield Rail Users Group felt we should postpone the Public Hearing, due to start on 21st October, pending the outcome in the Court of Appeal of the Marylebone case which wasn't due until November. There was talk of possible legal action, probably in the form of an injunction, if we didn't. They felt, with every justification, that the result might lead to changes in the procedure at Public Hearings, especially if the Court of Appeal came down in favour of cross-examination of British Rail. For our part, we were anxious to complete Huddersfield–Denby Dale before John Moorhouse moved to Lancashire so the decks would be clear for Settle–Carlisle in the spring.

Therefore I undertook informal soundings with both the local authority and user group. I put it to them that if they would not impede our Public Hearing, I would re-convene it at a later date if the Court of Appeal came down in favour of cross-examination. They agreed, so I was confident that the Public Hearing would proceed without the threat of injunctions or other forms of blocking tactics.

Second was an issue brought to my attention by transport consultant Mark Sullivan. He had been looking through his archives and discovered that at one time British Rail did provide financial information regarding closure proposals in accordance with recommendations made by Sir William Carrington in 1963. The practice had ceased in 1968 when the system of grant-aid for individual passenger services was introduced and figures published giving the long term cost of continuing a grant for a service and the short term effect of closure. However, as the grant-aid system no longer applied, we felt it would assist TUCCs to consider proposals for alleviating hardship if British Rail would revert to the practice of providing financial information as recommended by Sir William Carrington. Needless to say, we got no joy from British Rail on this.

Finally, just before the Public Hearing itself, we received – much to my astonishment and considerable annoyance – a request for copies of each individual objection! It came from Mr David Wharton-Street, the officious Provincial Sector manager at York. I had thought we'd seen this one off with my letter to the Chief Solicitor and Legal Adviser. So we held a brief committee meeting between sessions at the Public Hearing and members instructed Gerald Newton to send Wharton-Street an update of my earlier letter in the hope it would bury this one for good.

The result of the Marylebone case came on 22nd November when the Court of Appeal dismissed the call for cross examination of British Rail at Public Hearings. It was held that a public body set up to hear and report on objections to proposed ministerial decisions with a discretion to determine in advance the procedure of any public hearing it might hold may, having regard to the circumstances, disallow cross-examination and final submissions by counsel, in that it has no justifiable issue to decide and its criteria of procedural fairness differ from those of a trial. So that was that. Once again British Rail had escaped from the rigours of public accountability. On the other hand, at a more practical level, it would mean less likelihood of a posse of lawyers cluttering up the Settle–Carlisle Public Hearings.

For all their doubts regarding the competence of the TUCCs, the principal objectors realised that their call for a public enquiry was falling on deaf ears. Therefore they would have to make the most of the Public Hearings to present their case for retention of the Settle–Carlisle line. This point was taken up by Brian Sutcliffe, the FOSCLA chairman, in their November newsletter. In an impassioned plea to members he wrote:

"I must emphasise how important the TUCC hearings are to this association. We *must* make our presence felt and I have to ask you (assuming you are a registered objector) to give up time and money to attend one of the hearings. It is no good believing the other person will attend, we need as many members as possible. If this association cannot produce a high percentage of its members at the hearings we will have failed and through the media the public will be told we have failed. Please don't let this happen."

In the autumn of 1985, FOSCLA membership stood at 1,765. Of these, 46 were corporate members, ranging from the Bradford Civic Society to the Sheffield Passengers Association. Individual membership, although concentrated in Yorkshire, Lancashire and Cumbria, was spread throughout the country. There were also members overseas in Australia, Belgium, Canada, Cyprus, Eire, Germany, Hong Kong, South Africa, the United States and Papua New Guinea.

During the year ended 31st October 1985, membership fees generated just over £4,000. Another £1,700 came from the profit on sales of a wide range of merchandise. I was pleased to note the limited edition of 1,000 Matchbox 'T' Ford Parcels Vans had been selling well. There were only a few left and the price had risen from £8 to £10, so I was already showing a healthy profit on my two vehicles! With the addition of donations and a number of sundry items, income for the year totalled £6,173.

As would be expected, printing, postage and stationery were the largest items of expenditure at over £2,000. Almost £1,000 went on advertising – presumably on leaflets augmenting British Rail's promotion of the line – whilst there was a donation of £1,075 to the Joint Action Committee. With total expenditure of £4,760, FOSCLA had a healthy credit balance of £1,413.

The articles of association of the Joint Action Committee Ltd described the principal activity of the company as working for the retention, greater use and development of the Settle–Carlisle line in the interests of accident prevention, social justice, protection of the environment and the conservation of land and energy. Income for the year ended 31st October 1985 was £7,813. This was almost entirely from donations, including the £1,075 from FOSCLA who had two directors on the board, Brian Sutcliffe and Philippa Simpson. Transport 2000 (North Lancashire and Cumbria) were represented by Dr John Whitelegg and the Railway Development Society by Richard Watts. Other affiliated organisations included the Town Councils and Chambers of Commerce of Settle and Appleby, Kirkby Stephen Parish Council, the Ramblers Association and the Youth Hostels Association.

The Joint Action Committee's largest outgoing was just over £4,000 to TEST, the London based transport consultants retained to produce a report on the case for retention of the Settle–Carlisle line. The remaining expenditure was largely geared to maintaining the high profile established by the committee. It organised a number of public meetings and issued at least one news release a month in an attempt to keep the campaign in the public eye. Nevertheless, the total expenditure of £7,209 – including the TEST fee – was far removed from the envisaged budget of £55,000.

In simple cash terms the Joint Action Committee and FOSCLA had, between them, attracted support of just short of £13,000 during the year. Whilst the sum might appear small, it was probably the largest sum of money raised in a single year by user groups fighting a railway closure proposal. Moreover, virtually all the work done by the directors, the committee and ordinary members and supporters was on a voluntary basis. Indeed, it was the sheer dedication and enthusiasm of a hard core of twenty or thirty people, rather than the level of funds at their disposal, that provided the momentum for the campaign. Even so, when faced with the might of the British Railways Board – who would probably spend more on legal representation at the Public Hearings than the Joint Action Committee and FOSCLA would spend in a full year – it was very much a David and Goliath situation.

However, the disparity between the two sides was not as great as it seemed. For whilst the Joint Action Committee and FOSCLA had been calling the tune and had effectively mobilised their supporters to obtain the maximum number of objections, behind the scenes a third force was gaining ground as it marshalled its facts to derail British Rail's closure proposals. I refer to the Joint County Councils.

This was the label given to the alliance of Cumbria, Lancashire and West Yorkshire County Councils whose elected representatives had given the go-ahead for a team of permanent officials led by Cumbria to draw up a detailed case against closure of the line for presentation at the Public Hearings. Using the work undertaken by the PEIDA consultants as a base, they undertook further surveys and research. I had every confidence that, come the day, they would provide British Rail with some formidable opposition.

And what of British Rail itself? How were they coming along? Not very well judging by the revised 'Heads of Information'. It was heralded by Ron Cotton as a "properly printed document", and so it was; the trouble was that nobody had read the proofs! A correction slip was promised. The *pièce de résistance* was the map at the back which referred to such places as "Morecombe, Wigon, Hebben Bridge, Keignet and Whiteheaven!" Nor was that all. The

Cumbrian Coast Line missed Workington altogether whilst Settle Junction was at Hellifield! One would have thought British Rail could have come up with something a little better!

Meanwhile problems of a more immediate and practical nature had arisen. There was a good connection out of the 15.05 from Glasgow and 'The Clansman' from Inverness at Carlisle into the 16.35 departure to Leeds and Hull. As a result the Glasgow–Leeds journey took a respectable 4 hours 6 minutes. However, from May 1986 this was to change. British Rail, in its wisdom, was combining the Glasgow departure with 'The Clansman' at Motherwell which meant that the train would not arrive in Carlisle until 16.38 – just three minutes after the departure of the Leeds/Hull train!

This was ridiculous, but by no means the only example of inept timetabling at that time. I wrote to Ron Cotton pointing out that there was sufficient recovery time between Settle and Skipton (the up train was allowed 31 minutes whereas the down train did it in just 18 minutes!) to enable a later departure from Carlisle in order to maintain the connection. Fortunately, common sense prevailed and the departure was retimed to 16.46, but the damage had been done as it was too late to include the amendment in the timetable which showed a Glasgow departure of 14.20 to make the Carlisle connection.

That such a poor piece of timetabling had been seriously suggested only added weight to those who believed it was part of a deliberate ploy to deter long distance travel on the Settle–Carlisle line. Whether planned or just an unfortunate error, it reflected badly on British Rail, as did the decision to discontinue first class accommodation on the line from May 1986, thus discouraging business travel. This could have been a real money spinner had they introduced a first class day return fare. Ron Cotton was enthusiastic – for he could see a marketing opportunity a mile off – but his superiors simply didn't want to know. Moreover, the withdrawal of first class represented yet another broken assurance regarding the line on the part of senior railway management.

Of course, the real problem British Rail faced with the Settle–Carlisle line was that they had a success story on their hands. It was a most embarrassing one, too. For years they had derided those who advocated that the line had a future by saying it was surplus to requirements and had little potential for passenger growth. But the public – with a little encouragement from Ron Cotton – had proved them wrong. Thus a form of schizophrenia had set in within senior management circles. Whilst they relished the money the line was generating, they simply couldn't take the accompanying egg that was splattering all over their faces. Served them right, I thought.

Further confirmation of the line's continuing success came in the 'Yorkshire Post' of 19th December. Alan Whitehouse reported passenger loadings for 1985 were 20 per cent up on the previous year – itself a year of record growth – whereas over the same period patronage on British Rail's prime InterCity services had only increased by 4 per cent. As a subsequent editorial in the paper (27th December) put it:

"Impressive travelling figures on the threatened Settle to Carlisle railway link are not due primarily to the natural desire of many people to save this scenic line. Passengers have been ready and waiting throughout the years and only the determination of British Rail to close the route, it sometimes seems, has kept them away. Now that interest has once more been thoroughly aroused, passenger numbers are increasing markedly. Whether they will be enough to put the faceless planners of BR on the defensive is another matter.

The line which BR wants to scrap is at present, according to a report in the Yorkshire Post this month performing at five times a better rate than the highly favoured InterCity routes in passenger transit terms. A 20 per cent improvement in custom was registered on Settle–Carlisle over 1984, compared with four per cent on Inter-City trains this year. So the bureaucrats have been proved wrong in their opinion that the line was uncompetative. They may yet win by arguing that, while competitive, it is nevertheless unprofitable.

The man in charge of the line, Mr Ron Cotton, points out that it would take £15 million – nowhere near the profits from present business – to carry out necessary improvements. So all the bureaucrats have to do is sit back smugly and wait for the laws of economics to prove them right. In the meantime, what happens to all the revenue which the Settle–Carlisle link has proved it can gain, even during a wet summer like the last one when tourist enthusiasm might have been dampened? And what are the planners at BR headquarters doing to suggest ways of replacing that revenue?"

Just before Christmas, British Rail finally came up with their response to our 'Summary of Written Objections'. Whereas it had taken us little over three months to analyse and summarise the 14,897 objections, it had taken them just over a year to come up with the answers – many of which were a simple 'no comment'. Nevertheless, it did mean that we had the last piece of the jigsaw we needed to complete the documentation in readiness for the Public Hearing. Now it was up to us to fulfil our commitments and report to the Minister as soon as possible.

A great deal of preparation and planning goes into staging a Public Hearing. Immediately after the Christmas/New Year break, Rene Phillippo drafted the final summary of objections which included the points of objection and British Rail's response, where they provided one. A copy was then sent to each of the 2,000 objectors who had asked us to keep them informed of developments. We also sent them a form to complete if they wished to speak at the Public Hearing, asking them to indicate which venue – Settle, Skipton or Leeds – and what day and session (morning, afternoon or evening) they wished to take part in.

Meanwhile secretary Gerald Newton was busy finalising the arrangements regarding the venues: the Victoria Hall in Settle, Skipton Town Hall and Kitson College in Leeds. Then there was hotel accommodation to organise and meals to be arranged between sessions. In Skipton I was able to recommend a rather nice restaurant I knew called Oats, but elsewhere I just let him get on with it. We were lucky in that Gerald was a very good organiser. You just had to tell him what was required and he was busy on the phone sorting things out. He also had a new assistant in David Mallender, an agreeable young chap who was quickly learning the ropes.

Compared with most enquiries, we worked a comparatively long day at Public Hearings; allowing for three 2½ hour sessions each day with the exception of the final day when we dispensed with the evening session. But even with nine days and 24 sessions, I was acutely aware that we would have difficulty in fitting in everyone who wished to speak, especially as we also had to allow for the Joint County Councils and the Joint Action Committee, both of whom had indicated that they would require several hours to complete their evidence.

Gerald and myself met both organisations on an informal basis to see how best we could meet their needs and at the same time accommodate them in the limited time at our disposal. We estimated – correctly as it turned out – that there would be most demand to speak at Leeds, because of its accessibility. We knew, too, that a lot of individual objectors wished to speak at Settle.

Therefore, we arranged for most of the corporate objections, including the main presentations by the Joint County Councils and Joint Action Committee, to be made at Skipton.

I also suggested to both the Joint County Councils and Joint Action Committee that their evidence would have more impact if it were presented in segments of about 30 minutes between representations by ordinary objectors. Otherwise, if a single presentation went on for an hour or more, both objectors sitting waiting their turn and – more importantly – the lay North East TUCC committee members they had to convince might get bored. This was readily agreed by both bodies. Indeed, the Joint Action Committee who earlier had been vociferous in their demand for at least 7 days to present their evidence – something which, in all honesty, I felt they would have found hard to sustain – readily agreed to curtail their presentation to about 3 hours in six 30 minute submissions. The Joint County Councils agreed to follow suit.

The Joint Action Committee and FOSCLA had made every effort to make sure their members knew what the Public Hearings were all about. In their February 1986 newsletter, FOSCLA included a well researched fact sheet on TUCCs and the hearings. It included six useful hints for those speaking at the hearings:

1. It is much easier to speak from previously prepared notes unless you are used to public speaking.
2. Be relevant. The aim of the exercise is primarily to explain to the TUCC how you will be adversely affected if the Settle–Carlisle line were to close.
3. Although it is imperative to stress the hardship you will suffer, feel free to mention other reasons why you feel the Settle–Carlisle line should be retained and developed to its full potential.
4. Be concise. Do not ramble on unnecessarily; the TUCC will only get bored and the gist of your arguments for the line's retention may be lost.
5. Do not be afraid to put relevant questions to the British Rail officials present through the TUCC. They are not ogres, only people with a job to do. On the other hand do not use it as an opportunity to slam British Rail in general.
6. There is no need to be nervous. TUCC members will appreciate that many objectors are not used to speaking in public. They are not expecting prize-winning speeches.

Whilst also preparing for the hearings, the Joint Action Committee maintained their high profile media orientated campaign. On 5th March they launched their station re-opening campaign. Based on a report written for them by Johnathan Roberts of Transport 2000, it advocated that all the Dales Rail stations should be opened on a permanent basis, a project which also had captured the imagination of a number of local authorities headed by Cumbria County Council.

Following their final objectors co-ordination conference in Appleby on 10th March, the Joint Action Committee presented the TEST report 'Retraining the Settle–Carlisle Line' at a news conference. Among its recommendations was the introduction of an InterCity 125 service of four trains a day in each direction between Leeds, Carlisle and Glasgow, two of which would also serve Bradford. TEST maintained that, even without marketing, such a service would give a 55 per cent load and yield a 7 per cent return on investment which would pay for track improvements in 13 years.

The West Yorkshire Metropolitan County Council held their grand pre-hearings slam on Saturday 8th March when, in brilliant sunshine, the 'West Yorkshire Dalesman' left Leeds hauled by Class 5 steam locomotive No. 5305 to mark publication of Stan Abbott's book 'To Kill a Railway' which had been sponsored by the council. Public Transport Committee chairman, Councillor Wayne Jenkins, himself no rail buff, told 'The Guardian's' Malcolm Pithers:

"This is a fight to save a beautiful railway but also a fight for the rail network as a whole. The journey along the line is spectacular at any time. In winter it is not only one of the most exciting journeys in Britain but the rail line is one of the most necessary. Yet despite its value to the community in the towns and villages along its length, British Rail wants to close the line."

This, I felt, was but a trail for what we were going to hear in the weeks ahead.

Another special set forth from Leeds to the increasingly well used tracks of the Settle–Carlisle line on Thursday 20th March. Although only a DMU, it had been sponsored by the railway unions and amongst those on board were Jimmy Knapp of the NUR and Ray Buckton of ASLEF. They were joined by a party of the line's advocates ranging from churchmen to MPs, although the chap who attracted most attention from the massed banks of cameras was a very dapper suited Bill Owen – hardly recognisable as the same man who plays Compo in BBC TV's 'Last of the Summer Wine'.

Since the beginning of the year there had been a growing swell of optimism that there was now a real chance of saving the line.

There was no doubt at all that the campaign to date had been won by the objectors – thanks more than a little to British Rail's ham-handed approach from the beginning. But just as good campaigns do not necessarily win elections; so, too, there was no guarantee that the line's future was assured. Nevertheless, there was a growing confidence that it could be saved, not least because of the strength of the case that had been assembled for the Public Hearings. As Martin Flannery MP, a long standing proponent of the railway, told the 'Yorkshire Post': "The general opinion is that the tide has turned. We are not over-confident, but we are cautiously optimistic."

Certainly that was how I felt when, on the morning of Monday 24th March, I set out for the North Western TUCC Public Hearing in Appleby. It had been raining hard when I got up just after six and by the time I was walking back from the newsagent I noticed the rain was turning to sleet. By the time I got to Leeds station to catch the 09.03, it had been snowing hard for almost an hour. This had to be good news!

16

THE LOCAL AUTHORITIES IMPRESS

"In the absence of anything of substance from British Rail, the case of the Joint County Councils was virtually unanswerable."

I don't know whether it was fate or Ian McCaskill who decreed that the north of England would be subjected to a severe blizzard on the morning of Monday 24th March 1986. But whoever it was couldn't have picked a better day. Whilst most traffic on the roads of the Yorkshire Dales and the Eden Valley came to a standstill, the 09.03 from Leeds got through, although it was almost an hour late at Appleby. However, that we actually made it was one up to the Settle–Carlisle line which, as the headline in that night's 'Yorkshire Evening Post' put it, "Came Into Its Own!" It also reflected great credit on the railway community who invariably pull out all the stops on such occasions.

Sadly, such plaudits were not applicable to those responsible for the formation of the train, just a Class 31 locomotive and five Mark 1 coaches. It wasn't the extra traffic generated by the North Western TUCC's Public Hearings, although there must have been about 20 who plodded through the snow from Appleby station to the Grammar School, but simply that no one had told British Rail it was the week before Easter and the schools were on holiday. We had left Leeds with 169 passengers and a further 85 had joined at Keighley from where it was full and standing for the rest of the journey. Indeed, there were 267 on when we left Settle. It may have been cramped, but at least we made it.

Gerald Newton and myself arrived at the school – a modern complex of buildings in marked contrast with most of the historical town – just as David Maclean, the local MP, had finished his opening submission for the objectors. I was sorry to have missed him but was told he had gone down well. There were about 80 people in the body of the large assembly hall which had been appropriately decorated with numerous paintings by the pupils of trains on the

Settle–Carlisle line. They were to prove a poignant reminder of the line's heritage throughout the Appleby hearing.

The chairman of the North Western TUCC, Olive Clarke, and her new secretary, John Moorhouse, were strategically placed centre stage with four members of the committee on either side of them. Below and facing them was the table and chair used by objectors when making their representations. On each side of the hall and at right angles to the stage were two long tables, one for British Rail and the other for the media. Microphones were provided for the chairman, the objectors table and British Rail so that those in the body of the hall could hear what was being said, except on the all too frequent occasions when the PA system played up. At the back of the hall by the main entrance, the Joint Action Committee had their own table and display which provided the focal point for their activities.

This layout was more or less the standard one adopted at most Public Hearings. The only unusual factor related to British Rail. At previous hearings they were invariably headed by a divisional manager or chief passenger manager or even a deputy general manager, backed by anything up to a dozen subordinates. These invariably included one or two experts whose prime role was to beaver away through the timetable and provide their superiors with near instant answers to any timetabling idiosyncrasies objectors might include in their evidence.

On this occasion British Rail representation was just three: Ron Cotton, Michael Harrison QC – who reminded me rather of a young Rex Harrison (a relative, perhaps?) – and a young lad whose duties seemed to be to ply Messrs Cotton and Harrison with endless cups of tea. I later discovered that he was Mr Timothy Reardon, a solicitor from the British Railways Board. It isn't just the policemen who are getting younger!

By the time Gerald and myself had settled in and got our bearings – not least discovering the Reardon tea trail! – the opening statements from the Joint County Councils were in full swing. I was pleased to catch County Councillor Wayne Jenkins speaking on behalf of the West Yorkshire Metropolitan County Council – due to fade away into the sunset before our Public Hearing – and to note that he highlighted the 'Section 20'* implications of the Settle–Carlisle closure proposal on Passenger Transport Executive services within West Yorkshire. A most valid point as it could lead to reduced services on the Ilkley and Keighley lines – a good example of 'any user of any service affected'.

When the hearing adjourned for lunch, I alerted Ron Cotton to the overcrowding on the train from Leeds. He said he would get on the 'phone to someone. Whoever he spoke to managed to work wonders. The following morning the train was strengthened to 10 coaches – one could see it pass on the embankment across the road from the school – and I was pleased to note it was well loaded.

Our role at the North Western TUCC hearing was simply to observe. Therefore it was possible to be more relaxed. If one saw someone one knew, one could take one's leave and tiptoe from the hall down the corridor and pass the time of day over a cup of tea. However, I spent most of the time listening to the evidence – which was of an exceptionally high standard. Indeed, the three days in Appleby and the four days in Carlisle the following week – the hearing having been extended an extra day to accommodate a Saturday session – provided me with something of a 'dry run' to what I would hear the following month in Settle, Skipton and Leeds.

There were a number of issues which particularly interested me. First was the role of the QC engaged – no doubt at enormous expense! – by British Rail. Mr Michael Harrison himself defined it as one of offering assistance to the TUCC on the legal issues relating to the closure proposal. I was not quite sure whether this was altogether in accordance with the Act which referred to Public Hearings as being for the purpose of hearing objectors orally or "oral representations on behalf of the Board." I understood 'representations' to mean "a presentation of a view of facts or arguments" whereas 'assistance' suggested something extra. Moreover, if the committee required any legal 'assistance' the last place it should look to was British Rail.

That said, I rather enjoyed listening to Mr Harrison. As one would expect, he spoke with eloquence and aplomb and could bring a sense of occasion to the most mundane point. Nevertheless, I agreed with the chairman of the Joint Action Committee, Dr John Whitelegg, who said Mr Harrison's presence was intimidatory.

Then the objectors had a very good advocate of their own in Dr

* Section 20 of the Transport Act 1968 refers to the apportionment of the cost of local railway passenger services within the former Metropolitan County Council areas to the respective Passenger Transport Executives (PTEs).

Whitelegg himself. He effectively answered and dismissed most of Mr Harrison's legal points, particularly those relating to the status of diverted services on the Blackburn–Hellifield line. Indeed, the whole question of West Coast Main Line diversions, either by the Settle–Carlisle line or as proposed on the Cumbrian Coast line, played a large part in the North Western TUCC's Public Hearing. Nevertheless, I was determined that, so far as our own Public Hearing was concerned, Mr Harrison's role would be minimal.

This was because I was conscious that Mr Harrison was held in some awe, if not by the activists of the Joint Action Committee then certainly by the ordinary objectors to whom he was the senior legal man at the Public Hearing. This was particularly true when Mr Michael Shrimpton, an affable yet proficient young barrister, took up the cudgels on behalf of the Joint Action Committee. Although his exchanges with Mr Harrison were good natured and not without humour, there was always the deference one expects from a junior taking up an issue with a senior member of his profession. In fact, the barrack room advocacy deployed from the floor by Dr Whitelegg and Peter Horton was probably more effective. Then, quite apart from anything else, there would simply be no time for all the 'my learned friending' and other legal niceties at the North East TUCC's Public Hearing.

Secondly, I was interested to see what sort of show the Joint Action Committee put on. Here I was somewhat perplexed. For whilst Dr Whitelegg and Peter Horton, together with Keith Morgan of the Appleby Chamber of Trade, proved most adept at popping up with points of order, posing awkward questions and generally making life difficult for British Rail, I felt that their actual case for retention of the line – save on the question of diversions – lacked continuity and cohesion and never quite seemed to take off.

It wasn't that their case lacked substance, far from it because the two major reports which formed the basis of it – TEST's 'Retraining the Settle–Carlisle' and Jonathan Roberts's 'New Life in the Hills' were of an exceptionally highstandard. So, too, were their expert witnesses who, in addition to Mr Roberts, also included Dr Mayer Hillman of the Policy Studies Institute and co-author of 'The Social Consequences of Rail Closures' and David Joy of The Council for the Protection of Rural England. I believe the main reason for an apparent lack lustre performance on the part of the Joint Action Committee could be put down to one of comparison in that they were outshined by the sheer professionalism of the

Joint County Councils.

After the preliminary introductions by elected councillors at Appleby, the Joint County Council's case was expanded at the Public Hearing in Carlisle in six major presentations, each lasting about thirty minutes, under the following headings:

'The Effect of Local Communities'
'Hardship to Users of British Rail's Timetabled Services'
'Dales Rail'
'The Costs and Revenue Associated with the Line'
'Cost–Benefit Appraisal'
'Development Potential of the Line'

The papers were presented by a most capable team of officers headed by Cumbria County Council's director of engineering, David Lloyd. Others included Peter Robinson, group leader in the County Planning Department and, as I was later to discover, a most knowledgeable railway expert in his own right; and Alan Thompson, team leader (Transportation) in the Department of Highways and Engineering. The evidence they and their colleagues from West Yorkshire and Lancashire had assembled was formidable. So much so that, in the absence of anything of substance from British Rail, the case of the Joint County Councils was virtually unanswerable.

Each of the papers had been given to British Rail a week before the Public Hearing and copies were also made available to all the TUCC members who were taking part. The papers and the attached documentation were most comprehensive. Taking 'Hardship to Users of British Rail Timetabled Services' as an example, the package comprised:

A list of the contents.
Summary
1. Introduction
2. Numbers Using Regular BR Services
3. Origins, Destinations and Journey Purpose
4. Other Means of Transport
5. Availability of Alternative Public Transport
6. Times and Costs of Alternatives
7. Diverted Services
8. Conclusions

Appendix A: Description of Cumbria County Council's Survey Programme and Procedure

Appendix B: BR Timetabled Services Over the Settle–Carlisle Line in 1985

Appendix C: Train Loadings and Usage of Appleby and Settle Stations in 1985

Appendix D: Bus Services Operating in the Appleby Area in March 1986

Appendix E: Use of Buses for Sunday Possessions of WCML When the Settle–Carlisle Line is Available

Items 1 to 8 comprised the oral presentation, starting with "My name is David Lloyd, director of engineering, Cumbria County Council..." and finishing with four concise single sentence conclusions. In between there were some 4,000 words plus a number of tables which were fully explained although not read out in full. Above all, it was phrased in easy to understand language. I was very impressed. As one who had done his own share of grumbling about local authorities over the years, this quite restored my faith in them. I felt the case presented by the Joint County Councils could not be faulted.

Up against such a formidable case and an excellent team of advocates, Ron Cotton was cast in a hapless role. Nor was there anyone he could really turn to for support. Apart from legal issues, of which there were relatively few, Mr Michael Harrison QC was little more than a passenger, as was solicitor Timothy Reardon. As a consequence Cotton was largely on his own and ran into a fair amount of flak, especially when he made the fatal flaw of questioning the Joint County Councils' cost–benefit analysis. Although a man of many talents, this simply was not his subject – and it showed.

Nevertheless, he lasted the course well and, given that his was essentially a solo performance, he got through largely unscathed. Moreover, he had a disarming way of treading through the minefield of questions put by the Joint Action Committee by simply refusing to answer or discuss any issues other than those he considered related to hardship. This annoyed objectors who were frustrated that British Rail could get away so lightly. However, notwithstanding the occasional question from chairman Olive Clarke, there was little she could do to satisfy objectors.

Mrs Clarke had a good public hearing. She went out of her way to make objectors feel at ease and had obviously been well briefed by John Moorhouse on the more complex issues of the proposal. I was pleased to learn that the text of her opening statement was very similar to that I had used for my recent hearings. It was one of those occasions where one positively welcomed plagiarism!

As a footnote to my visits to Appleby and Carlisle for the North Western TUCC's Public Hearing, the following diversion provides an interesting insight into the apparent paranoia amongst certain people within British Rail regarding the Settle–Carlisle line and my involvement in it. The previous August, Eastern Region general manager Frank Paterson initiated a 'Service Excellence Award' for railway staff worthy of some special form of recognition. It comprised a certificate and a £10 voucher, the latter which could be exchanged for cash by the recipients. A number of people outside British Rail who travelled extensively by train, including Barry Flaxman and myself, were asked to participate with senior railway management and nominate staff for the award.

I was happy to co-operate as it enabled some form of recognition to be made to those on the 'shop floor' of the railway who were often working in difficult circumstances. Between August 1985 and May 1986 I nominated about 40 awards with Frank Paterson's enthusiastic support. Two went to stationmen Paul Holden (Appleby) and Ken Keen (Settle). The third was a collective award to 'The Skipton Guards' who worked the line and had always impressed me for their helpful attitude, especially on my journeys to and from the North Western TUCC's hearings when they pulled out all the stops regarding overcrowding and late running.

Unfortunately my plaudits were not greeted with universal approval within British Rail. In an internal memo, the area manager at Preston, who was responsible for the Skipton guards, acidly remarked that he could not help wondering if the signalmen on the Settle–Carlisle line would be the next to be honoured – "They are almost the only people left!" The quality of service manager at Manchester was equally peeved. In a memo to the British Railways Board he expressed his concern "at the way the Award system was progressing" and called for urgent discussions on the matter.

However, the final word belongs to the Skipton guards themselves. In a letter of thanks, they told me that the £10 would be donated to the British Rail childrens home at Derby – something that should have made the area manager at Preston and the quality of service manager at Manchester feel very small indeed.

17

SETTLE IN THE SPRING

"If we didn't object to the Settle–Carlisle closure – and he told us they were going to close it – then British Rail would spend £7 million on the Cumbrian Coast Line, replacing track and widening bridges. It would ensure the future of the coast line. I told Mr Brazier the answer was no. I would always object to any rail closure in Cumbria."

County Councillor William Cameron, 14th April 1986

Attending someone else's Public Hearing into a railway closure proposal is far more enjoyable than chairing one's own. Olive Clarke and John Moorhouse had done a good job steering the North Western TUCC through their seven days in Cumbria. Indeed, it was hard to believe this was the same TUCC which had given us so many headaches in the past. Perhaps they had caught the consumer bug after all. Certainly there was no doubting the success of their hearing. Now it was our turn and we had something to live up to.

The hearings in Appleby and Carlisle had been relatively leisurely affairs, so much so that the timetable allowed twenty minute tea breaks during the morning and afternoon sessions. They had sat for just over 40 hours during which they had heard about 130 submissions which averaged about 20 minutes each. This included time for British Rail to answer points raised by objectors and, of course, the break for tea. By contrast, we would have to allow for some 270 submissions during the 60 hours at our disposal. This indicated an average of little more than 13 minutes for each submission – quite the most taxing schedule I'd faced. Certainly there would be no tea breaks!

Such conditions impose an enormous strain on the chairman. Quite the most difficult task is that of 'pacing' the hearing so that everyone gets an opportunity to say what they want to in the limited time available. Several weeks beforehand, secretary Gerald Newton drew up a list of those wishing to speak at each session from which I chose the running order. A copy was then sent to each prospective speaker. On my copy I added a margin in which I inserted the time each speaker should start his submission. This became my 'form card' for the hearing. I knew that I had problems if I was running more than 15 minutes late and if we were running over 30 minutes late I was in dead trouble.

Another responsibility the chairman has is to cajole and encourage speakers so that their objections make a favourable impact. Mind you, one can overdo this. I recall that at Settle I dropped a real *faux pas* when, adopting my best bedside manner, I endeavoured to make an unlisted speaker feel at ease with his microphone. He turned out to be Jonathan Porritt, the director of Friends of the Earth and one of the most lucid and accomplished broadcasters in the country!

Having chaired too many closure hearings for my own liking, I had evolved an almost telepathic form of communication between the chair and the objectors table whereby I could – usually – steer an objector who had overshot his or her time towards a speedy conclusion. I hope the look of delight on my face when the objector said "... and finally, chairman ..." didn't give the game away! Nevertheless, there was no doubt that the word 'finally' grew to have a warm glow about it.

Someone who kindly proposed a vote of thanks to me at the end of an earlier hearing said I always endeavoured to ensure those attending – except, perhaps, British Rail – had a good day out! Whilst I made no conscious effort to foster this, I was aware of the importance of maintaining everyones interest throughout the hearings. The most constructive role I as chairman could play was, as the old theatrical adage said, to 'keep it moving'.

Then three day hearings – and we had three of these within the overall Settle–Carlisle Public Hearing – evolved a pattern of their own. Day one presented few problems as everyone was fresh and raring to go. The final day benefited from something of an 'end of term' feeling. It was the second day which could be difficult, especially by the time one came to the evening session when patience could become exhausted and tempers frayed; both on the part of objectors and the committee.

That we managed to get through the Settle–Carlisle hearings relatively unscathed – I never overran a session by more than ten minutes whilst we actually concluded at Leeds two minutes ahead of schedule – was due to the measure of co-operation and goodwill extended by the Joint County Councils, the Joint Action Committee, Ron Cotton of British Rail and, above all, score upon score of individual objectors who, appreciating the problem we had of endeavouring to put a quart into a pint pot, were helpfulness itself.

Those who rambled on a bit were invariably balanced by others whose contributions were brief and to the point. Indeed, I only recall two objectors – both gricers – whom I had to gently admonish for overrunning their time; and this was because they were tending to bore the committee – who, sadly perhaps, were not really interested in timetable intricacies – and other objectors.

Overall, the job of chairman at a Public Hearing is a rather lonely one. Again in theatrical terms, one has to combine the role of impresario with that of director and a leading supporting player on stage around whom the 'stars' of the production – that is to say the objectors and British Rail – deploy their talents. Whereas for committee members a hearing can provide an interesting break from routine and perhaps, even, a good day out which affords an opportunity for some modest socialising, the chairman is on duty all the time.

A Public Hearing also requires a lot of preparation and homework, especially if, like me, one does one's own research. Whilst most of this will be done prior to the hearing, there are always major submissions to study and plans to be made for the following day. Whilst I was always aware I would encounter many people at a hearing who would know far more than me about specific aspects of the closure proposal, for example – diversions, I tried to make sure I had a comprehensive knowledge of the proposal and its background. This meant that all the documentation had to be studied. It enabled me to pick out points which I could put to British Rail if objectors did not do so.

Monday 14th April 1986 dawned cold, damp and blustery and became more gloomy and wet as the day progressed. So much for my idyllic thoughts of Settle in the spring. I travelled on the 09.03 from Leeds with several members of the committee. There were also a sprinkling of journalists on the train so I was kept pretty busy providing them with background and recording the odd radio interview. We arrived at Settle station spot on time at 10.00 and moved straight over to the Victoria Hall where our Public Hearing was due to open half-an-hour later.

At the hall people were starting to arrive and there was time to have a chat with one or two I knew and get the 'feel' of the room before we got the show on the road promptly at 10.30. It was bitterly cold, especially on the stage where the committee was ensconced and where there also seemed to be a howling gale. Gerald Newton had to organise a supply of travelling rugs for the lady members and a number of electric fires to augment the hall's central heating.

It is a requirement of any successful public meeting for the chairman to establish authority at the outset, if only to allow him or her the flexibility to run the show the way they wished. Therefore I felt my opening address to be of some importance and went to considerable trouble in drafting it, especially in view of the controversy surrounding the Settle–Carlisle line. It was important, too, that I set an example and kept my opening remarks brief. Therefore everything I wanted to say had to be compressed into ten minutes.

There were about 130 people present in the body of the Victoria Hall when I opened the Yorkshire TUCC's Public Hearing. After explaining the TUCC's role was to represent the views of rail users and our prime responsibility was to report to the Secretary of State for Transport on the hardship involved if the line closed, I emphasised that the many other issues involved would also be considered by the committee and any strength of public feeling on them would be conveyed to the Secretary of State who would make the final decision regarding the future of the line.

I then turned to three specific points. The first was that whilst it was arguable whether any of British Rail's closure notices fully met the requirements of the Transport Act 1962, we felt that those who wished to object had ample opportunity to do so, save that since September 1984 (the last date for objections) the line had attracted many new users who would have liked to lodge objections had it been legally possible for them to do so. This would be brought to the Secretary of State's attention.

The second point related to use of the Blackburn–Hellifield line (which, of course, was incorporated in the Settle–Carlisle closure proposal) by diverted passenger services. Following the North Western TUCC's Public Hearing we had agreed with them that diverted services were passenger services in accordance with the Act so, should British Rail wish to completely close that line at a later date – it was being retained for freight and diversions – it should initiate a further closure proposal under the Act. This was the old one of when is a train not a train? When it is a diverted service, so far as British Rail were concerned. However, as the Act referred to all railway passenger services and there were no exclusion clauses, we felt we were on firm ground.

Finally, in what the press described as a "stinging rebuke", I criticised British Rail for failing to substantiate its case for closure with the relevant financial information. Indeed, I had not come across a closure proposal where the information provided was so scant – and I said so, recalling that the data provided for the closure of Filey Holiday Camp station in 1977 was far more comprehensive than that for 'England's Greatest Historical Scenic Route.' I also added that I took exception to British Rail's response to our request for information as it appeared to stipulate how we should conduct the Public Hearing and what should appear in our report. That, I stressed, was "an impertinence" as it was the TUCCs and not British Rail who were responsible for the hearings and the subsequent report.

Michael Harrison QC responded for British Rail. He said they were at the hearing to "assist the committee on the issue of hardship". Declining to comment on our decision to consider non-hardship issues, other than to say British Rail took the view that they were not covered by the Act, Mr Harrison said that in view of this they did not intend to respond to questions on non-hardship issues. To this I retorted that under the Act the committee was obliged to 'consider the objections' and, as the grounds for objection were wide open, this included consideration of issues other than those solely relating to hardship. That, I hoped, would put Mr Harrison in his place.

Before I could reflect in any glory of having won my first legal encounter with Mr Harrison, on points anyway, I was embroiled in a slanging match with a Mr Robert Leakey of Giggleswick who was sitting at the front of the hall. Although not an objector, it appeared he'd been engaged in a long one man war of attrition with the Department of Transport against the road lobby. Quite why he had it in for us, I'm not sure. After all, he should have been on our side for we were pro-rail. But in a 'point of order' he questioned the credibility of the Public Hearing and as good as accused me as being a Government lackey.

I suppose it was quite amusing in a way, but for the fact he was deadly serious. However, I was far from amused as I was up against the clock and he was wasting valuable time. He kept going on and it took my threat to call upon the services of the local constabulary to shut him up so we could continue with the hearing.

John Watson opened for the objectors. In a perceptive and often witty submission, the local MP outlined how closure of the line would adversely affect his constituents and provided some useful figures to back his case. On tourism, he said the Settle–Carlisle line was an attraction in itself. To close it would be remarkably short-sighted. To do so to save public money whilst other Government departments were spending money to encourage tourism would be "the economics of Lewis Carroll."

He said it was quite clear the crucial decision within British Rail to close the line was taken on 6th January 1982 at the meeting of the Railway Executive Group in London. Such a meeting could be forgiven for believing Giggleswick station was in Giggleswick. However, it wasn't. It was in the middle of nowhere. Giggleswick station, said John, was the sort of place people only go to when they are lost. It was unstaffed. There was no ticket office, telephone or taxi service. The single shelter faced the prevailing wind.

The reason British Rail were seeking to close the line related to negotiations with the Treasury over the Public Service Obligation (PSO). He asserted that British Rail would have stressed that reductions in the PSO could only be achieved at the expense of reductions in the network. But the PSO was cut. Had British Rail done nothing, their bluff would have been called and their future negotiating position weakened. So a cut had to be made and the Settle–Carlisle line, being long, rural and northern, was chosen.

I felt John had hit just the right note. It was a copy book submission and one which was expected from an MP of his calibre.

The next speaker was Councillor William Cameron of Cumbria County Council. A craggy yet genial advocate with a twinkle in his eyes, he recalled the formation of the Joint County Councils steering committee in 1983 and the commissioning of the PEIDA Report which concluded that although considerable capital expenditure was required on the line, British Rail's 'wanton neglect' of it during recent years had advanced the case for closure.

He summarised Cumbria's objection which was on five main grounds: Hardship to those living in or requiring access to the region, particularly to Appleby. The termination of Dales Rail. The increase in journey times between Leeds and Carlisle via Carnforth. Loss of jobs in Cumbria with little prospect of alternative employment. And the loss of the diversionary route for the West Coast Main Line, the alternative via the Cumbrian Coast

Line or the use of buses would result in hardship. This, too, was another excellent submission.

Ron Cotton replied for British Rail. On diversions, he confirmed that if there was a blockage on the West Coast Main Line between Carlisle and Carnforth, trains would be diverted via the Cumbrian Coast Line; whilst if the blockage was between Carnforth and Preston, trains would be diverted via Settle-Junction, Hellifield and Blackburn. He said that whereas diversions via the Settle–Carlisle line added 1 hour 40 minutes to journey times, those via the Cumbrian Coast Line would involve an extra journey time of up to 2 hours 40 minutes. On an average weekday, 72 passenger and newspaper trains would be involved. On Sundays there would be 44 trains.

Responding to an earlier request from the North Western TUCC, Cotton went into some detail regarding the work required to make the Cumbrian Coast Line suitable for use by Mark 3 Inter-City coaches which were currently banned from the line due to narrow tunnels and sub-standard track clearances. It was because of this that even the local DMUs had bars fitted across their windows so people could not lean out. By cutting back station platforms and operating single line working on the sub-standard double track between Maryport and Carlisle it would be possible to accommodate services comprising Mark 3 coaches.

Mrs Olive Clarke, who was present as an observer from the North Western TUCC, remarked that it was unfortunate no details of the cost of diverting the service over the Cumbrian Coast Line had been included. I agreed. Therefore, we were all rather surprised when Ron Cotton – after earlier refusing to disclose any financial information – blandly replied that the overall cost of the work involved was £100,000. There were gasps of astonishment. I don't think anyone believed it. I doubt if he believed it himself. The figure seemed too pat. He added that the Railway Inspectorate had passed the proposals and agreed to the use of Mark 3 coaches on the coast line. Nor would the windows have to be barred. Passengers would have to make do with a warning instead.

Then came a bombshell from Councillor Cameron. He said he had listened to Mr Cotton with some incredulity. The Cumbrian Coast Line was often blocked by landslips at Parton. During periods of high tides the line at Siddick was often washed away leading to closure of the route. However, his main bone of contention was the figure of £100,000 for the cost of upgrading the coast line for use by diverted services.

"I was offered £7 million if my council would not object to the Settle–Carlisle closure," said Councillor Cameron. He then explained how, in 1981, senior British Rail managers had promised to spend £7 million on improvements to the Cumbrian Coast Line if Cumbria County Council would not object to the closure of the Settle–Carlisle line. This was dynamite.

Outside the Public Hearing he provided more details. The proposal had been put to a group of Cumbria councillors at a lunch by a British Rail team headed by the then Preston divisional manager Tom Brazier. "If we didn't object to the Settle–Carlisle closure – and he told us they were going to close it – then British Rail would spend £7 million on the Cumbrian Coast Line, replacing track and widening bridges," Councillor Cameron told journalists covering the hearing. "It would ensure the future of the coast line. I told Mr Brazier the answer was no. I would always object to any rail closure in Cumbria."

Ron Cotton declined to comment other than to say it was unfortunate such issues should be dragged up after the person concerned – in this case Tom Brazier – had retired. That, of course, was a problem with British Rail. People seldom stayed in any position sufficiently long to enable them to account for their decisions. I felt it rather shabby they had set up Ron Cotton as the fall guy when the person who should have been facing the music and carrying the can had got off scot free. Nor was it Tom Brazier I had in mind, for he was one of the few people within British Rail to have been candid on the issue from the beginning. The person who should have been facing the music was, of course, Mr J J O'Brien.

Following the excitement generated by Councillor Cameron, the hearing settled down to a more predictable pattern. The chairman of Lancashire County Council's Highways and Transport Committee, Councillor George Slynn spoke up for Clitheroe and the Ribble Valley. The case for Appleby was put by Mr Keith Morgan of the local Chamber of Trade whilst Dr Judith Allinson explained how students from all over the country travelled by train to visit the Malham Tarn Field Centre near Settle.

Rounding off the first session, County Councillor Beth Graham, who was speaking as chairman of Settle Town Council, emphasised the importance of the railway to the town, especially with regard to tourism. Two surveys had highlighted the impact of closure of the line. It was not just that 13 per cent of all visitors to the town arrived by train, a further 36 per cent of all visitors travelled on the Settle–Carlisle line during their stay. Most significant of all was that 32 per cent of visitors said the line was their main reason for visiting the town. It was by far and away the most popular attraction in the area. She also took a swipe at British Rail for their 'closure by stealth' policy for the line.

When Ron Cotton denied there was any 'closure by stealth', Councillor Graham referred him to the letter Sir Peter Parker had written to Ben Ford MP in 1981 which said British Rail had no plans nor desire to close the Settle–Carlisle line. Yet, said Councillor Graham, documents showed that plans for closure existed. It was, she added, difficult to accept statements from British Rail unless its representatives were under oath.

I rather liked that. So I put it to Ron Cotton that there seemed to be a credibility gap so far as British Rail and the Settle–Carlisle line was concerned. To his credit he accepted that there had been one. However, he implied that they were 'good boys' now! All in all it had been an interesting and eventful first session.

There was plenty of interest in the sessions that followed. That afternoon David Lloyd presented the first of the six statements on behalf of the Joint County Councils. But for an occasional addition or update, they were the same excellent submissions which had been made at the North Western TUCC hearing. Then Dr John Whitelegg's lucid exposition on the financial case for retention of the line suggested that the Joint Action Committee had got its act together.

I warmed to the amazement of David Stuttard, representing the Borough of Pendle, at the decision to discontinue first class on the Settle–Carlisle line from May which would discourage business travel. Ron Cotton replied that there was no demand for it, to which I retorted this was only to be expected as there was a 660 per cent surcharge for the privilege of a first class day return journey between Leeds and Carlisle. What was required, I added, was a competitively priced first class day return fare – a point Ron Cotton subsequently agreed with me on, although it was more than his job was worth to have said so at the hearing.

Mr J R Tardiff of Nottingham was one of many who bemoaned the re-routing of the Nottingham–Glasgow service, pointing out that the journey between those cities now took an extra 38 minutes than when the trains ran via the Settle–Carlisle line. Moreover, British Rail's proposals for travel to Appleby via Penrith and thence by 'dedicated' bus was unacceptable as it reduced the amount of time spent there by almost half.

From Ian Taylor we learnt a great deal about one of British Rail's success stories – 'Red Star Parcels'. His family firm of agricultural engineers used Settle station to send machine parts all over the country. During 1985 they despatched 278 parcels from Settle at a cost of £2,199. In addition they received 292 parcels which had cost senders £2,309.

Ron Cotton replied that whilst Taylor's business represented 53 per cent of parcels despatched from Settle, it should be seen in context as the parcels business only contributed 6 or 7 per cent of the revenue taken at the station. This was most interesting as, on the basis of the figures provided by Ian Taylor and the percentages provided by Ron Cotton, it was possible to calculate that Settle station took some £60/70,000 in 1985. This was backed by more Red Star data from Peter Lawrence.

Opening the second day of the hearing in Settle, I suggested British Rail should revert to the procedure of providing financial information to back the case for closure in accordance with the 'Carrington Recommendations' (see page 177) and asked Mr Michael Harrison QC if he would ask his clients to reconsider their position as:

"The absence of financial information meant the committee was forced to clutch at straws to assess the substance of British Rail's case, be they in the columns of newspapers, between the covers of 'leaked' British Rail documents, in representations from objectors or, indeed, from the asides made by the British Rail representative (Ron Cotton) in an unguarded moment. The previous day figures ranging from £100,000 to £7 million had been quoted as the cost of upgrading the Cumbrian Coast Line to enable diversions from the West Coast Main Line to take place."

Mr Harrison, in a characteristically gracious response, said he noted what I had said and would seek instructions and report back. Fair enough. I don't suppose he could have said anything else. Nevertheless, I was under no illusions that his clients would change their tune and they didn't. Even so, it was worth a try.

A recurring theme was the inadequacy of Giggleswick as an alternative to Settle if the line closed. No one put this better than Mrs Christine Lawrence who made her submission accompanied by her two exceptionally well behaved children. She spoke of her fears regarding the remoteness of Giggleswick station and the access to it by a "lonely, long and unlit road." Moreover, the Settle by-pass would create additional access difficulties as people would have to cross a busy unlit road when it was built.

Following the evening session of the second day, one of my members, Mrs Shirley Shaw – who had kindly been ferrying me between the Victoria Hall and our headquarters at the comfortable Falcon Manor Hotel – ran another member, John Blezard, and myself down to Giggleswick station so we could sample the walk back to Settle. The car park – if you could call it that – was in a frightful state and I was rather worried about the springs of Shirley's Audi as she manoeuvered it amongst the pot holes.

Nor did the station itself impress. It was a simple country halt comprising a couple of low platforms, one of which had a bus stop type of shelter. The light strategically placed above the timetable was not working so it was impossible to check train times, whilst the light adjacent to the track crossing was adjusted so it didn't illuminate the crossing. Perhaps the wind had blown it askew. Walking briskly, it took us 20 minutes to get back to Settle. Fortunately it had stopped raining or we would have been soaked. Above all, our little excursion proved that objectors had not been overstating their case when it came to the total unsuitability of Giggleswick as an alternative to Settle.

At the opening of the third and final day in Settle, John Blezard and myself reported on our fact finding mission to Giggleswick station. John added that improvements should be effected immediately, irrespective of the future of the Settle–Carlisle line. I also took the opportunity to put in a good word for Ron Cotton. Whilst at the receiving end of much criticism, there were also many plaudits for his work in promoting the line. The committee endorsed this praise.

Our three days in Settle proved to be both interesting and enjoyable. Indeed, at times, they could even be said to have been entertaining. Any chill in the Victoria Hall due to the insufficiency of the central heating system was more than compensated by the warmth of those attending the hearing. Notwithstanding a considerable amount of repetition in the submissions, they seldom palled. This was largely due to the variety of the evidence, both in its content and presentation.

In addition to a couple of half-hour presentations by David Lloyd on behalf of the Joint County Councils and a most knowledgeable discourse on bus substitution from Richard Watts for the Joint

Action Committee, we had the benefit of a teach-in from Morag Simpson, an economist at Leeds University who also acted as a consultant to the World Bank.

After explaining to us the methodology of sensitivity analysis – the identification of those items of benefits and costs which most effect the possible results of an investment project – she said the PEIDA report concluded that over a 20 year period the financial cost-benefit appraisal resulted in a negative net present value of £19.6 million. The PEIDA update in 1986 indicated a reduction to £17.5 million, whilst the Joint County Councils had arrived at a figure of £13.7 million. Mrs Simpson's estimate brought the total down to £8.3 million. Whilst all a bit beyond me, it certainly gave one food for thought.

So, too, did Mr J L Lonsdale of the Yorkshire Dales National Park who emphasised the importance of Dales Rail which had developed into a thriving and integrated transport service. He referred to the listed structures on the line like the Ribblehead Viaduct and said the National Parks had a statutory duty to secure the conservation of these, as had British Rail. I put this last point to Mr Harrison who replied that British Rail had no statutory obligation to maintain listed structures as such, although they were under an obligation not to damage them. They also had obligations under Common Law to maintain them so they were not dangerous to third parties.

The writer David Joy, speaking as secretary of the local branch of the Council for the Protection of Rural England, drew the committee's attention to a report prepared for the Countryside Commission by the Centre for Environmental Interpretation. This defined heritage as 'a broad term to describe those resources of scientific, scenic, historical and cultural interest which link with the past and yet have such attraction that they are highly valued and judged to be worthy of conservation for future generations.' The report said railways and their structures should satisfy the following criteria to be judged part of the national heritage:

● represent great engineering achievement in the national context.
● exhibit particularly important railway architecture.
● involve important construction techniques.
● mark a significant stage in the development of the rail network.

● have had a significant role in the development of the environment and the communities in the areas through which they pass.
● have a landscape setting which makes the line or features an
important aspect of the townscape or countryside.

The Settle–Carlisle line, said Mr Joy, satisfied all of these
criteria. I felt this was a particularly good point.

The director of Friends of the Earth, Jonathan Porritt, in an
eloquent plea on behalf of the cycling fraternity, had the committee
in fits of laughter when he maintained only 12 bicycles could be
conveyed between England and Scotland on a winter Sunday! By
contrast there was nothing to laugh about as Mr A K Little, a
psychologist from West Sussex who could only travel long distances
by train due to a severe locomotor handicap, put the case for disabled users equally eloquently. He had a champion in North Western TUCC member Pat Entwhistle who strongly rebuked Ron Cotton for the non-provision of facilities for the handicapped on the
projected bus service between Appleby and Penrith.

The potential of the Settle–Carlisle line as an attraction for overseas tourists was stressed by Christopher Thompson, course director of the International Summer School in York. Three American
organisations he represented had placed £15,000 of advertising in
up-market journals which made special reference to rail tours on
the line. The response had been beyond expectations. Mr
Thompson also suggested that part of the large volume of tourist
travel between London and Edinburgh should be diverted via the
line.

Looking back, it was the diversity of the submissions that made
our three days in Settle so absorbing. Among the 70 or so individual
objectors who spoke was John Spencer Gilks, one of the country's
foremost authorities on railways. He made the novel point that if
the Settle–Carlisle line closed, he was not satisfied that the money
saved would be spent in a manner equally beneficial to him as a
taxpayer. Then, time and again, the importance of the line to the
finely balanced tourist dominated local economy was emphasised.
Bernard Houghton of Settle's Golden Lion Hotel spoke for many
when he said that any reduction in tourism would have a "devastat-
ing effect" on the town.

Then there were a number of delightful characters, like Mr
Cameron who restored string instruments at his home in Selside
and travelled throughout the country by a combination of bike and

train. He took the committee on a travelogue which seemed to end at Haymarket! As for Tom Crowther of Morecambe, he had evolved a variation of the Richter Scale to evaluate hardship. It ranged from 'Increase in Journey Costs' at 20 and 'Reduction in Time Available at Destination' at 30 to 'Closure of Stations En-Route' at 90 and, the ultimate hardship of 'Closure of the Line' at 100. Thus was born 'Crowthers Hardship Scale'.

After Settle, we had four days to re-charge our batteries before we opened at Skipton Town Hall. Then it was on to Leeds. What else, I wondered, would be in store for us.

18

FIGHTING TALK IN SKIPTON

"It behoved everyone to strain every nerve, fight tooth and nail, and explore every channel to preserve the pride and glory of our country for this and future generations. We must not be complacent. The battle will not be won until we see such headlines in the press as 'Settle–Carlisle Line Saved!'"

E C Swinburne Garrett.

Following the four day break, the North East TUCC Settle–Carlisle Public Hearing resumed at Skipton Town Hall on Monday 21st April for a further three days. It was a bright sunny, albeit chilly morning. After arriving off the 09.03 from Leeds and checking the arrangements in the hall, I had time for a wander round some of the stalls in the High Street. There I bumped into Ron Cotton. After passing the time of day, I asked if he had been told that the re-routed Nottingham–Glasgow service, which had been the start of the whole saga, was to be withdrawn in May 1987. He hadn't, so I warned him that I would probably refer to it.

When we had been at Settle, Councillor Beth Graham had strongly criticised the absence of senior British Rail management at the hearing. I took up this point in my opening address at Skipton and, turning again to the Filey Holiday Camp station closure, recalled that British Rail had been represented by two senior managers and three subordinates. In making this observation, I emphasised I was not questioning Ron Cotton's ability. "Indeed," I added, "it could be argued that he ranked as a giant alongside some of today's senior British Rail managers."

Another legacy of our stay in Settle was an assurance from British Rail that, if the Settle–Carlisle line closed, they would upgrade Giggleswick station with an additional shelter, a British Telecom phone and a British Rail phone to the nearest control so passengers could enquire what had happened to their trains if they didn't turn up. Ron Cotton had said he would also consider providing a bus service between Settle and Giggleswick station. I sincerely hoped we would not have to put these assurances to the test.

Then followed Michael Harrison's set piece, in which the QC explained British Rail were only prepared to comment on hardship as they considered other issues to be outside the remit of the TUCCs. To this I once again replied this was not the case. It was becoming a bit like 'Oh, yes it is!' and 'Oh, no it isn't!' in pantomime with neither of us budging an inch. However, I was able to back my position with an extract from a letter Sir Robert Reid had sent to an MP, in which the British Railways Board chairman had stated "the whole issue would be considered by the TUCCs."

Max Madden, the able Labour MP for Bradford West opened for the objectors by quoting from an article by Alan Whitaker in the 'Telegraph & Argus' which said: "If British Rail thought the Settle–Carlisle would be easy meat, then they've certainly misjudged the mood of the travelling public and have had a rude awakening. The dubious methods used to achieve their objectives have alienated British Rail who now find themselves in a corner."

Mr Whitaker's article should be formally considered by the committee, said Mr Madden. For British Rail stood accused at the Public Hearing of wanton neglect of the Settle–Carlisle line. It had re-routed services away from it and there had been minimum maintenance and marketing. He called for investment and imagination from British Rail and a commitment to the railways from the Government. The line should remain open to support local communities, assist in employment and economic recovery and in the expansion of tourism.

I felt Max's submission hit just the right note. I knew him from the days of the Common Market debate, whilst he had been very helpful and supportive in opposing British Rail's illegal closure of the Wortley Curve which had severed the direct Bradford–Wakefield route used by the 'Bradford Executive' to King's Cross.

The evidence that followed was also of a high standard. Among the many contributions I recall was that of Jack Smith from Burley-in-Wharfedale who praised Dales Rail – "that splendid innovation much appreciated by all walkers and among people living in the Dales." It would be a great loss if it was discontinued, he said. The same was true of steam excursions, yet British Rail were pricing them out of the market. With the restoration of through express trains as well as a local stopping service, the line would become a paying proposition.

Mr D H Watson of Bradford raised the question of 'closure by stealth'. In December 1982 he had written to British Rail complaining of the re-routing of the Nottingham–Glasgow service. Yet the reply he received dated 9th February 1983 stressed that the change did not imply they were anxious to ensure closure of the Settle–Carlisle line. However, the 'Telegraph & Argus' of 29th August 1983 gave details of a leaked British Rail document dated August 1981 which outlined plans to close the line. Mr Watson also dismissed the alternative Leeds–Carlisle service via Carnforth as a non-starter.

Up to now we had not heard a great deal about this service, possibly because so few people would choose to use it. David Lloyd, for the Joint County Councils, had said their survey had indicated that, if the line closed, 74 per cent of existing users would not make the journey at all and, of the remainder, only 15 per cent would use alternative rail services. I felt the final estimate to be on the generous side. Certainly British Rail were living in cloud-cuckooland if, as Ron Cotton had suggested, they expected to retain between 25 and 33 per cent of users.

But what really fascinated me was the timetable for the projected service via Carnforth. No one had taken it up so I decided to do so myself. The question I wanted answering was why, even when taking into account the time taken for the engine to run round from one end of the train to the other, the journey of 13 miles between Carnforth and Oxenholme was scheduled for no less than 51 minutes! Ron Cotton replied that, apart from the engine change, the train would have to wait for a path on the West Coast Main Line. As a consequence it would be standing for over half-an-hour in Carnforth Down Goods Loop!

I could hardly believe my ears! Surely British Rail were not serious. I put it to Ron Cotton that this was some form of joke. It wasn't. "You'll have to put on a cabaret or floor show to keep the passengers amused," I retorted. "Words almost fail me." Then came the vital question: "Will passengers be allowed to use the facilities (toilets) when the train is standing in Carnforth Down Goods Loop?", I asked. "We do frown on people using them in sidings and stations," replied a straight-faced Mr Cotton to an outburst of laughter in the hall.

The comedy interlude over, I turned to the decision to discontinue the re-routed Nottingham–Glasgow service in 1987. So much for the innovation that was going to bring so much new business and open new travel opportunities following its removal from the Settle–Carlisle line. The Joint Action Committee chairman, Dr John Whitelegg, recalled that the Nottingham–Glasgow service had been amalgamated with the Manchester–Glasgow service for 'commercial reasons'. Obviously these had proved unsound. From past experience he had no faith in the diverted service via Carnforth if the Settle–Carlisle line closed. Not only were the timings atrocious, the service – if introduced – would be transient in itself. The proposals were totally unacceptable on any grounds whatsoever.

Opening the afternoon session, John Lark of Great Yarmouth said the fact he had travelled such a long distance demonstrated his concern at British Rail's decision to close the Settle–Carlisle line. The same point was made by Gordon Keers of Aberdeen who referred to money spent by Scot Rail on unnecessary cosmetic alterations to stations. He felt it would have been better spent on Ribblehead Viaduct. The last time he had travelled on the line, the train windows were very dirty. This was symptomatic of management that wished to close the route.

Indeed, Keers felt British Rail were trying to reduce income. Dirty trains was one symptom. Another was frequent timetable adjustments and poor connections. The current timetable was so bad that, when returning from Leeds on the 16.05, there was an hour to wait in Carlisle for a connection to Glasgow. This arrived too late to catch the last train to Aberdeen. Undaunted, he planned to take the 16.52 from Skipton (ex 16.05 Leeds) to Carlisle. From there he would fly with Air Ecosse to Dundee where he would get a train to Aberdeen!

For the Joint County Councils, Earl Peel – who had spoken in a recent House of Lords debate on the line – said it struck him as absolutely crazy to allow something that was irreplaceable to be destroyed. Colin Pepper from Keighley remarked that although his use of the line was largely for pleasure, it should be exploited for its strategic importance as the direct link between West Yorkshire and South West Scotland.

Then it was the turn of FOSCLA to present what was almost a hearing within a hearing. It was opened by their chairman Brian Sutcliffe who introduced Peter Shaw, probably the most knowledgeable of all Settle–Carlisle objectors, who provided the best submission to date on diversions. During the Easter weekend 92 trains had been diverted over the line to accommodate planned engineering work on the West Coast Main Line. He had details of every train involved. Nor were there any doubts about Shaw's data, for he was known to set up his small tent by the side of the line for days at a time to undertake his research.

With FOSCLA president Russell Harty unable to be present, Brian Sutcliffe's 'star' objector was Bob Cryer, the MEP for Sheffield and former Westminster member for Keighley. He said the Public Hearing should mark the halt of the 'closure by stealth' philosophy expounded by British Rail. The Settle–Carlisle line was far too important a railway to be consigned to a few remnants to be gazed upon by passing motorists.

After summarising a multitude of points made by scores of other FOSCLA members unable to attend the hearing, Bob – someone else I knew from the Common Market debate – said that in 1982 British Rail received £177 million under the Public Service Obligation grant for expenditure on track, viaducts and underbridges. They failed to spend all that amount. "The situation was that they were saying there was a problem, yet failed to spend the money to put it right," he claimed. When he questioned this, British Rail had told him that strikes had prevented all the expenditure planned. However, the strikes concerned ASLEF and during them the viaducts would have been available for full possessions for repair work. Failure to undertake it demonstrated the lack of faith on the part of British Rail which had deliberately run down the Settle–Carlisle line to justify the closure proposal.

Dales Rail founder Colin Speakman spoke for the 50,000 strong Ramblers Association and the influential Yorkshire Dales Society. He opened with some useful thoughts on 'hardship'. As defined by the Shorter Oxford English Dictionary it meant: 'the quality of being hard to bear, hardness, severity, hardness of fate or circumstances; severe toil or suffering, extreme privation.' Not to be able to reach England's finest fell-walking country and being denied part of one's birthright was 'hardship' in the deepest sense, he said.

The feeling that the Yorkshire Dales were a natural hinterland of the towns and cities was something built into the very consciousness of West Yorkshire people, said Colin Speakman. The late J B Priestley had captured that feeling. Writing of living in his native Bradford he had said:

"You caught the fever when you were quite young, and it never left you. However small and dark your office or warehouse was, somewhere inside your head the high moors were glowing, the curlews were crying, and there blew a wind as soft as if it came from the middle of the Atlantic. That is why we did not care very much if our city had no charm, for it was simply a place to go and work until it was time to set out for Wharfedale or Wensleydale again."

This affinity between West Yorkshire people and the Dales was enhanced by the Settle–Carlisle line which provided the link between the industrial and residential West Riding and some of the finest walking country in England, continued Mr Speakman. Nor was walking a minority pastime. The Countryside Commission's recent survey of outdoor leisure pursuits showed it to be by far the most popular activity.

Turning to tourism, he said it was most significant that Lord Young saw a major role for British Rail in its development. Speakman wondered that if the argument were about the National Gallery, York Minster or Hadrian's Wall, how long it would take for the laughter to stop if it were suggested they should close because maintenance costs were too high. Yet the Settle–Carlisle line was a national monument on the same scale. No other European country would contemplate the destruction of such an asset. If the incomparable Monsieur Voltaire were alive, he would doubtless be writing to his fellow countrymen that not only do the English shoot their Admirals, they are also hell-bent on destroying their national monuments!

In the evening a new dimension regarding the importance of the line raised its head – that of national security. The Mayor of Skipton, Councillor Claire Brooks, resplendent in her magnificent chain of office, opened her submission by covering the familiar territory of employment, tourism, diversions and access to the North Pennine communities. She then warned that the frequent blockages on the West Coast Main Line could seriously hamper the defence of the country and interfere with supplies to NATO forces at times of international crisis if the Settle–Carlisle line was closed.

Recalling the intensive use of the line during the Second World War in the run-up to D Day, she said: "British Rail's proposals are effectively achieving the KGB's goal of hampering NATO supply lines. This must constitute severe hardship, not only for users of the line but for every citizen of the United Kingdom." This was fighting talk from a champion of the people. Nor was that all, for she then proceeded to make submissions on behalf of the Skipton and Ripon Liberal Association and herself. A case of three for the price of one.

The Mayor was followed by Bradford solicitor Mr T M Walsh. He warmly welcomed the TUCCs decision to consider issues other than hardship. British Rail, in attempting to narrow the issue had not come to the hearing with 'clean hands'. Were it a court of criminal jurisdiction, he felt they would stand indicted by the public on prima facie evidence in respect to the line under the Companies Act of asset stripping, of fraudulent accounting, of perjury and of contempt. He used the expression 'contempt' because "not only did British Rail attempt to put forward fallacious arguments towards the closure of the line, but they made the biggest insult of all to our intelligence – both the committee's and mine – in expecting us to believe what they said."

This was strong stuff. The pressure was maintained by former FOSCLA chairman, David Burton. He considered the issue of Ribblehead Viaduct to be a red herring and recalled that between 1980 and 1983 he had collected waste paper for fund raising purposes. As a consequence, a "railway dossier" had come into his possession which set out in great detail the procedure for closing the Settle–Carlisle line. The procedure had been vigorously followed.

Ripon dental surgeon Adrian Morgan calculated British Rail were spending £306 million to cut 15 minutes off the London–Edinburgh journey. This worked out at £340,000 per second. The expenditure required to return to the running time of 15 years ago on the Settle–Carlisle line worked out at £6,250 per second – better value for money! As for the projected Leeds–Carlisle service via Carnforth, it would add an additional £19,000 a year in fuel costs alone. He said British Rail were custodians of our national network. If they did not wish to care for it, they should step down and let someone else take over. Their case for closure was undoubtedly weak. Why else did they need the assistance of a QC at the Public Hearing?

And so the evening progressed. Martin Calvert of Leeds – a frequent champion of the line via the correspondence columns of the 'Yorkshire Post' and other papers – said British Rail's slogan 'We're Getting There' was quite catchy. But what they were advocating was 'We're Getting There the Long Way Round!' He wanted to travel to Appleby via Settle, not Carnforth. It was not just a case of getting there, but how you got there that counted.

Rounding off what I thought was probably the best days evidence we had heard so far, broadcaster and teacher John Bushell spoke of the tremendous educational potential of the Settle–Carlisle line. Then we were driven over to Ilkley in a blizzard where we were booked into the Craiglands Hotel for two nights.

I awoke on Tuesday morning to a Christmas card scene from my bedroom window. However, the roads were clear and we resumed the Public Hearing promptly at 10.30 when I was able to give some financial details regarding the cost of recent repairs to a viaduct. Unfortunately, the information related not to Ribblehead but to the Durham Viaduct on the East Coast Main Line. The fact it had come via Ron Cotton following comments made by an objector at Settle just underlined the stupidity of British Rail's embargo on financial information regarding the Settle–Carlisle line.

The first submission came from Dave Morton, the policy co-ordinator for the City of Bradford. He said that since the re-routing of the Nottingham–Glasgow service the area's service to Scotland had disappeared. One had to conclude the changes were designed to kill off business travel by rail between the largest city in Scotland and the centre of the wool textile industry to help the case for closure of the Settle–Carlisle line. The image of Bradford had changed. Much of the smoke and grime had gone. It was now recognised as one of Britain's fastest growing tourist centres and a gateway to the Yorkshire Dales. The council was concerned at the tactics employed by British Rail in its attempt to close the line. If they were allowed to succeed, it would sound "the death knell" for other lines serving Bradford.

Other major submissions came from the Joint County Councils and Transport 2000. For the former, Mr C Emslow summarised the success story of Dales Rail. Of the 4,800 passengers carried in 1985, 49 per cent were from West Yorkshire and 28 per cent from Lancashire. The main purpose of 80 per cent of West Yorkshire users and 90 per cent of Lancashire users was to gain access for walks in the country, although significant numbers of residents along the line used Dales Rail to make shopping trips to Leeds and Carlisle.

For Transport 2000, Jonathan Roberts said it was the first time they had presented evidence at national level at a railway closure hearing. This was a clear indication of the importance they attached to the future of the Settle–Carlisle line. The advent of the Channel tunnel would increase the potential for both tourist and freight traffic.

Jonathan Roberts then spoke on behalf of the Joint Action Committee. His case was based on two papers he had played a major part in drafting: TEST's 'Retraining the Settle and Carlisle' and 'New Life in the Hills', copies of which were submitted to the committee. He called for a semi-fast Leeds–Carlisle service and introduction of a local service to stop at all the Dales Rail stations which should be reopened on a permanent basis. This latter point was already being considered by British Rail and the local authorities and was likely to commence in the summer, yet another bizarre twist to the whole saga.

Introducing his paper 'The Costs and Revenue Associated with the Line', Alan Thompson for the Joint County Councils estimated that in 1985 £0.9 million of revenue from timetabled British Rail services should have been allocated to the Settle–Carlisle line. To this figure should be added contributions from diverted services and charter trains. If the line were to close, he estimated that British Rail would lose £0.8 million from timetabled services alone. Therefore, there seemed little case for closing the line when its financial performance was so much better than much of the network.

Highspot of the afternoon was the submission on behalf of the Joint Action committee by Christopher Loudon Wallis on the 'Condition of the Structures'. The son of Barnes Wallis of bouncing bomb and 'The Dam Busters' fame, in a Freudian slip of the tongue I introduced him as Christopher Barnes Wallis and was half expecting the sound of Eric Coates' 'Dam Busters March' to burst forth over the PA as he strode to the front of the hall. He had an impressive background which included 13 years of bridge design with British Rail prior to forming his own company to restore historic buildings.

Chris Wallis recalled that towards the end of his railway career in 1980, British Rail had said the Barmouth Viaduct on the Cambrian Coast Line was not economically repairable and could only be replaced, otherwise the line would have to close. He therefore made his own investigation which disproved this. However, his conclusions were not accepted and he felt British Rail were giving biased or false technical information to back their case for closing the line.

"I am proud of my profession and do not approve of falsifying engineering technical information," said Mr Wallis. The public had to be able to trust the information given by civil engineers. There-fore he had made his own report public. Subsequently the Bar-mouth Viaduct was repaired, largely as he had suggested and at a quarter of the cost of replacement. Therefore, when he first read reports coupling proposals to close the Settle–Carlisle line with the poor state of Ribblehead Viaduct, he felt this could be another case of British Rail's 'Barmouth method' of taking the largest struc-ture on the line and finding seemingly incurable faults which could only be rectified by expensive replacements.

He had closely examined viaducts at Ribblehead, Dent Head, Arten Gill and Crosby Garrett. At Ribblehead scaffolding had been in position which enabled him to take the leading dimensions and inspect the condition of the masonry in the spandrels and the tops of the piers. Then, with the aid of a blackboard, Mr Wallis gave the committee a detailed description of Ribblehead Viaduct, its construction and his assessment of its current condition. He explained that thermal expansion and contraction, not the pressure of ballast and train loadings as claimed by British Rail, had caused the separation of the spandrels from the arches.

Mr Wallis said the track ballast on the viaduct varied in depth between two and three feet below the sleepers. It covered a deck of stone slabs supported on four internal diaphragm walls, parallel to the spandrels and resting on the arches. Each wall was almost directly beneath a running line. The stone slabs were laid to fall from the arch crown to the water drainage spout through the centre of the spandrel over the pier and must have been waterproofed with asphalt. The leaking of the waterproof membrane by move-ment of the spandrels, and possible differential movement between the stone slabs, was the cause of the viaducts present malaise. Thus British Rail's recent singling of the line to the central position was not necessary.

The piers were founded on bedrock and were completely stable, continued Mr Wallis. The limestone of which they were made was very strong, roughly twice the strength of the strongest concrete. To reach such a great strength, the limestone – a sedimentary rock – must have been very heavily compressed beneath the ground. Gradual relief of this external pressure would relieve the triaxial compressive stresses, which could allow expansion and cause hair cracking. Water and frost would open the cracks so they became visible. If the compressive pressures in the pier were very high, this could be dangerous. In practice they were not, a point Mr

Wallis proved with detailed calculations.

The Ribblehead Viaduct's problems had been caused by water seeping through the masonry from the deck. For many years the railway engineers had applied first-aid treatment instead of identifying and correcting the fault. However, all was not lost, for the technique of stablilising and waterproofing old masonry was now fully understood and had been proved many times in practice.

Mr Wallis said he had approached Colcrete Ltd, who were specialists in this type of work, and on the information he had provided they had submitted an estimate for repairs to Ribblehead of £900,000. This compared with British Rail's estimate of more than £4.2 million.

I thanked Mr Wallis and told him that he had given us a great deal to think about. It really was quite an eye opener. For British Rail, Ron Cotton accepted that the evidence presented was Mr Wallis's professional opinion. Nevertheless he would convey the evidence to British Rail's engineers for consideration.

Following a brief interlude from the former Vicar at Kirkby Stephen, the Reverend Rigg, who recalled the difficulty of arranging cremations in Carlisle during the winter and suggested British Rail might provide a special funeral parlour coach, we were in the midst of another learned submission, this time from Claus Meyer of the National Council on Inland Transport. Like many beforehand, he said the information provided by British Rail was insufficient for proper consideration of the proposal. In particular there was no 'Origin and Destination Survey'. This should be mandatory. Fortunately surveys had been undertaken by the Joint Action Committee and, on the basis of these, Mr Meyer estimated contributory revenue for the line to be £1.23 million.

One of the best individual contributions that afternoon came from John Turner of Derby. His personal involvement with the line began in 1959 when, as a student teacher, he assisted with a London school party to Loch Lomond. They had travelled from St Pancras and he had been "completely bowled over by the experience" which was enhanced by a fast, efficient service worthy of the route. Having witnessed the closure of the direct service between Derby and Manchester where a once busy main line was wantonly and speciously destroyed on narrow cost-accountancy grounds, it would be a tragedy if the same thing happened to the Settle–Carlisle line.

Mr Turner said the line was part of the technological and cultural heritage of the country. If destroyed its spectre would return to haunt British Rail as surely as Euston's Doric Arch still does today. Future generations would not thank us if we allowed institutions like the Settle–Carlisle to disappear because of a lack of social and political will. It was for this reason he had travelled 120 miles to add his voice to the proceedings. In a day that had been dominated by a multitude of facts and figures it was good to hear someone speaking from the heart.

Someone else who undoubtedly did was Mrs Ann Stephenson of Doncaster. She came from a railway family and asked people to imagine the outcry if York Minster or the Tower of London were threatened by closure – "the very idea was unthinkable!" Yet 72 miles of railway which ran through some of Britain's most magnificent scenery was to be tossed aside. She challenged British Rail to "show us you're getting there!"

Indeed, it was to prove something of a 'Ladies Day'. Others who spoke included Mrs Gillian Fox, a mother with two young children, who stressed the advantages of rail travel. Children didn't have to be confined to a seat whilst the provision of toilets was most helpful – except in Carnforth Down Goods Loop! Mrs Jenny Morgan of Appleby spoke on behalf of parents who took their children into Carlisle for medical treatment, and Mrs E Day of Bolton recalled holidays spent in a cottage directly below Arten Gill Viaduct.

That evening it was the turn of Philippa Simpson, a town planner who was also a director of the Joint Action Committee. She presented a particularly well researched paper on the 'Neglect of the Long Distance Through Passenger Using the Settle–Carlisle Line'. I was glad that someone had really got to grips with this angle as it was in danger of being neglected amid all the talk of diversions, bikes, Red Star parcels and Dales Rail. Yet the line was primarily built to take express trains over the hills at speed.

Later, in a separate personal submission, she strongly criticised facilities – or the lack of them – at Giggleswick station. It was not the sort of place any lady would wish to travel to on their own, especially after dark. There was, she added, something "rather spooky about it" – and I don't think she was thinking on the same lines as Dame Edna Everage!

The sense of irritation at British Rail's continued refusal to answer financial queries and their inability to come up with replies to other quite innocuous points was seldom far from the surface. That evening it boiled over and tempers began to fray. Ron Cotton, who up to now had shown commendable restraint under pressure, began to display signs of that 'we know what's best for you' arrogance that those who have dealings with British Rail encounter from time to time. Part of the problem was he had nobody to help him. Both Michael Harrison QC and the young solicitor from the British Railways Board were little more than passengers. I doubted if either of them could have found their way around the railway timetable.

Things came to a head when Peter Horton of the Joint Action Committee asked if Mr Cotton had contacted the Social Services Department regarding arrangements for the disabled on the projected Appleby–Penrith bus. Mr Cotton replied that he had not had the opportunity to do so. I retorted that I felt Mr Cotton should have more support so he could promptly respond to issues raised at the hearing. "Couldn't the young gentlemen be delegated to chase up the Social Services people," I asked Cotton, referring – not too patronisingly, I hope – to the solicitor-cum-tea boy. "Do you know who he is," Cotton replied. "He's Mr Timothy Reardon, a solicitor from the Board." Of course I knew. "But surely this doesn't prevent him from lending a hand," I replied.

When we resumed the following morning, tempers were back on an even keel. The session was largely confined to completion of the remaining submissions from the Joint County Councils and the Joint Action Committee. But first Councillor Beth Graham presented the formal case for Craven District Council. It was another well researched presentation highlighting the importance of the Settle–Carlisle line to the local economy, especially with regard to tourism where there were over 2,100 jobs in Craven representing almost 5 per cent of the total population. She also commended Lord Young's report on 'Pleasure, Leisure and Jobs'.

Councillor Graham said a recent survey by a local holiday cottage agency of customers in Wharfedale, Wensleydale and Swaledale showed that the most popular 'wet weather activities' for visitors were trips to: (1) – the Jorvik Centre in York; (2) – the National Railway Museum, also in York; and (3) – a ride on the Settle–Carlisle line. Despite the fact the first two involved a journey to York, not even the Minster was as popular as a ride on the Settle–Carlisle line. Yet, following the fire, nobody had suggested the Minster should not be rebuilt on the grounds of its lack of tourist appeal.

For the Joint County Councils, Peter Robinson presented his paper on the 'Development Potential of the Settle–Carlisle Line'.

He opened by stressing it was part of the neglected Leeds–Carlisle–
Glasgow InterCity route. Leeds–Glasgow journey times compared
very unfavourably with those on similar InterCity routes. Rail journey times were also most unfavourable compared with those by
air or car.

Mr Robinson said there was considerable potential for improved
access by rural communities to the large towns and cities, and for
recreational purposes in reverse. The line was a unique part of our
national heritage and provided a strong complement to the major
elements of the dramatic landscape through which it passed. He
felt there was enormous potential for continued innovation to tap
new markets and called for a development plan to guide the marketing and management of the line.

In his concluding statement for the Joint County Councils, David
Lloyd drew together the main points which had emerged. There
would be severe hardship on the local communities if the line closed
whilst, in spite of the poor quality of the existing service, through
travellers would suffer hardship to a greater or lesser degree as a
consequence of increased journey times. Three-quarters of users
said they would no longer make their current journeys.

Mr Lloyd said all the proposed diversionary routes were less
satisfactory and the Joint County Councils had severe reservations
about use of the Cumbrian Coast Line which was unable to meet
existing commitments. He poured scorn on British Rail's proposals
for improvements at Giggleswick and "very much regretted"
British Rail's refusal to participate in considerations of costs and
revenue, and to respond to quite reasonable questions on a wide
range of matters, although he exonerated Ron Cotton for blame
in this direction. He added that British Rail's stance was likely to
strengthen the resolve of the councils to press for public enquiry.

There was little doubt in my mind that if anything could tip the
scales of Ministerial decision making in favour of retention of the
line, it was the excellent evidence submitted by the Joint County
Councils. They had set a new standard for local authority participation in opposition to railway closure proposals. For my own part,
I couldn't thank them enough. David Lloyd, Peter Robinson, Alan
Thompson and solicitor Richard Claydon, together with John Carr
who looked after the West Yorkshire end of the 'combined operations', had been most helpful to the committee and myself.

In the last major presentation for the Joint Action Committee,
Chris Ryan came up with yet another submission, albeit a good

one, on diversions. Of the four alternatives to the Settle–Carlisle line, single line working on the West Coast Main Line was only applicable for minor work on the adjacent track, the East Coast Main Line was only suitable for end to end journeys, whilst bus substitution was generally unsatisfactory even when the number of passengers involved was small. As for the fourth option, he said that he and his colleagues had listened "with incredulity and astonishment" to Ron Cotton's plans for the Cumbrian Coast Line which offered no permanent solution to the clearance problem, involved extended journey times, and was potentially dangerous.

Ron Cotton replied – more in sorrow than in anger, I felt – that the number of diverted trains had to be related to the number of days in a year they would occur. The Civil Engineer had indicated these were likely to decrease and there could be some years with no planned blockages. The Chief Inspecting Officer had given clearance for use of the Cumbrian Coast Line by Mark 3 coaches so the proposals were not dangerous.

Dr John Whitelegg summed up for the Joint Action Committee. He said the evidence presented at the North Western and North East TUCC Public Hearings had set a new standard which would alter the character of subsequent closure hearings. Unfortunately, his main impression of them was the "pathetic response" from British Rail who had imposed hardship on hundreds of people attending the hearings by failing to supply them with satisfactory answers to questions which arose from deeply felt worries. This attitude was raucousness beyond belief and understanding.

He simply did not believe the figure of £100,000 quoted for the Cumbrian Coast Line diversionary works. As for Giggleswick station, British Rail were testing people's patience and credulity by suggesting it as an alternative to Settle, whilst the idea that passengers on the projected Leeds–Carlisle service should spend 40 minutes waiting in Carnforth Down Goods Loop was beyond belief!

In between all the 'heavyweight' objections, there were a number of worthwhile individual contributions. Inspired, perhaps, by the Mayor of Skipton, Claire Brooks, the previous evening; the strategic importance of the Settle–Carlisle line at times of international crisis was raised by a number of speakers. Indeed, Mr C Morrow of Chorley said the main reason for keeping the line was for use during hostilities. Mr Mills of Harrogate pointed out that closure would reduce rail links to the north by a third. He added that whereas the East and West Coast Main Lines were easy to

pick out from the air, the Settle–Carlisle line blended more into
the natural contours of the country through which it passed.

Mr S Harrison of Bradford spoke as a director of a successful
railway company, the Ravenglass and Eskdale. For business travel
between West Yorkshire, Carlisle and Scotland, a fast direct service
was essential. With a bit of imagination the line could become one
of British Rail's assets. He called for scenic tours, more steam
specials, dining car specials on weekend summer evenings and historical excursions. The scope was endless.

I was pleased to see Graham Nuttall, with his dog Ruswarp
sitting obediently under the objectors table – although the latter
refused my offer of a Spillers shape! Graham said British Rail had
manipulated services to achieve the closure of the Settle–Carlisle
line by stealth. He applauded the decision of the TUCCs to consider
and report on issues other than hardship. As for the projected
service between Leeds and Carlisle via Carnforth, this could be
under threat as the service could run just as easily via the Copy Pit
Line and Preston.

Ron Cotton said that "to the best of his knowledge" there were
no plans to run a Leeds–Carlisle service via Preston – but then he
had no knowledge that the re-routed Nottingham–Glasgow service
was coming off until I told him! Nevertheless, he was inclined to
agree with Graham that it would make greater economic sense to
do so as it would take in Bradford, Halifax, Burnley and Blackburn
as well as Preston. An interesting point, I thought.

However, it was left to veteran Bradford railway cognoscente E
C Swinborne Garrett to capture the public mood as effectively as
anyone. He said British Rail had pulled out all the stops to bring
about the closure of the Settle–Carlisle line. Yet, in spite of all the
efforts to run it down, more passengers were being carried and it
was making a profit. What sense was there to close a line that could
be a money spinner, asked Mr Swinborne Garrett. In a positively
Churchillian conclusion he exclaimed:

"It behoved everyone to strain every nerve, fight tooth and nail,
and explore every channel to preserve the pride and glory of our
country for this and future generations. We must not be complacent. The battle will not be won until we see such headlines in the
press as 'Settle–Carlisle Line Saved!'"

19

THE LEEDS MARATHON

"The Settle–Carlisle railway is something very special – something most countries would give a great deal to possess. Today we value parts of our heritage which were not fully appreciated before. Let it not be said at this century's end that we flung away as surplus to our needs a jewel which was unique and could never be replaced."

Gary Waller MP

By the time the North East TUCC Settle–Carlisle Public Hearing arrived at Kitson College, Leeds, on Saturday 26th April, we had heard close on 180 submissions. During our visits to Settle and Skipton we'd evolved a pattern that was a little like BBC Television's 'Antiques Roadshow'. The secretariat – Gerald Newton and David Mallender – were the advance party and set up our stall in the respective halls. Then the committee members or 'experts' arrived – and when it came to diversions, Red Star Parcels, tourism and bikes they could hold their own against any specialists. My role, I suppose, was that of Hugh Scully!

There was no doubt that Leeds would prove my greatest challenge when it came to beating the clock. At Settle and Skipton we had averaged about 28 submissions a day. In Leeds we would have to increase our productivity to 40 a day if we were to fit everyone in. Notwithstanding the extra hour a day we had allowed, it would be a daunting task to speed things up so submissions averaged out at about 11 minutes against the 14 minutes or so at the earlier sessions. And whilst Leeds was largely reserved for individual objectors, there were still a number of local authorities to be heard.

Wayne Jenkins, chairman of the West Yorkshire Metropolitan County Council's Public Transport Committee until its dissolution on 31st March, opened the batting for the objectors. In characteristic fashion, he lambasted British Rail's incompetence in its handling of the Settle–Carlisle case and warned that, if the line closed, the hardship would flow back into West Yorkshire and threaten the Bradford–Keighley service through "the dreaded Section 20 extortion racket."

For Leeds City Council, Councillor Neil Taggart, chairman of the Passenger Transport Committee, said that as long ago as December 1981 he had successfully moved a motion at a full council meeting opposing British Rail's decision to re-route the Nottingham–Glasgow service as it heralded the closure of the Settle–Carlisle line. People from the Upper Dales visited Leeds, the regional capital, which was a major shopping, educational, medical, legal and cultural centre. For Leeds people, the Upper Dales represented a major recreational facility. Easy access was essential to enhance the quality of life and for many the line was the only way of travelling beyond Settle as only 52 per cent of Leeds households had access to a car.

Stephen Waring, a well known rail user and articulate speaker from Halifax, poked fun at British Rail's 'Heads of Information'. When he read it he could hardly believe his eyes. The good news was that there would still be through trains between Leeds and Carlisle via Carnforth. The bad news was that journey times would be almost an hour slower than in 1973. British Rail's response to the suggestion that the re-routed service would not last long was "a dead give away" as it stated: 'It is not correct to suggest that the proposed diverted services will not last long. These through services will become an integral part of the British Rail timetable and will be judged on their overall results in exactly the same manner as any other service.'

In other words, said Mr Waring, if the re-routed through service failed to carry sufficient passengers to justify its existence, it would suffer the same fate that would befall the Nottingham–Glasgow service via Miles Platting which was to be taken off next year without any public consultation like the present Public Hearing.

Another West Yorkshire objector, Derrick Joanes of Menston, cited poor timetabling as contributing to the run down of the Settle–Carlisle line. Quoting the example of the Sunday service, he said that whilst there were good connections from Bradford and Shipley to Carlisle, the afternoon return service provided no connections for passengers returning home. Yet the return service passed through Shipley without stopping just seven minutes before an Ilkley–Bradford train stopped at Shipley. By the simple expedient of allowing the train from Carlisle to stop at Shipley, the vast potential of the Bradford area could have been served by a perfect connection. This could only be described as "closure by incompetence!"

There was no sign of incompetence on the part of objectors that Saturday morning. We were moving along at such a brisk pace that we were well in front of the clock and had time for a coffee break. Afterwards there was a useful contribution from Peter Mann of Bingley. Peter J Walker for Transport 2000 in Cleveland spoke of the superiority of rail travel and emphasised that the Settle–Carlisle line was the direct route between Leeds and Glasgow. Lee Regardsoe, hot off the 08.45 from King's Cross, pointed out that closure of the line would deprive British Rail of revenue on the East Coast and West Coast Main Lines as he would no longer travel north.

Andrew Connell of Appleby provided a humorous interlude by explaining how he used the line for journeys to Halifax Town home games – and they needed all the support they could get; whilst Graham Lund of Kilmarnock perceptively remarked that it was at best woolly minded or at worst an example of shocking duplicity to appoint Ron Cotton, one of British Rail's best marketing men, to promote a line it wished to close.

With so much 'recovery time' in hand, I had to let British Rail get into the act. Ron Cotton answered or fudged a number of points submitted earlier by the Joint Action Committee. One positive response was that the projected bus between Appleby and Penrith would accommodate wheelchairs.

Then Michael Harrison, the QC acting for British Rail who I had been able to shunt into a siding for most of the hearing, decided the time had come to claim centre stage. Reiterating points he had made during earlier sessions regarding British Rail's role in the Public Hearing, he explained in a meticulous if rather long winded way that he felt the TUCCs consideration of the objections should be read with a view to the TUCCs reporting function in relation to hardship. Yet it had been apparent that what was taking place was a consideration of the merits or de-merits of the closure of the Settle–Carlisle line. It was his submission that this was not the function of TUCCs as there was no power under the Act for the TUCCs to report to the Minister on what he would call 'non hardship' matters.

I replied that there were a number of interpretations of this part of Section 56 of the Transport Act 1962 and we had now heard

British Rail's. However, the fact remained that TUCCs were bound
to consider the objections and the grounds for objection were wide
open. Moreover, there was nothing in the Act to preclude the
TUCCs from drawing the Minister's attention to issues other than
hardship.

I was conscious that my riposte lacked the charm and flow of
Mr Harrison's legal niceties which, although a delight to the ear,
were now in danger of scuppering my timetable. Even so, I welcomed the intervention by John Carr of the West Yorkshire Passenger Transport Authority for I was aware that I could get out of
my depth if I became involved in an extended legal discourse with
Mr Harrison.

John Carr said the Joint County Councils were aware the evidence had gone somewhat wider than the conventional interpretation of hardship. Everything turned on the interpretation of Section
56(9) of the Act. His interpretation was that the TUCCs function
was to hear and consider objections. The statute did not say what
matters should be incorporated within those objections – indeed,
it would be impossible to prejudge what could be considered as
valid grounds for objection. The statute then said the TUCCs must
report on hardship, but no limitation was placed on them to prevent
them from reporting on anything else. Certain TUCCs had tradi-
tionally taken a wider view and this was something the Joint County
Councils supported.

John had said it all. Moreover, he could not have timed it better
as it was lunch-time. During the afternoon any doubts regarding
the breadth of national interest in the Settle–Carlisle line were
dispelled. After Dr Hugh Porteous of the Sheffield Passengers Association and innovator of the phrase 'closure by stealth' had delighted us with his experiences of trying to get to Settle via Giggleswick, there were contributions from people who had especially
travelled from Coventry, Halstead, Weybridge, Norwich, Ipswich,
Chelmsford, Gateshead, Nottingham, London and HMS Chal-
lenger (Scotland), plus those from nearer the line in Leeds, Bradford and Sheffield.

Indeed, the submissions that afternoon were amongst the best
of the whole hearing. If I pick one as representative, it has to be
that of Mr R E West of Norwich. He said closure of the Settle–Carlisle line would severely restrict access to the area by those who
did not own a car. His family used both scheduled and Dales Rail
services, the latter being particularly useful as they served more

stations. Closure would mean people like himself would effectively be prevented from reaching some places. Others would have to use cars which would increase congestion on busy, narrow roads. Bus services were already being cut back and experience in East Anglia had shown that services which replaced the train were likely to be short lived.

Mr West felt that, instead of closing the line, British Rail should increase services on it. Dales Rail had proved the demand was there. People had more leisure time and the fastest growing leisure activity was walking. Moreover, British Rail should not lose sight of the fact that for visitors like himself, they would not only collect his fare on the Settle–Carlisle line but also between Norwich and Leeds.The full potential of the line was not being realised. An improved service would benefit the region, those like him who wished to visit it, and British Rail who could substantially increase their revenue from the line if only they had the will to do so.

Whilst Mr West's submission varied little from many others, it was his presentation that made it so poignant. For he was blind and read his evidence in braille. As Malcolm Pithers recorded in 'The Guardian', Mr West "was making a plea for the line to be saved because he takes his family on walks through some of the most beautiful countryside in the north, which he knows he will never see."

The evening opened with another excellent objection from an MP, Gary Waller, the Conservative member for Keighley and secretary of his party's backbench transport committee. After explaining the adverse effects closure of the line could have on local services as a consequence of the Section 20 funding arrangements, he said he was not one who stood for investment in transport whatever the circumstances. There were projects within West Yorkshire which he would not defend. He continued:

"However, the Settle–Carlisle railway is something very special – something which most countries would give a great deal to possess. Today we value parts of our heritage which were not fully appreciated before. Two or three decades ago buildings were torn down in Bradford and other cities which we now mourn. Let it not be said at this century's end that we flung away as surplus to our needs a jewel which was unique and could never be replaced."

Mr Waller had, in four simple sentences, encapsulated the whole heritage case as effectively as anyone throughout the hearing.

The submissions that followed were also of a high standard.

Roger Smith of Manchester, an old hand at the game, said that as British Rail assured the Government it could maintain the network and improve the quality of its service, and had found funds to repair the Barmouth Viaduct and by-pass the Penmanshiel tunnel, they must have some other reason for wanting to close the Settle–Carlisle line.

He understood from press reports that British Rail would only respond to points regarding hardship at the Public Hearing whereas, under the Act, grounds for objection were not limited. This stance did not square with that of its spokesman who said: 'We are completely open about our case on the Settle–Carlisle line,' which they wished to close because it lost money and would cost a lot to repair. Yet they refused to provide information or answer relevant questions. It was, said Mr Smith, as silly as if a doctor said to a patient: 'Yes, I know you've got angina but all you can discuss is the weather!'

Then it was time for youth – in the form of two of Roger's teenage sons – to take a bow. Daniel Smith said he believed trains were a very important method of transport. He wished British Rail agreed! Instead of trying to close the line, they should be co-operating with thousands of people like him who wanted it retained and improved for everybody's benefit, now and in the future. Samuel Smith explained that he did not enjoy long car or bus journeys as he suffered from travel sickness. Moreover, there was room for his bike in the train. What he wanted was a better service with proper connections from Manchester – not closure.

The theme of youth continued as Miss D Brown of Leeds, a teacher, told how her school used the line for travel to an outdoor pursuits centre near Settle.Afterwards many of the children brought their parents to see the wonders of Pen-y-ghent, Ingleborough, Whernside and Wild Boar Fell from the train.

Among others who spoke was Mr Feather of Shipley who used Dales Rail to visit friends at Hawes. Mr Parry of Selby said services on the line were far worse than when it opened 110 years ago. Mr J D Wood of Chesterfield said the case for keeping the line open was because it was the best and most direct route between Yorkshire and South West Scotland. He suggested that two of the Nottingham–Glasgow trains should revert to the line, leaving 'The European' to run via Manchester. It was left to Mr M Blake of Horsham to claim British Rail was meekly bowing to the demands of the influential road transport lobby, something that was strongly refuted by Ron Cotton.

Rounding off a long but rewarding day, Richard Watts of the Joint Action Committee referred to the extended stops in Carnforth Down Goods Loop if the Settle–Carlisle line closed. He understood National Express were operating a Leeds–Glasgow Rapide service complete with reclining seats, hostess service, light refreshments, video films and a chemical toilet. If the line closed the alternative rail service between Leeds and Glasgow would take 5 hours 7 minutes. The Rapide was doing it in 5 hours flat.

When we re-convened on Monday morning, it was the turn of the City of Sheffield to put its case. Probably the most pro-rail of all British cities, it was still smarting over the loss of the Woodhead line. In a most accomplished presentation, Mrs Marion Marsh, a transportation planning officer, outlined the strategic value of the line as part of the missing InterCity link between Leeds and Carlisle. She emphasised its tourist potential and said that if British Rail had adopted a more positive approach towards the line, its future would not be so bleak. There was need for a development plan involving all the interested local authorities which would guide the development, marketing and management of the line.

The Leeds City Council's case was developed by Councillor Mrs Elizabeth Nash, chairman of the Leisure Services Committee. She was also a member of the Yorkshire Tourist Board which had shown a surprising lack of interest in the Settle–Carlisle line since it became a live issue. Mrs Nash was anxious to promote the line because of its valuable two way traffic in and out of Leeds. It had an important role to play in developing the city as a tourist centre.

For Calderdale, Councillor David Shutt – a Halifax accountant I knew from the Five Curves closure – said his council objected to closure on the grounds of hardship and inconvenience that would be caused to Calderdale residents travelling to Carlisle and Scotland, and seeking access to the Yorkshire Dales. The alternative services proposed for travel between Leeds and Glasgow increased journey times by 16 per cent on the East coast Main Line – which was more expensive – or 22 per cent via Carnforth. This deterioration in journey time was "nothing less than astounding." He supported the call for a long term development plan.

John Rodgers of Leeds said that although his use of the line was solely for leisure purposes, such was the pleasure and enjoyment he derived from it, its closure would cause him considerable hardship. He charged British Rail of deciding to close the line back in 1979 when they failed to waterproof the Ribblehead Via-duct. From Leicester, John Armstrong criticised British Rail's dis-missive attitude towards leisure users and the way they attempted to dismiss Dales Rail as an 'unofficial' service and had claimed the massive increase in usage of the line was due to people having 'one last look' before it closed.

This point was later developed by Dr Robin Sisson, a master at Bradford Grammar School. Whilst it was possible some people may have come to pay their 'final respects', many more new users had been won for the line. This latter category had not come to witness the death of the Settle–Carlisle, but rather to make it "a way of life."

An aspect of hardship we had not encountered before was explained by Laura Wyles, of the Yorkshire Wildlife Trust. Since 1975, the trust had leased a disused limestone quarry from British Rail which was adjacent to the Settle–Carlisle line. It contained many interesting plants, as did the embankments, cuttings and ver-ges alongside the line which also provided good cover for small birds. When railway lines closed and the land was sold, the wildlife interests were usually lost to agriculture, tipping, industrial use and roads. Therefore she wished to see the line remain open under British Rail.

The afternoon session was opened by two Dales Rail stalwarts. Peter Davies was also a knowledgeable rail enthusiast who had undertaken many surveys on the line which he had submitted to MPs and the TUCCs. He felt the line was even more important today than when it was built by the Midland Railway. Les Watson explained how his company, North Country Travel of Otley, had been formed to organise rail excursions for those wishing to walk in northern England. Closure of the Settle–Carlisle line would seri-ously undermine his business.

Due to ill health, Mr W M Williams, a former theatrical designer and scenic artist, found the train was the only satisfactory way he could travel. He painted along the line and its closure would lead to the loss of virtually the whole of his recreational facility and a constant inspiration to his work. FOSCLA's Peter Shaw, in a per-sonal submission, said his principal hobbies were cycling, hiking, camping, photography and railways; all of which could be amalga-mated into one by use of the Settle–Carlisle line.

Peter Shaw also provided some useful background regarding the line's viaducts. When in use, they had to be maintained to standards

set by the Railway Inspectorate. Following closure, a viaduct clas-
sed as a listed building would still have to be maintained by the
owner – British Rail. However, those viaducts which ranked as
ancient monuments – Ribblehead, Dent Head, Arten Gill and
Smardale – were the ultimate responsibility of the Department of
the Environment and it would be they, rather than British Rail,
who would have to foot the bill for any repairs. Thus the savings
that could accrue to British Rail could be considerable if the line
closed.

Probably the most novel submission of the whole Public Hearing
was made by David Smith of Sheffield in association with the National Council on Inland Transport. It certainly had the greatest
visual impact for he presented the committee with two large albums
packed with photographs covering every aspect of the Settle–Carlisle line. In particular, they captured in superb colour many of the
views that could only be enjoyed from trains travelling over the
line. To back his pictorial case he submitted a 34 page booklet
which concluded:

'It is hoped that this objection has demonstrated many of the
visual reasons for retaining and developing the potential of the
Settle–Carlisle line.The ground-swell of public opinion has been
enormous, far exceeding any previous railway closure proposal. In
that respect alone the closure proposal should be withdrawn by
British Rail and certainly by the Government. Despite the need
to remedy the neglect of many years, the amount of money needed
to bring the route back to first class order is very small compared
with the cost of a small length of urban motorway or even the
interest payments on the Humber Bridge.'

Robin Hood – yes, really! – told us that his family ran a small
caravan and camping site near York. Many visitors came simply
so they could travel on the Settle–Carlisle line, something that had
been made easier by starting trains at York during the summer.
Also from York, Walter Lee had difficulty in getting his 'bike to
Scotland via the East Coast Main Line'. Therefore he left York at
09.00, arrived in Carlisle in time for lunch, and then caught 'The
Clansman' which got him to Inverness for dinner. Paula Sneyd of
Huddersfield put in a plea on behalf of young people without jobs.
They were dependent on public transport to get into the country.

David Symes had come all the way from Chelmsford to object
to the closure on the grounds of British Rail's Machiavellian man-
oeuvring behind the scenes and because he was not a car owner. He

accepted his appearance might not make any difference to the outcome, but even if all hopes faded he would be able to say he did his best to ensure justice was done. Mr Symes called for a full Public Enquiry into "this whole sordid business" so all the relevant issues could be brought into the full light of day. Another long distance traveller, Christopher Allen of St. Albans, spoke of improvements on Scot Rail as a good example of investment in tourist areas which should be followed on the Settle–Carlisle line; whilst Mr G Duddle of Leicester, a regular user of the line, proved a veritable walking timetable and highlighted many connectional shortcomings.

Perhaps the nicest touch of all came from John Gilham of York. Neither he, nor his wife Carol, drove; so his family were dependent on public transport. Therefore they were not among those who only used the railway when it was convenient to them and their cars the rest of the time. Mr Gilham confided that he had proposed to his wife on the summit of Ingleborough and their first visit to the Dales National Park had persuaded them to settle in York because of its accessibility to the magnificent walking country and a landscape they found beautiful and stirring.

Nigel Roberts, a senior planning clerk with the West Yorkshire PTE, opened the Monday evening session. He had been involved in the promotion of Dales Rail and added his name to those who called for a development plan for the Settle–Carlisle line. Mr C Lunnon of Worksop spoke of the close parallel between the Settle–Carlisle and the Bern–Lötschberg–Simplon route in Switzerland. Both were scenic mountain routes with a busier line nearby, but there the comparison ended. The Swiss promoted their route with splendid posters and, instead of considering closure, had recently upgraded it from single to double track. He suggested that intelligent use of the Settle–Carlisle line could enable 'The European' to arrive in Carlisle over 90 minutes earlier in time to provide a service to Northern Ireland via Stranraer and the West Highland Line via Dumbarton.

Humberside rail user Mr T R Haywood of North Cave made a wry observation on progress when he recalled that the 1934 journey time between Leeds and Carlisle was 2 hours 4 minutes against the current time of 2 hours 31 minutes. He was supported by Mr G M Carter of Loughborough who concluded the crux of the matter was that the Settle–Carlisle line existed and people had shown they wanted to use it. It behoved Government and British Rail to ensure it was not relegated to a dotted line on an Ordinance Survey map marked 'Course of Old Railway'.

It was left to Dr Peter R Beeley from Leeds University to provide the keynote address that evening. Whilst he concurred and sympathised with those who based their objections on loss of service, he looked at the Settle–Carlisle line in a much broader sense for future generations of users. He based his thesis on the idea it was not just another railway line but a true national asset. It should be accepted as such by Government, local authorities and, above all, British Rail.

Although the line was a monument to the greatest industrial age, he did not see it in terms of railway enthusiasm, worthy though that was, but rather in terms of Britain as an industrial nation. The Settle–Carlisle was not just a line – it also offered scenic travel and an inspiring experience through journeys on it. He didn't want to see the line associated with steam which was a thing of the past. Rather he wished to see it electrified with fast trains plying up and down it with, perhaps, an occasional steam train as a reminder of the past. The Settle–Carlisle line was history but it was living history and the identity of the present time was strongly associated with it.

Dr Beeley's case was echoed by several subsequent speakers including Barry Slaymaker from Harrogate – "abandonment of the line would be akin to national vandalism such was the heritage it conveyed to the country as a whole" – and Dr D L Barnard of Leeds – "Ribblehead Viaduct was unique. Who would sanction allowing the Mona Lisa to go mouldy because it cost too much to keep it restored? British Rail should be the proud guardian of such a masterpiece as Ribblehead. It was the 'Jewel in their Crown'."

Then, all of a sudden, the mood of the session changed. One of my members, John Blezard asked for leave to speak which , of course, I granted. He had obviously been greatly influenced by his visit to Giggleswick the other week for he launched into an indictment of the stations inadequacies. This not only upset Ron Cotton, which didn't matter, it also had Michael Harrison on his feet. This upset me, but only because I'd had a private bet with myself that I could get through the day without a murmur from him – and would have done so but for John's outburst. Mr Harrison felt it was poor form that a member of the committee should express his views in such a forceful manner. So I had to remind Mr Harrison that it was a free country and if John wished to have his say, so be it. Ever since John has been known as The Earl of Giggleswick!

There were a couple of solid submissions from the West and North Yorkshire branches of Transport 2000. Then Steve Wiltshire, a British Rail employee who is unlikely to have enhanced his career prospects by being a regular objector to closure proposals, said the objections received by the TUCCs only represented the tip of the iceberg.

In the absence of any financial information from British Rail, it was left to Mr A J Flockton to point out that if it cost £6 m to repair Ribblehead, this worked out at £150,000 a year or £410 a day over 40 years.By some creative accounting he got the figure down to £154 a day and calculated that, as it cost £3.75 to travel from Settle to Appleby, it only needed 43 people to cross the viaduct each day to cover the cost of its repair. Time, I felt, to call it a day!

There was a feeling of spring in the air the following morning, certainly so far as the committee were concerned. It was not just the last day in Leeds but the final day of the Public Hearing, something that had hung over us for almost 5 years. Truth to tell, we'd had enough. I think that went for most of the objectors, too. Certainly there was no doubt Ron Cotton would be glad when it was all over.

The session opened with a couple of heavyweight submissions. Professor Paul Fairest, chairman of the Friends of Dales Rail, encapsulated the many individual points made earlier by other speakers. Wilf Proudfoot of the National Union of Railwaymen had based his text on that used by Jimmy Knapp at Appleby. He didn't pull any punches when he referred to the "extraordinary story of leaked documents, contradictory letters of reassurance to MPs and a secret closure plan partly implemented before its existence became known." British Rail had been "less than honest" in their approach to the closure of the Settle–Carlisle line, concluded Mr Proudfoot. He could say that again!, I thought.

There was a doughty objection on behalf of the Youth Hostels Association and the Council for the Protection of Rural England by veteran walker Margaret Petyt who had used the line for over 65 years. I particularly liked her reference to "the gem that is Appleby." Claire Nash put a good case for Leeds Friends of the Earth whilst Mr S H Sneyd, whose daughter had spoken the previous day, drew attention to the many medieval castles – like Pendragon Castle at Mallerstang Common – which could be seen from the line. This was a new angle in support of the Settle–Carlisle.

Nor should one neglect the influence of Lady Anne Clifford, too.

Mr D Wilson, a marketing executive, declared: "Thank God for Dales Rail." It proved there was a market – a walking market, a rambling market, and there could well be a diner market with restaurant car specials. A man after my own heart! He regretted that everything about British Rail was so negative and devious and drew attention to the way Hellifield station had been allowed to go to "rack and ruin". He felt it was an obvious headquarters if the Settle–Carlisle line were to be promoted as a marketing entity. It had parking facilities and did and could have an engine shed and a "wonderful dining room".

In a particularly good submission, Mrs Audrey Marlow said that although she lived in Leeds, she was a native of Cumbria and used the line to visit relatives. In addition to the personal hardship she would suffer, she stressed the importance of restoring the Nottingham–Glasgow service to the line and extending it to London for the benefit of overseas tourists. She drew particular attention to three aspects of the line's scenic attractions: the beauty of the winter scene in the High Pennines, that some of the finest views could only be seen from the train, and the contrast between the grandeur of the fells and the calm and peace of the Eden valley.

Examples of hardship that hit the pocket and resulted in additional journey time came from Mr G Brown referring to his journeys from Huddersfield to Appleby. At present the journey via Leeds took 2 hours 18 minutes and cost £9.20 return. Under the proposed alternatives, the journey via Manchester would take 3 hours 57 minutes at a cost of £15.30 return, and via Leeds and Carnforth 4 hours 19 minutes for about £15.00 return. So far as Huddersfield was concerned, the facts spoke for themselves.

Rounding off the penultimate session, Councillor Eddie Scott, a member of the West Yorkshire Passenger Transport Authority, endorsed the objections lodged by the Joint County Councils and various district councils. He deplored the run down of the line, the crunch having come with the re-routing of the Nottingham–Glasgow service, and went through the familiar arguments of how closure of the Settle–Carlisle line would have an adverse spin-off effect on local Section 20 supported services.

Opening the final session, Russell Ogden for Barnsley Metropolitan Borough Council, and another old hand at Public Hearings having been involved in the battles of Goose Hill–Wath Road and The Five Curves, emphasised how closure of the Settle–Carlisle

line would create direct hardship for Barnsley folk wishing to visit
the Yorkshire Dales and Cumbria for leisure purposes. The recreational opportunities offered by the line should be viewed in relation to tourist and leisure promotion elsewhere in South and West
Yorkshire.

Then came a delightful submission from Mr A J F Wrottesley
of London. A former member of British Rail's legal department
and author of a number of books, including the definitive study of
the Midland and Great Northern Joint Railway, he said he was
speaking as a private objector. He explained that his daughter's
'in-laws' lived near Hawes and that she had been to the Malham
Field Centre near Settle. All the family agreed with him that the
area was full of charm and interest.

In the absence of the railway, Mr Wrottesley said it would be
much harder for long distance visitors to reach the district. Noting
that it was proposed to improve Giggleswick station, he assumed
some expenditure would be involved. And whilst the bus service
between Penrith and Appleby might be valuable to a passenger
from London like himself, the existing trains on the Settle–Carlisle
line came through to Leeds from Hull and York. What a roundab-
out journey was now apparently suggested from York to Appleby
via Leeds, Carnforth and Penrith.

Long experience over the years with railway, coach and bus
travel had indicated that on a number of occasions the 'substitute'
road facilities were found after a time not to pay and were reduced
or withdrawn altogether, leaving the particular area with no public
transport at all. As for the Cumbrian Coast Line, he dismissed it
as an alternative route, not least for its length and an awkward
tunnel. Making the tunnel suitable would be a formidable undertaking.

An amusing diversion was provided by Mr J F Sayer of Wetherby
who had been a user of the Settle–Carlisle line for 60 years and
deplored any suggestion that British Rail should close it. "Heaven
knows, they've made every effort to do so. They've put every 'crap'
engine on the line," he exclaimed. Since January he had been on
three trains which had failed.

It was good to see and hear the ladies shining at our final session.
Miss C Zilahi of Downham Market said that when she was first
invited to spend a holiday in Appleby she had been amazed and
entranced by the views of the Pennine landscape from the train.
Although she used the train to gain access to the area for walking

and cycling, the rail journey was no mere preliminary to the holiday – it was part of it. If British Rail closed the line she would stay at home and explore East Anglia on her bicycle so British Rail would lose her fare to Leeds as well.

Miss Diana Sandy of Hull travelled regularly to visit her parents at Kirkby Stephen. She could leave Hull at 07.40 and be in Appleby at 10.45. If the line closed her journey would be quite horrendous. Challenging British Rail management to stand up and fight for the Settle–Carlisle line, she said she would back them "every inch of the line" if they demonstrated they were fighting to improve services. She added it was time there were some women on the British Railways Board. They would know how to run an efficient service for the customers rather than an inefficient service for the Government.

Miss H Brown frequently travelled from York to visit her brother and his family in Motherwell.She strongly objected to the idea of being routed via Carnforth on the congested West Coast Main Line. She was also an enthusiastic user of Dales Rail and took her bike to "get to the parts the regular walks don't reach."

A former military railway operator, Dr George Huxley, said none of the three closure notices fully complied with the Act. Therefore the proposal was incurably flawed and should be withdrawn. He endorsed the House of Commons Select Committee on Trade and Industry report on 'Tourism in the United Kingdom' which recommended that regional Tourist Boards be instructed to investigate whether British Rail could make more use of existing railways as tourist attractions.

Dr Huxley said the fact no direct grant had been made to secure the infrastructure on the Blackburn–Hellifield and Settle–Carlisle lines was evidence of a serious lack of foresight and intellectual capacity in the higher levels of the Treasury and the Department of Transport. Settle–Carlisle was a test case, not simply for rail users or lovers of steam locomotives, but because it raised fundamental questions about the goodwill, competence and wisdom of central government.

For the Yorkshire Branch of the Railway Development Society, secretary Denis Bradbury dismissed the alternative service via Carnforth as it involved increased journey times, higher fares to Appleby, and travel on the West Coast Main Line with its poor record of punctuality. As for Giggleswick as an alternative to Settle, with its low platform, insufficient shelter from the elements and the long, lonely and – at night – unlit road, it was all like a horror story worthy of an 'X' certificate Hammer film.

He commended the classic work by Houghton and Foster 'The Story of the Settle–Carlisle Line' in which there was a vivid account of the part played by the railway during the winter of 1947. It should be compulsory reading for those concerned at the British Railways Board and the Department of Transport "as they loll in their overheated London offices." If the Settle–Carlisle closed, it would be yet another tombstone in British Rail's graveyard, a mausoleum to be erected beside that of the Woodhead line. But British Rail would need a new slogan instead of 'we're getting there', as they had nearly got there so far as rail closures were concerned. He suggested a far more appropriate slogan would be a line from Shelley's poem 'Ozimandias' which read: 'Look upon my works ye Mighty and despair.'

After that there was little more to be said. There was a competent discourse on behalf of the Cyclists Touring Club from Ronald Healey, and an impassioned plea by Gerald Garside for the line's retention as it provided the severest continuous test for steam locomotives. Further criticism of the lack of promotion by Mr R Fickling and a final reminder of British Rail's 'closure by stealth' and its failure to respond to many of the points made by objectors from Mr D C Leal of Leeds completed the submissions from the floor.

Then it was time for a final word from Ron Cotton. So far as engine failures were concerned, Eastern Region had assured him there was no question of "clapped out" engines being used on the Settle–Carlisle line. The failure rate was broadly in line with that on other routes. He reiterated that diversions by the Cumbrian Coast Line had been agreed with the Railway Inspectorate, that the bus service between Appleby and Penrith would accommodate wheelchairs, and that it was likely there would be a new local service to the Dales Rail stations sponsored by the local authorities. His thanks to the committee and myself for the way we conducted the hearing was endorsed by Michael Harrison who added that my sense of humour had helped smooth the way.

After a final word from Richard Watts of the Joint Action Committee who joined the chorus of thanks – I always made a point of letting an objector rather than British Rail have the last word from the floor – it was time for me to wrap the proceedings up.

I said that we were at the end of a journey which had started

almost 5 years ago when we learnt of the decision to re-route the
Nottingham–Glasgow service. During the 9 days of the Public
Hearing we had heard some 480 submissions (here I had obviously
got my sums wrong for the actual figure was about 290 – that no
one corrected me then or since can only be because it seemed that
we had listened to at least 500 submissions!). This ranked as a
record in the history of railway closure proposals (and still did at
290), as befitted that which had generated more objections than
any other proposal.

After thanking the committee – "who now go to sleep counting
Red Star Parcels instead of sheep" – for their stamina and persever-
ance, and the secretariat for the splendid back-up, I recalled that
British Rail's case for closure had been that the Settle–Carlisle line
was expensive to operate and maintain, and that heavy expenditure
was required on 5 viaducts and bridges. It was unfortunate they
were unwilling to substantiate their case with the relevant figures.

Indeed, I continued, the only figure of any substance to slip
through their net was the £100,000 for the cost of ungrading the
Cumbrian Coast Line. I was wary of this figure as it appeared too
pat. Had it been £112,000 or even £88,000 I'd have been more
convinced. Nevertheless, I commended Ron Cotton – "marketing
man that he is" – for resisting the temptation of pitching it at
£99,000!

Turning to Ron Cotton, I congratulated him on having what I
termed as "a good Public Hearing". Unlike the Lone Ranger –
and he'd been very much on his own – he'd had to operate within
a somewhat restricted ranch. Nevertheless, his role had been unusual to say the least – that of endeavouring to close the line he
had been promoting with some skill. I continued: "Someday,
perhaps, the real Ron Cotton will stand up. Indeed, there were
times when I felt he almost did; restrained only by his sense of
duty and, perhaps, the influence of Mr Harrison, the eminent silk
retained to mind British Rail's legal interests".

I thanked Mr Harrison "whose eloquence we enjoyed, even if
we did not always agree with what he was saying".Finally, turning
to the objectors, I said:

"I cannot recall a Public Hearing where the committee has had
the benefit of so much comprehensive and constructive evidence.
That of the Joint County Councils has done much to compensate
for the absence of information from British Rail. We have been
impressed, too, by the detailed contributions from the Joint Action

Committee and their distinguished experts. But, above all, we have admired the quality of the contributions from the individual objectors who have come from all over the country to publicly endorse their support for the line.

For myself, I can only add that it has been a privilege to chair the proceedings which have always been full of interest and which at times were both moving and touching. And whilst I have no idea what the eventual outcome of it all will be, of one thing I am certain. It is that all those who took part in this Public Hearing – at Settle, Skipton and here in Leeds – can hold their heads high and say 'We did our best to save the line'."

With that it was all over at 16.58 – two minutes ahead of schedule.

20

THE REPORT

"On the basis of the undoubted hardship that closure of the line would cause, together with the strength of the commercial case presented for its retention, the committees strongly and emphatically recommend that consent to British Rail's proposal to close the Settle–Carlisle line be refused."

> North East and North Western TUCCs Joint Report, 12th December 1986

There was no doubt it was an enormous relief to have got the Public Hearing out of the way. That we had managed to do so without any filibusters, lawsuits, injunctions or riots owed much to the inherent good sense of everyone involved and, perhaps, a little to my 'stage management' from day one back in May 1981. Indeed, the only two occasions when I had been obliged to raise my voice related to unauthorised interventions by a lone anti-roads campaigner whose views – including the allegation that I was in the pocket of the Department of Transport! – were sufficiently eccentric and off course to be disregarded.

I recall a *faux pas* I made way back in 1981 when interviewed by BBC Radio Sheffield at the end of the first three day Huddersfield–Sheffield hearing. When asked if I was relieved it was all over, I had replied that it had been hard work "sitting down" listening to all the complex evidence. That was, of course, quite true. It had been hard work, although I made it a rule to avoid all reference to the sedentary position when asked similar questions on subsequent occasions.

Whilst the Public Hearing had been quite an ordeal, it had also been a most rewarding experience; not least because I had got to know a great many agreeable people – albeit only fleetingly. That things had run so smoothly was even more surprising when one considered that the overall mood of the hearing had been of frustration, anger and resentment towards British Rail. This was directed to them in their corporate capacity rather than to their representatives at the hearing. Even so, I shudder to think what sort of reception Jim O'Brien would have got should he have put in an appearance. Suffice to say that we had all got through relatively unscathed.

There had been other compensations, too. From my vantage point centre stage, I had enjoyed an all embracing view of the proceedings. I could see people coming and going and watch various little dramas taking place at the back of the halls as there were no footlights to obstruct my view. Then, amid all the passion and frustrations, there were many lighter moments – quite apart from some of my exchanges with Ron Cotton. I recall an elderly chap who fell fast asleep one morning at Skipton. It wasn't until I'd called someone to speak three times that I realised who he was, for he suddenly awoke and went on to present one of the most sprightly submissions of the hearing. Then, not even British Rail could keep Cupid at bay. Notwithstanding the discourse on diversions and Red Star Parcels, I could see romance was blooming. Nor was it just a case of 'holding hands in the back seats of the TUCC Public Hearing'! I know of at least one 'brief encounter' that became a permanent attachment.

However, any complacency at having run the gauntlet of the Public Hearing proved short lived. There was a report to be written and I was aware that much of the work would fall on my shoulders. First the committee – or those members who had participated in all the sessions at Settle, Skipton and Leeds – had to meet and reach their conclusions. Indeed, it wasn't until 11th June, some six weeks after the end of the hearing, that we were able to get together. At least, this meant that there had been plenty of time for sober reflection.

I opened the meeting by explaining that we had to see if we could agree, in broad terms, the conclusions to our report. That is to say we were, in effect, starting at the end and working backwards! We already had a draft 'on ice' covering the first part of the report, incorporating the history of the line and the background to the proposal including the controversy surrounding the re-routing of the Nottingham–Glasgow service. I had prepared this some eighteen months earlier as an 'insurance' in case the old Yorkshire TUCC had been forcibly removed from consideration of the proposal. The middle section of the report was simply a case of recording everything we had heard at the Public Hearings. However, it was the conclusion that was of prime importance and to which we had to direct our attentions.

Therefore, we had to agree an assessment of the hardship which would be caused if the line closed and put forward our suggestions for alleviating that hardship. This was obligatory in accordance with the Act. We could also make any comments we considered appropriate. This was where we could really go to town and put forward any positive suggestions of how we felt the Settle–Carlisle could be more effectively run – assuming, of course, we felt it should be retained. Therefore, my first task was to seek the views of each member.

It very quickly became apparent that the committee were of the unanimous opinion that the line should be retained and a report should be drafted to that effect. This was good news as it avoided any possibility of a minority report or a watering down of the majority conclusions to meet the requirements of the minority. Quite how our views would fit in with those of our North Western colleagues was, of course, another matter. We would cross that bridge when we came to it.

So far as hardship was concerned, this didn't present too many problems. We had already evolved a complex 'sliding scale' which we had used for the second Huddersfield–Sheffield closure proposal. Based on additional journey times and other factors, it ranged from the 'Extremely Severe Hardship' which would be caused to disabled passengers unable to use alternative bus services, to 'A Degree of Hardship' for those travelling on an occasional basis for recreational purposes. However, given the Settle–Carlisle line's unique status as 'England's Greatest Historical Scenic Route' – I derived considerable pleasure in quoting from British Rail's publicity to get the message across! – surely some special category of hardship was called for. In the end I came up with 'Unquantifiable hardship' for all those for whom the loss of the 'most spectacular main line in England' would, in aesthetic terms, represent hardship every bit as great as that affecting those whose primary use of the line was to get from one place to another.

It was agreed that I should endeavour to come up with a summary of our views which, when agreed, would provide the basis of our detailed comments and conclusions. It involved me in a great deal of reading and research, not least picking up any items of relevant information British Rail had let slip at the Public Hearings or in correspondence, to back the case for retention of the line. I was particularly fortunate in the help I received from three members of the committee.

Bill Butler of Whitley Bay had, until his retirement, been director of the North East Tourist Board. Throughout the Public Hearing he quizzed objectors and Ron Cotton on any number of tourist related issues. Nor was that all for, in between sessions, he would make sorties into the local tourist offices to check if publicity material for the line was on display. And if it wasn't he wanted to know why! Indeed, when it came to tourism, if Bill didn't know about it, it wasn't worth knowing. Therefore we gave him a free hand to compile the section on tourism in the knowledge he would turn in a professional job.

Retired polytechnic principal Chris Bridger was also a barrister. I had appreciated his moral support at the Public Hearing during my exchanges with Michael Harrison QC. Chris was to prove his worth again in beefing-up and embellishing my somewhat pedestrian prose. For example, where I had written: "On the basis of the financial evidence submitted at the Public Hearing by objectors, especially by the Joint County Councils, the committees were convinced...", Chris amended it to read: "On the basis of the financial evidence submitted at the Public Hearing by objectors, most notably that provided authoritatively by the Joint County Councils, which was not challenged by British Rail, the committees were convinced..." It read so much better.

Finally there was Fred Fieldhouse, the longest serving member on the committee. A former transport manager with a large industrial group, Fred was a member of the Chartered Institute of Transport and an excellent proof reader to boot. He also felt very strongly about British Rail's handling of the Settle–Carlisle issue; so much so that he had submitted a personal memo on the subject to David Mitchell, the public transport minister.

Our efforts culminated in the summary which forms Appendix 2 to this book. It provided the framework for our detailed comments and conclusions. These were split into sections under the following headings:

Settle
Appleby
Through Services
Diverted Services

At the end of the summer our summary and the detailed comments and conclusions were sent to John Moorhouse, the North Western TUCC's secretary. We hoped he would be able to incorporate much of our work in his draft which would pave the way towards the joint report we were committed to deliver to public transport minister David Mitchell before Christmas. This, in fact, was what eventually happened; although there was one major problem and a number of minor issues that took some resolving.

The minor points largely concerned emphasis or the choice of words. I remember one phrase regarding diversions on the Cumbrian Coast Line which seemed to upset our North Western colleagues. We had concluded that item by stating that: "It struck the committees that British Rail's whole approach to the diversionary potential of the line was somewhat akin to that of 'It'll be alright on the night!'" The North Western committee didn't like that and wanted it deleted. In the end we compromised with "...British Rail's approach to the diversionary potential of this line lacked credibility and was somewhat haphazard."

More serious was the disagreement that developed over that part of 'The Strategic Role of the Settle–Carlisle Line' which referred to the well documented controversy surrounding British Rail's antics prior to the formal announcement in August 1983 that it proposed to close the line. We were particularly concerned that the 'lack of candour' on the part of British Rail before the announcement should not go unrecorded. For their part, the North Western TUCC wanted no reference to it at all. After enjoying their consumer orientated glory at the Public Hearing, they appeared to have retreated into their non-controversial shell. It seemed that, when the chips were down, they lacked the courage to say "boo!" to British Rail!

As a consequence, the North Western TUCC insisted that the 18 relevant paragraphs were prefixed with a statement to the effect that they did not wish to be associated with the contents, or words to that effect. I wasn't over happy about this but if the North Western committee wished to score a blatant 'own goal' – for that was how many would see it – then it was up to them. Once again it was a legal mind that came to the aid of common sense. Bill Meikle, a Newcastle solicitor and something of a rail buff as well (he coined the phrase 'The Pathetic Pacer' for the new generation DMUs!), was unhappy about the North Western TUCC's phraseology, especially as the section to which it referred was historical rather than subjective. Therefore he suggested the following prefix:

'Please note that paragraphs 221–238 relate to matters with which the former Yorkshire Area TUCC were concerned and therefore these paragraphs do not form part of the North Western TUCC's submission.'

Bill's amendment was agreed by both committees and the final hurdle to agreement of a joint report was cleared. There had been some give and take on both sides, although I don't think we gave anything of substance away. Perhaps the most surprising thing of all had been a potential row over Bill Butler's excellent tourist appraisal. The North Western draft limited tourism to a single paragraph and relegated Bill's report to an appendix. I said that simply wasn't on and that was the last we heard of it.

By the beginning of December, the report was almost ready. After the joint introduction which provided the background history and details of the proposal, the report separated into two sections: that relating to the North Western TUCC's consideration of the objections and Public Hearing which totalled 85 pages, and our own which ran to about 350 pages. The report then came together again for the joint conclusions and comments of both committees.

It had been no easy task summarising everything that had been said at the Public Hearing and I wish there had been more time to do it justice. I was particularly anxious that our effort should capture the flavour of the individual contributions. Needless to say it involved much burning of midnight oil to meet the December deadline, as I had promised David Mitchell that he would have the report by Christmas. However, the person who deserved the lion's share of the credit was Rene Phillippo who typed it all.

It was then left to Gerald Newton and David Mallender to collate it all, add the 86 appendices and bundle them all together. I'm told the whole package weighed 22 kilos. It was despatched from York by Red Star Parcels. I can't say I was sorry to see the back of it.

Even so I was relatively satisfied with the outcome of it all; not least because it struck me as a most constructive document. We didn't just say that the Settle–Carlisle line should be retained and leave it at that, but tried to take the matter a stage further. Bill Butler's appraisal of the relationship between the line and the expanding leisure and tourism market was the result of much painstaking research and represented a positive approach.

This was developed further in the section on the line's future where we stressed that its success was dependent on it embracing both InterCity and Provincial passenger services together with traffic from the parcels and freight sectors rather than becoming bogged down in the 'robbing Peter to pay Paul' philosophy of British Rail's sector management structure. For example, it struck us as ludicrous that some freight trains were subjected to longer journeys and higher operating costs simply to avoid using the line. We emphasised, too, that – as Ron Cotton had proved – the line was a marketable product with long term growth potential so long as the will to go out and sell it was there and suggested the creation of a new post of Director (Settle–Carlisle Line) with wide powers to market, promote and operate the line.

One of the more ridiculous aspects of the railway closure procedure as it has developed over the years is that whilst TUCCs are allowed to publish a summary of their conclusions after the report has landed on the desk of the Secretary of State for Transport, the full report is not issued until after the Minister decides to consent or withhold his consent to British Rail's proposals. This may be anything up to two years after he has received the report.

Therefore, we were now in a position to publish our comments and conclusions on the Settle–Carlisle proposal, many of which were highly subjective, yet we could not publish that part of the report which simply recorded who had said what at the Public Hearing – which was common knowledge anyway for those who had been present. No doubt there is a good reason for this but for the life of me I cannot fathom what it is.

We had agreed with the North Western TUCC to hold concurrent but separate news conferences in our respective patches to announce the results of our deliberations. Both were timed to start at 10.30 on Wednesday 17th December, theirs in Appleby and ours in Settle at the Falcon Manor Hotel. In addition to journalists, we had invited representatives of the Joint County Councils, the Joint Action Committee and, just to show there was no personal ill-feeling, Ron Cotton of British Rail.

Indeed, the gathering seemed more like a re-union than a news conference! So much so that I wasn't really prepared for the googly pitched by Alan Whitehouse of the 'Yorkshire Post'. Referring to the 18 paragraphs of the report which the North Western TUCC had sought to exclude, he asked if I thought British Rail had lied to MPs and others during the run-up to the closure proposal in 1981 and 1982. Whilst I felt they had, I didn't feel it was the occasion to go beyond what was in the report which referred to British Rail's 'lack of candour' at the time. So, taking my cue from Cabinet secretary Sir Robert Armstrong, I simply replied that I felt British Rail had been "economical with the truth". That seemed to satisfy everyone.

However, the joker in the pack proved to be Ron Cotton. He blandly disclosed that British Rail had just submitted its own case for closure of the Settle–Carlisle line to the Secretary of State for Transport. It was largely financial and based on the latest engineering and operating appraisal, but its contents were to remain secret. To this my retort, as recorded by Michael Parkin of 'The Guardian', was:

"This closure proposal created unprecedented opposition from the public. If the Secretary of State agrees to closure without publication of British Rail's report, then all hell will be let loose!"

In any case, I added, someone would probably leak it soon anyway!

We didn't have long to wait, for a couple of days later on 19th December, Alan Whitehouse had a piece in the 'Yorkshire Post' which claimed that British Rail's 'secret report' contained an astonishing U-turn:

"Instead of following the usual BR line, and presenting the route as a worthless drain on finances, it says there is now only one stumbling block to keeping it open.

Until the report was submitted to the Transport Secretary, Mr John Moore, two days ago, British Rail had always maintained that the Settle–Carlisle line was a redundant asset. It was not needed for the future network.

And rail chiefs have always strenuously denied that the scenic route – said to be England's finest train ride – was proposed for closure because of the crumbling Ribblehead Viaduct.

Now, they are effectively telling Mr Moore that all this has changed, and the only hurdle in the way of keeping the line open is a £15 million bill to repair the viaduct and set right years of neglect to track and signals."

What a turn up for the book! I suppose I should have been astonished but somehow I wasn't. By now I had ceased to be surprised at anything which involved British Rail. It simply went to underline that one couldn't believe a word they said from one day to the next.

Of far more importance was the actual business on the line. What sort of year was 1986? So far as I had been concerned, it had been a year in which I had spent far more time listening, talking and writing about the line than actually travelling on it. Nevertheless, it had not prevented me from joining the inaugural journey of the new 'Dalesman' Skipton–Carlisle service sponsored by the local authorities. This was very much a gala occasion and there was quite a crowd of us on the 06.30 from Skipton, including Councillor Claire Brooks, her sister Councillor Beth Graham, Sheffield Euro-MP Bob Cryer and Jonathan Roberts of Transport 2000 who had strongly advocated the need for such a service at the Public Hearing three months earlier.

On the return journey from Carlisle the official party was augmented by a Cumbrian contingent headed by Councillor William Cameron and including Peter Robinson and Alan Thompson, whilst Mrs Olive Clarke and John Moorhouse were there for the North Western TUCC. We all alighted at Settle and proceeded to the Victoria Hall where Cumbria had organised a very good spread. The overall mood was one of cautious optimism and modest self congratulation. We all hoped the new service would take off although Dr John Whitelegg acknowledged that there was a risk that it might take some time to become firmly established.

In the event it proved an instantaneous success with holidaymakers and within a month there were reports of overcrowding. Whilst there were few takers for the 06.00 from Skipton – when my wife and I joined it on Thursday 27th August en-route to Langwathby, we had the train to ourselves until Kirkby Stephen where two joined whilst a further 10 got on at Appleby – the 09.00 from Carlisle was well supported whilst the 12.20 from Skipton was the most popular train of all with loadings approaching 200 on many days.

However, later in the year I had occasion to travel on the 17.42

from Carlisle to Skipton. It was the last Monday in September so the peak of the holiday season was over. Therefore it would be interesting to see the level of local support. Frankly I was rather disappointed. Although there were a number of students returning home to stations in the Eden Valley – and bearing in mind that Appleby, Settle and Skipton had the option of the 'fast' 16.46 – the loadings struck me as poor:

	Join	Alight
Carlisle	23	–
Armathwaite	0	3
Lazonby	0	4
Langwathby	0	0
Appleby	2	3
Kirkby Stephen	0	1
Garsdale	0	1
Dent	0	5
Ribblehead	0	0
Horton	0	2
Settle	0	1
Long Preston	0	0
Hellifield	0	0
Gargrave	0	0
Skipton	–	5
Total	**25**	**25**

I was glad that the public transport minister had not chosen this train for one of his fact finding journeys!

Overall, though, 1986 had been another good year for the Settle–Carlisle line. Boosted by the new local 'Dalesman' service, passenger figures were up for the third consecutive year. Then the year had ended on an optimistic note with the publication of the report of the North Western and North East TUCCs which had been generally well received.

Of all the comments on the report, two particularly pleased me. The first was an observation in the 'Craven Herald' that "the report is a reasonably lively one." Coming from such an august and sage publication I felt that was praise indeed. But most of all I appreciated the comment made by Cumbria's Peter Robinson who knows more than most when it comes to railways. Quite apart from our conclusions, the thing he liked about the report was that it was "so readable." That not only made my day, it all but made my year!

21

SACKED!

"I am cross about the decision because the overtones are that he was not reappointed to the job because he had become a thorn in BR's side. If this was the case, then that was every reason to make sure he was reappointed. It is his job to be a thorn and some TUCC chairmen are not."

John Watson MP (as reported in the
'Yorkshire Post' of 27th March 1987)

By all accounts, 1987 should have been the year of decision for the Settle–Carlisle line. Certainly, David Mitchell, the minister for public transport who would advise the Secretary of State for Transport on the ultimate decision, had been adamant on a number of occasions that he would not take long to make up his mind. He had suggested that it might be only three or four months following receipt of the TUCCs report before he came to a conclusion. Whilst I felt this time scale to be on the optimistic side – on the basis of earlier closure proposals one or two years was par for the course – a decision during 1987 seemed a certainty. It might even dovetail into the anticipated General Election. If so the omens had to be good.

Indeed, there was a mood of quiet confidence amongst all those who wanted the line to be retained. Even obdurate journalists who had followed the case from the beginning were quoting odds of between 3 to 1 and 5 to 1 that the line would be saved. Meanwhile, the year had opened with a row about British Rail's failure to publish its financial case for closure; although, to their credit, they moved quickly to rectify this omission.

Unfortunately, the figures they provided were so limited that they only added fuel to the flames of discontent. Even Brian Sutcliffe, the normally urbane and restrained chairman of FOSCLA, blew his top! He accused British Rail of publishing figures which were out of context, of exaggerating operating costs, gures which were out of context, of exaggerating operating costs, and of failing to take into account the increased level of revenue being generated by the line. "This is just another example of BR's dirty tricks department trying to sabotage the future of the line," he told the 'Yorkshire Post', adding that FOSCLA would be sending its own figures to the Secretary of State for Transport to help him make up his mind.

Brian Sutcliffe was right. British Rail's 'Settle–Carlisle: The Financial Case for Closure' was little more than a press release and, in accountancy terms, was hardly worth the paper it was printed on. Indeed, these were the only figures it provided:

Balance Sheet of Settle–Carlisle

Immediate Outlay	£3.5 – £5.1 million
(Ribblehead and Radio Signalling)	

Ongoing Annual Costs

1. Infrastructure (renewal & maintenace)	£0.95 million
2. Train operating costs	£0.80 million
3. Interest and depreciation on rolling stock	£0.21 million
	£1.96 million
Current Revenue	£1.00 million

I'd never seen a balance sheet like it before in my life!

The interest and depreciation figure related to "new Sprinter units." If the Class 150/2 Sprinters introduced on the North Trans-Pennine service were anything to go by, they were totally unsuitable for the Settle–Carlisle line (just as they were for journeys between Scarborough and Liverpool, and Hull and North Wales). For a start, I would have thought that stock which provided passengers with a good view of the passing scenery, preferably with Widney type sliding windows for the benefit of the Ribblehead photocall, was a must. Indeed, I had formally suggested to Ron Cotton that two sets of Mark 2 Open Saloons (TSOs) be painted in Midland Railway maroon, labelled 'Settle–Carlisle' and apportioned to the line. Failing that, Mark 1 stock – preferably with Commonwealth bogies – would do. Anything other than the dreaded Sprinters!

Following pressure from MPs and others, British Rail provided FOSCLA with a copy of the complete report advocating closure. With the aid of this, their legal advisor Edward Album, an eminent City solicitor with innumerable contacts in the business world, arranged for international chartered accountants Coopers and Lybrand to draw up an estimate of costs and revenues for the next ten years based on British Rail's own figures. This exercise showed the line in rather better light, moving into profit of about £200,000 in 1993 and rising to a healthy £282,000 by 1997.

Perhaps the most interesting if least reported aspect of British Rail's submission was the 'Civil Engineering Report' and in particular Appendix C on the Ribblehead Viaduct. Reading this I detected a trace of paranoia on the part of the drafters when they referred to other reports and articles published during the past five years which usually "cast British Rail in the role of iconoclast" (Whose fault was that?, I asked myself!). The appendix appeared to lack confidence and frequently resorted to underlining or capitals – or both – to get its message across.

However, its great omission was that it made no reference at all to the case put by Christopher Wallis at the Public Hearing (see pages 216–218). He had implied the cost of repairing Ribblehead would be £0.9 m and provided a quote to back his case. A copy of Mr Wallis's paper had been handed to British Rail at the hearing so they should have had sufficient time to digest it. Therefore, I would have expected them to have either endorsed or, more likely, refuted his claims.

Could it be that they were unable to dispute what Wallis had said? After all, he was an experienced bridge engineer who had been employed by British Rail for many years. Moreover, his diagnosis, certainly so far as the Barmouth Viaduct was concerned, appeared sound. That British Rail chose to ignore the Wallis solution suggested to me that it might be too near the mark for comfort. For if Wallis was right, it reduced the cost of repairing Ribblehead by between £1.8 and £3.4 million and all but destroyed the case for closure.

On 11th February David Maclean MP initiated another adjournment debate on the Settle–Carlisle line in the House of Commons. He opened by referring to the "unique" report of the North East and North Western TUCCs which "strongly and emphatically recommended that consent to British Rail's proposal to close the Settle–Carlisle line be refused." He said he intended to "put on record on the Floor of the House some of the comments from the Joint TUCCs report which make up that emphatic recommendation." He did and it was very flattering to read some of one's own prose between the covers of Hansard. Mr Maclean also called for the Government to commission a firm of internationally renowned structural engineers to carry out a full study of the Ribblehead Viaduct and other structures on the line.

Replying for the Government, David Mitchell agreed there was a need for independent scrutiny of British Rail's estimates, not that he suggested there was any deception by British Rail, but because he recognised the widespread unease and the feeling that the estimates should be subject to an independent check. He proposed to discuss the matter with the Joint County Councils.

David Mitchell also placed on record the "appreciation of the whole House" of the work the TUCCs had done. That was nice of him. He stressed that the Government needed to establish whether contributions for the upkeep of the line would be available from sources other than the Public Service Obligation grant and assured MPs that no decision would be made until "we have given the most careful consideration to all the relevant evidence." So it now seemed that an early decision could be discounted.

February also saw the departure of one of the central characters of the Settle–Carlisle saga – Ron Cotton. Like many of the more able British Rail managers, he opted for early retirement. I was sorry to see him go, both at a personal level and because I knew the line would miss his promotional flair. Indeed, the omens for the future of its day to day management were not good as it was to come under the Provincial sector of Eastern Region at York, a body not noted for an abundance of promotional or, indeed, other talents.

However, Ron Cotton did leave one useful legacy in the form of two 8 coach sets of Mark 1 Commonwealth bogied Carlisle based stock for the May 1987 timetable. Moreover, they would be hauled by Class 47 locomotives. This ranked as a marked improvement on the rag-bag assortment of stock the Eastern Region had provided for the past five years. Even so, I would remember with affection the sight of the two ubiquitous Class 31 locomotives as they arrived from Hull at the head of 10 coaches which formed the morning train from Leeds.

Not quite such good news was the May timetable itself. Whilst the two additional trains were undoubtedly welcome, the stopping pattern struck me as going over the top to provide a local service at the expense of through travel. Although there would still be a Glasgow connection at Carlisle out of the first morning departure from Leeds, now timed for 08.42, the good connection out of the mid-afternoon departure from Glasgow was lost. Thus a journey from Glasgow to Leeds via Settle–Carlisle which currently took 4 hours 1 minute would take 5 hours 6 minutes of which over 3 hours would be spent in a DMU! As a consequence travel between Leeds and Glasgow was now faster by the East Coast Main Line. This is something which should have been resisted at all costs, if only for psychological reasons.

Whilst the new timetable would undoubtedly appeal to the rucksack and walking boots brigade, it was less attractive to the larger, albeit more fickle market of those making end to end journeys largely for the sake of a ride on the line. Moreover, by timing the mid-morning departure from Leeds at 10.42 rather than, say, 11.30, it missed the first Leeds arrival from Bristol and Birmingham and, on Saturdays, from London. These connections had provided a lot of patronage on the extra summer Saturday services. Moreover, because of the distances people travelled to gain access to the Settle–Carlisle line, this was very good for British Rail in revenue terms.

Likewise the Sunday service, which used to leave Leeds at 11.30 – a most sensible time on a Sunday! – and allowed about 1½ hours in Carlisle, was retimed to depart at 09.33 to give over three hours in Carlisle. This was far too long for there is little to do there on a Sunday and there is a limit to just how long one can spend wandering round Texas Homecare!

Following closely on Ron Cotton's retirement, March saw another departure from the Settle–Carlisle scene – namely myself! Being aware that my period as chairman of the North East TUCC expired on 31st March, I had asked the Department of Trade and Industry in November if they could indicate by the end of the year whether or not they wished me to carry on for a further term. Given the amount of work involved, this did not strike me as an unreasonable request. All I sought was three months notice so I could make the necessary arrangements regarding a number of business commitments in 1987 and beyond.

I heard nothing until I was summoned to London on 3rd March by Lord Lucas, the Parliamentary Under Secretary of State for Trade and Industry responsible for consumer affairs. From his attitude and tone it appeared he'd been got at. This did not surprise me as I was aware a number of senior managers within British Rail were already relishing my imminent demise.

Lord Lucas asked if I would find it "the end of the world" if I wasn't re-appointed. I replied quite truthfully that I wouldn't. After all there are other things in life than being a TUCC chairman. However, I added that some of the North East TUCC members might be disappointed; to which he replied that if he asked every member what they thought he would get as many different answers. I felt that a little unkind but didn't press it, saying that all I sought was a decision one way or the other. He said he'd let me know by the end of the week although I had little doubt my time was almost up.

Settle–Carlisle only came up once during our conversation when Lord Lucas said "I suppose I should thank you for the report" which struck me as rather backhanded when one considered all the work it had involved. But then he probably didn't realise I had drafted most of the report myself – or perhaps he did and that was why he wasn't particularly enthusiastic about it! He queried my partisan attitude towards the line, so I had to explain that TUCCs were there to represent the views of rail users and they hardly wished to see the line close.

I have to confess that, over the years, what few dealings I had with the Consumer Affairs Division of the Department of Trade and Industry did little to inspire confidence in the machinery of government. My impression was that they neither understood nor were particularly interested in the work of the TUCCs. We were there so lip service could be paid to the Government's commitment to consumers and so long as we kept our heads down and didn't rock the British Rail boat, they were quite happy. Unlike the Department of Transport, they never sent anyone to our Public Hearings and when we sent them copies of our reports on closure proposals they just passed them on to the Department of Transport who already had their own copy.

At least you knew where you were with Transport – they were hand in glove with British Rail and tended to look upon TUCCs as something of an irritation. Indeed, David Mitchell had made it quite clear that he saw the role of TUCCs to be "generally supportive" to British Rail which suggested that we were little more than a rubber stamp for British Rail decisions – including their proposal to close the Settle–Carlisle line! Needless to say, that was not how I saw things at all. However, if that was how they wanted it, I was glad to be on the way out.

Contrary to Lord Lucas's expectations, North East TUCC members were upset when I told them of my impending departure. There was talk of mass resignations and they all but declared UDI!

Deputy chairman Barbara Ashwin told the 'Yorkshire Post' that the whole committee was "utterly dismayed" and sought a meeting with Lord Lucas to get him to reverse the decision. Barry Flaxman, chairman of the TUCC for Eastern England, accused British Rail of organising my dismissal. "They will be hoisting flags at the York headquarters, thinking they can take it easy. It is a tragedy that British Rail can succeed in putting pressure on the Government in this way," he said.

Alan Whitehouse of the 'Yorkshire Post' reported that news of my 'sacking' had dismayed campaigners fighting for the controversial Settle–Carlisle railway. He continued:

"Mr Towler is the second major figure connected with the line to disappear within a month, and the protest groups are now seriously concerned for the scenic route, which is waiting a Government decision on whether it will close.

It is an open secret that Mr Towler is disliked by many senior British Rail figures, who have seen him as a thorn in their side for almost all the eight years he has been chairman. He challenged the legality of the closure notices for the Settle–Carlisle line forcing two amendments.

He made it plain several times that he believes British Rail massaged the figures to prove their case for closure. On other fronts, he has complained loudly about the quality and timekeeping of train services."

'The Times', too, had the story. Transport Correspondent Rodney Cowton wrote:

"One of the men who led the struggle to save the historic Settle–Carlisle railway line may pay with his job. Mr James Towler, has been told that his position as chairman of the North East TUCC will not be extended when it expires at the end of the month.

One source said: 'James Towler prepared a splendid report arguing the case for keeping open the line which was adopted by the North East and North Western TUCCs and sent to John Moore, the Secretary of State for Transport. This caused British Rail a great deal of embarrassment and has almost certainly stood in the way of his reappointment.'"

There was no doubt that Lord Lucas's decision caused something of a furore at the time. MPs of all parties including John Watson, Max Madden and Richard Wainwright took up the issue and questions were asked in the House. Dr John Whitelegg, chairman of the Settle–Carlisle Joint Action Committee said I was "one of the few leaders of a consumer organisation that has ever defended consumer interests" whilst Brian Sutcliffe of FOSCLA added that I always "fought for the interests of the ordinary passenger".

There was support, too, from the National Union of Railwaymen. Frank Edwards of the Leeds City branch told the 'Yorkshire Evening Post' that his members had no doubt that if I had not been so dedicated to my job, many lines would have been closed. He said that "the Settle–Carlisle line owes its existence at this moment to the work done by Mr Towler." That was kind of him and, whilst he was probably stretching it a little, there was more than a grain of truth in it.

Harry Mead, writing in the 'Northern Echo', recalled that in the 30 years he had been familiar with TUCCs, it was only under my "breezy, but intelligent leadership" that any committee had commanded attention across a full range of rail issues. He went on:

"The recent news of Jim's sacking means that rail users between Berwick and Sheffield are losing the best champion they have ever had. The unbudging attitude of the Department of Trade and Industry, responsible for the TUCC appointments, confirms a suspicion that watchdogs which bite, and maybe even those that just watch, are not welcome."

It was left to Alan Whitaker to remark in the Bradford 'Telegraph & Argus' that I would probably be best remembered for my rousing battles with British Rail over their controversial plan to close the Settle–Carlisle line. I have to say that I was very touched by these and all the other many kind words that were directed towards my efforts, from members of my committee, local authorities, rail user groups and many individual rail users. In all I received over 100 letters and it was almost as if I were in the position of reading my own obituaries!

But life goes on and the parting of the way became inevitable following Lord Lucas's rejection of an attempt by David Mitchell to defuse the situation by offering me a place as an independent member of the Central Transport Consultative Committee. Such a move, concluded Lord Lucas, would not be in the interest of the North East TUCC as it would "inhibit" the new chairman of that committee. As the 'Yorkshire Post' succinctly put it, the whole thing had developed into a 'Whitehall farce'.

From the 1st April I was just an ordinary rail user with no statutory responsibilities for the Settle–Carlisle or any other line. Who knows, I might have to write to British Rail and complain about their services. And if I was not satisfied with their reply, it would be open for me to take up the matter with the North East TUCC. That might be fun. However, my 'retirement' from any formal role relating to rail user issues proved shortlived for, within a matter of days, I was invited to become chairman of the Yorkshire area of the Railway Development Society and was elected a vice-president of the RDS at national level at the end of the month. Another case of 'as one door closes another opens'.

At the beginning of April, Cumbria County Council gave a presentation to David Mitchell and civil servants at the Department of Transport on behalf of the Joint County Councils. In many respects this was an update of the evidence they had presented to the TUCC Public Hearings in the spring of 1986, particularly with regard to the new local Dalesman service. This had done well and up to the end of January had averaged 50 passengers per train. A revenue balance sheet was even more encouraging. It indicated that from a (£24,000)/£153,000 profit/(loss) in 1987/88, profitability of the line would grow to £330,000/£562,000 by 1996/97 – the wide variation in the annual figures being due to the level of charges to be made for diversionary services on the revenue side, and interest and deprecation on the costs side.

The omens for the line looked good and were further enhanced at the end of the month when David Mitchell himself was unable to find a seat on the 'Dalesman' when he made a fact finding trip on the line. There is nothing like a bit of overcrowding to emphasise the problems of success! Afterwards Stan Abbott reported in 'The Independent': "A decision to close the line is seen as unlikely in the run-up to a general election and it is believed the outstanding obstacle to a reprieve is a means of saving face for British Rail which has been determined to close the line despite a near four-fold increase in passengers".

Back on 'the line', the mood of optimism continued into May. To mark the introduction of the new timetable of 5 trains a day each way, Provincial sector marketing manager, Paul Prescott, told a meeting of local authority and media representatives in Settle that he felt the line was a "wonderful product" and he looked forward to returning in a year's time to "fly the flag". However, the chap who would be flying the flag in the meantime, York-based Mark Causebrook, the Provincial line manager for North Trans-Pennine and West Yorkshire services, was less sanguine. He maintained the line should be closed. Perhaps this was why it took two months for the first of the splendid colour posters designed by Cumbria County Council showing a Class 31 locomotive heading a six-coach train on Arten Gill Viaduct to go on display at Leeds. Even then it was only because I persuaded an assistant station manager to put one in the redundant 'roller blind' departure panel on the concourse. Already, Ron Cotton's flair and initiative was being missed.

Nevertheless, there was still general confidence that the line would be reprieved, perhaps during the run-up to the General Election. This was encouraged by reports that a consortium of civil engineering firms had presented a plan to save the line by funding the essential repairs for Ribblehead Viaduct which British Rail maintained it could not afford. Such a move would undoubtedly appeal to the Government.

The June General Election came and went. I had a wry smile to myself when I learnt that Lord Lucas was amongst the ministers who had been 'sacked'. There was yet another change at the helm of the Ministry of Transport with Paul Channon taking over as Secretary of State from John Moore who moved to Social Services. David Mitchell remained as minister responsible for railways.

In the middle of July the all-party House of Commons Transport Committee announced their support for the Settle–Carlisle by re-commending that the Government should safeguard the line's future by sanctioning a one-off grant to repair the Ribblehead Via-duct. In a report on the financing of rail services, the committee stated that even if the line were closed, the cost of maintaining the viaduct would have to be met. They felt this was one case in which payment of a specific grant would be appropriate.

At the end of the month there was a flurry of speculation that, as part of a package that would both save the Settle–Carlisle line and get British Rail off the hook, the line would become Britain's first privatised main-line railway. If this meant that the line would not be closed it had to be good news. Moreover, given British Rail's lack of enthusiasm for the line, there might be something to be said for letting someone else run it. If so, certain safeguards were essential – the most important being that it must be retained and developed as part of the national rail network. The sanctity of the network was paramount. Then the line would have to con-tinue to be subject to the provisions of the Transport Act 1962 – amended as necessary – so that it could not be closed without recourse to a further Public Hearing.

Developing these themes in an interview with Ruth Pitt on Yorkshire Television, I remarked that it said little for British Rail senior
management that they wished to opt out of running a line that
appeared attractive to private investors. However, it was vitally
important that any new owners were not allowed to let the line
degenerate into a 'Thomas the Tank Engine' fun railway. The Settle–Carlisle line was 'England's greatest historical scenic route' and
was built to carry trains 'over the hills at speed' as well as to serve
the local communities. So it must remain.

My observations were also taken up by the 'Yorkshire Evening
Post'. This prompted one reader to suggest I should be made chairman of the British Railways Board! It was an amusing thought.
Not so amusing were reports in August that the line was likely to
close. In the 'Yorkshire Post', Alan Whitehouse wrote that consent
to closure might incorporate a 'stay of execution' clause so that
the line would remain open for a further 12 months to allow private
companies to put in bids for it. I didn't like the sound of this at all
as it looked as if it could all end in a classic fudge. In many respects
this would be the worst of all possible conclusions.

Concerned at the effect of rumour and counter rumour, David
Mitchell wrote to the Joint County Councils saying that he was
anxious to put an end to the uncertainty surrounding the line's
future as quickly as possible. "But before I can advise the Secretary
of State on his final decision, I must be absolutely clear about how
much financial support is available from Cumbria County Council
and the other local authorities," stated Mr Mitchell. Had the Minister and the Department of Transport taken a leaf out of British
Rail's book over the Goole swing bridge and moved into the extortion racket? As Cumbria's Councillor Bill Cameron said: "It does
not seem reasonable that the Minister should be holding a gun to
the heads of the local authorities." I agreed.

At a meeting with FOSCLA representatives in August, David
Mitchell stressed that no money would be forthcoming from either
British Rail or the Government to fund capital expenditure on the
line and earlier reports that it was to be privatised were denied.
Whist Mr Mitchell told Brian Sutcliffe and his colleagues that he
did not want to close the line, the terms he was imposing for its
retention made closure all the more likely. Indeed, he seemed to
be moving the goal posts.

As the summer slipped into autumn, the clouds of gloom and
despondency grew darker and rumours abounded that it was now

only a matter of weeks, or possibly even days, before an announcement would be made that the line was to close. Whilst business during the summer had been brisk – particularly at Settle and Appleby plus a number of the Dales Rail stations where local FOSCLA groups were strong on the ground – time and again I saw the 08.42 pull out of Leeds with far too many empty seats for my liking. Then, at the beginning of November there was a ray of hope when it was learnt that the Settle–Carlisle line was to be the subject of a feasibility study into a multi-million pound job creation scheme under the Manpower Services Commission.

The scheme was the brainchild of civil engineering contractors J Jarvis and Sons Plc who had become the first national managing agent to be appointed by the Manpower Services Commission in the construction industry. Plans included the development of Hellifield as a park and ride centre and a couple of new stations at Langcliffe and Helwith Bridge. Over half the cost would be born by the Manpower Services Commission, but contributions would also be sought from British Rail, the local authorities and other sources including English Heritage. The move was warmly welcomed by Dr John Whitelegg of the Joint Action Committee who said it offered a chance of saving the line without "muddying the waters with talk of privatisation or Mickey Mouse railways." But he warned: "While we are very excited, we are also aware there are several points at which the project could become unstuck."

To round off a year of rumour, counter rumour and continuing uncertainty – ingredients destined to undermine any business – the 'Yorkshire Post' of 12th December carried a piece by Alan Whitehouse which said British Rail chiefs had admitted that the Ribblehead Viaduct was not collapsing after all and was safe for the foreseeable future! This was in marked contrast with the official predictions made in 1981 when it was claimed the viaduct only had a life of three to five years.

A British Rail spokeswoman said: "That information is now out of date. When it was quoted, we thought there was a serious structural fault on the viaduct. That has subsequently proved not to be the case." So, was this a tacit agreement on the part of British Rail that Chris Wallis was right after all? If so, it meant that as the main plank of the case to close the line was the money required to repair the viaduct, the case for closure appeared more spurious than ever. Once again it all rested on Ribblehead.

22

BETRAYAL!

"The Government's plan is both a betrayal of honest enthusiasm and an abdication of social responsibility. It stinks."

From the editorial in the 'Yorkshire Post', 17th May 1988

With the arrival of 1988 there was one thing we could be sure. So far as the Settle–Carlisle line was concerned it simply had to be the year of decision. But what decision? At the outset the odds appeared about evens.

Characteristically, the year opened with yet another twist to the long running saga which, in theatrical terms, would soon be entering its '8th Great Year!' It became known that English Heritage, the Government-sponsored historic buildings and monuments commission headed by Lord Montagu of Beaulieu, had offered the Department of the Environment £1 million towards the cost of repairing the Ribblehead Viaduct; not just for saving what was termed an ancient monument, but because they also saw the Settle–Carlisle line in the wider context of an "economic lifeline for the historic towns and communities of the area." This had to be good news. But why had the offer been languishing on a Whitehall desk since May the previous year? Was it because it might prove an embarrassment to a Department of Transport anxious to close the line?

Not such good news was the landslip between Garsdale and Kirkby Stephen at Mallerstang on 5th January following a period of incessant rain. This caused a stretch of the up line to be closed for a short period whilst repairs were effected. And top marks to British Rail's civil engineers who quickly filled the gap with thousands of tons of ballast. Would they have gone to all this trouble if the line were to close later in the year.

At the end of January, public transport minister David Mitchell

– under constant pressure from MPs to announce a decision on the Settle–Carlisle line – wrote to the local authorities asking if they were prepared to put up more money to save the line. It was said the figure he had in mind was £500,000, a point confirmed by Keighley MP Gary Waller who said that if the councils came up with that sum the Government would find it "very difficult" to close the line. Mr Mitchell proved less circumspect, saying that the Government had to be "absolutely clear about all the local authorities commitments to the line" before a decision on its future could be made. This, he added, would be a "very important factor" in the decision making process.

I never knew quite what to make of Mr Mitchell, even though I'd met him a number of times. A former wine merchant, he had entered Parliament in 1964 where he initially was active in the small business lobby. After spells at the Northern Ireland office and the Department of Industry, he was appointed an Under Secretary of State for Transport in 1983 and Minister for Public Transport in 1986. A firm proponent of the view 'that the men from British Rail knew best', he had a consistent track record of defending them from Parliamentary criticism, not least from his own backbenchers.

During the row in 1986 about the British Railways Board's decision to withhold punctuality statistics from the Central Transport Consultative Committee, he came down firmly on the side of British Rail and worked hard to persuade the official rail watchdog to accept the Board's revised tabulations. These included the nonsensical notion that trains arriving five minutes late were on time! Try telling that to someone who has just missed a connection!

On the other side of the coin, David Mitchell had built up a reputation for being a pro-rail minister with a genuine interest in railways. Indeed, he was said to be something of a 'gricer' and seldom missed the opportunity of a ride on the footplate. He probably ranks as the only minister ever to have savoured the delights of a ride in the cab of a humble Class 31 locomotive over a section of the South Trans-Pennine route. In a personal capacity he was a supporter of the North Yorkshire Moors Railway.

Therefore, if anyone in the Government had the inclination to save the Settle–Carlisle line it was probably David Mitchell. But did he have sufficient weight and clout to carry his senior colleagues so that, come the day, he would be able to deliver? I had my doubts, certainly if his attempt to get me on to the Central Transport Consultative Committee as an independent member was anything to go by.

But to return to the more immediate problems facing the local authorities at the beginning of 1988. Were they in a position to meet Mr Mitchell's reputed target of £500,000? Understandably, they felt rather peeved at the position they had been manoeuvred into. They felt they were being 'set up' to bail out the Settle–Carlisle line. As Bill Cameron, chairman of Cumbria County Council's transport committee, put it: "I am convinced that all this is geared to making the local authorities the scapegoat for closure."

This feeling of frustration regarding just what the Government was after prompted Councillor Michael Simmons, the chairman of the West Yorkshire Passenger Transport Authority, to write and ask David Mitchell exactly what level of financial support he sought from the local authorities. Councillor Simmons explained: "As recently as December 1987, it appeared the Minister was saying: 'increase operating subsidies or the line will close.' Now he seems to have shifted his ground and to be saying it is far more important that the authorities help to find the cash to repair Ribblehead Viaduct."

A vital constituent in any local authority funded package would be North Yorkshire County council. After all, the Ribblehead Viaduct was situated within its boundaries, albeit in that part of the county which used to be part of the West Riding of Yorkshire. For years the council had resolutely refused to fund any significant contribution to British Rail, firmly believing that such projects should be financed from the Public Service Obligation. Such a policy did not strike me as unreasonable, save for the fact that other counties throughout the land had relented from such a stance under pressure from British Rail. The North Yorkshire case was admirably summarised by Alliance Councillor Nigel Watson who, at the beginning of March, claimed: "The Government was using a combination of blackmail and shirking their own duties to try and put an unfair burden on local authorities at the same time as telling them to tighten their belts on spending."

The charge of 'blackmail' was subsequently repeated by representatives of all parties. Councillor Keith Lockyer (Conservative) described the position as one of "double blackmail" as Cumbria and other councils were claiming that as part of the line was in North Yorkshire, they would only pay up if North Yorkshire made a contribution. "I don't like having a pistol pointed at my head," he said, adding that the council had no duty to maintain British Rail's structures.

Although there was still some mileage left in the North Yorkshire cliffhanger, council leader John Clout hinted there could be a satisfactory outcome when he remarked: "If the other local authorities do find the resources, North Yorkshire would not want to be left in the invidious position of odd man out."

More ready financial support came from FOSCLA who pledged £15,000 over three years towards the £500,000 target set by David Mitchell. In addition they had already contributed £1,500 towards the cost of the splendid 1987-88 posters and leaflets designed by Cumbria County Council whilst a further £1,500 was earmarked for British Rail who were to provide leaflets for 1988-89. As an example of practical enthusiasm this was a magnificent gesture. At their annual general meeting in Skipton on 19th March, the general consensus was that so long as North Yorkshire came up with its share of the £500,000, a reprieve for the line was on the cards.

This sentiment was endorsed on 22nd March when the report by J Jarvis and Sons plc, the civil engineering contractors, and the Manpower Services Commission was published. Said to have the personal backing of industry secretary Lord Young, it saw a bright future for the line as the Settle–Carlisle Tourist Corridor or Heritage Trail. However, it was emphasised that it was not a blueprint for a Disneyland of the Dales.

Titled 'A Feasibility Study on the Training, Employment and Enterprise within the Settle–Carlisle Corridor' and compiled by Michael Brooks-Rooney, the report called for a joint interface between the Government, British Rail, local authorities, tourist boards and the private sector to fund the restoration of the line and develop new attractions. These included the refurbishment of Hellifield station as a sort of 'base camp' for the line complete with tourist office, a Victorian buffet and bar, a video room and extensive car and coach parking facilities.

Other projects involved the rebuilding of the Hoffman line kiln at Langcliffe near Settle where a new station or halt would be provided, and the opening of further tourist offices at Garsdale, Kirkby Stephen and Appleby. The cost of these projects – but not including work on Ribblehead Viaduct or the track and signalling – was put at £4.6 million of which £3 million would come from the Manpower Services Commission. The report also called for the appointment of a Settle–Carlisle management committee and a business opportunities manager – I wonder if they had Ron Cotton in mind? – and estimated that usage of the line could be increased from 300,000 journeys a year to 750,000 within three years.

The following day came news that a letter, leaked to Labour transport spokesman Robert Hughes MP, suggested the Cabinet was split over how to save the line. Mr Nicholas Ridley, the Environment Secretary, had evidently written to the Secretary of State for Transport, Paul Channon, on 8th March stating that whilst he agreed with the general view that the Settle–Carlisle line should remain open, he had a number of qualifications. He continued:

"But I feel that in reprieving the line, we must establish in people's minds that it is now seen as a leisure and heritage-based enterprise and not as a transport matter. For this reason – and in fairness to British Rail themselves – I do not feel they should be left with the job of running the line."

Mr Ridley was said to agree the Government had to meet the cost of repairing the Ribblehead Viaduct and other sections of the line but that this should be covered from resources earmarked for heritage rather than the public transport budget. He added that he was disappointed the Government had not yet found a private organisation or trust to take on the line.

What was one to make of all this? Mr Hughes was in no doubt. He told John Petty, transport correspondent of 'The Daily Telegraph':

"The fact is that everyone in Government has now accepted the fact that the line should not be closed but it is the Environment Secretary who is delaying action because of his obsession with privatisation. By giving in to these delaying tactics, the Transport Secretary has, yet again, allowed himself to be bullied into putting Government ideology before the needs of the travelling public."

However, Judy Jones of the 'Yorkshire Post' reported that rail-buff MP Robert Adley was less sceptical and expressed his delight at the contents of the letter. "It is entirely appropriate that a wholly exceptional solution has to be found for a wholly exceptional problem," he added. This struck me as worthy of W S Gilbert himself!

I wasn't enthusiastic at Mr Ridley's intervention. When it came to privatisation he ranked as an extremist. Indeed, he would probably privatise the air we breathe if he thought he could get away with it! Moreover, he seemed to be advocating that British Rail should be let off the hook for its neglect and run down of the line. This, in itself, undermined its attraction to the private investor, a factor emphasised by the reference to an absence of any private body willing to run the line. Then, quite apart from anything else, the question of the future of the line was one for transport secretary Paul Channon – aided and abetted by David Mitchell – rather than Mr Ridley. However, the fact that the Government appeared resigned to reprieving the line was encouraging.

After the Ridley diversion it was just a case of waiting for North Yorkshire. Fortunately they didn't keep us in suspense for too long and on 11th April they agreed to contribute £120,000 to the local authorities' kitty. Understandably there were a number of conditions, one being that the line should be operated by British Rail and not privatised – an interesting caveat as the county was under the firm control of the Conservatives. Council leader John Clout said he felt it would have been wrong not to participate. "We would be quite rightly blamed if all the work done so far came to nought because North Yorkshire County Council refused to change its stance and make a contribution," he added.

The North Yorkshire decision meant that the target of £500,000 set by David Mitchell had been met. This was an enormous relief and reflected great credit on all concerned. The contributions ranged from £165,000 pledged by Cumbria County Council to £1,000 from Calderdale Metropolitan Council, and included the £15,000 from FOSCLA. Amongst the conditions of the offer was that the line should be maintained and operated by British Rail for 20 years and it was emphasised that it was intended to be a 'one-off' payment and should not be seen as a precedent. It would also mean that current revenue support provided by Cumbria and the district councils would cease when the existing agreement ended in July 1989.

These conditions did not strike me as unreasonable, given it was ratepayers money which was involved. As Cumbria's Councillor Bill Cameron, the prime architect and driving force behind the line-saving package, put it: "We have shown British Rail and the Government how to run the line. We have proved its viability and once again demonstrated our commitment to safeguarding the future of this magnificent railway."

Barring any last minute slip-up, it looked as if the future of the Settle–Carlisle line was assured. Now it was simply a case of waiting for Mr Mitchell to brief his Secretary of State, Paul Channon, so that a suitable announcement could be made in the House of Commons. Whilst not yet time for splitting open a bottle of champagne,

I felt that even the most cautious could prudently put one on ice. Another month or so and it should be all over.

How wrong I was! Indeed, I shall not forget Monday 16th May 1988. It was a bright sunny spring day and I'd spent the morning in Harrogate on business. On returning home that afternoon I was surprised to hear the telephone ring. I say 'surprised' because British Telecom were having problems with the line and we were unable to take incoming calls. I lifted the receiver, expecting to hear a click followed by a buzzing, but was astonished to hear Alan Whitehouse of the 'Yorkshire Post' at the other end. After congratulating him on getting through, he came straight to the point.

"I thought you should know that David Mitchell is about to make a statement in the House of Commons saying that the Government is 'minded' to consent to British Rail's proposal to close the Settle–Carlisle line, but that the final decision will be deferred until November in case any private body wish to take it over," said Alan.

I was shattered! Indeed, it took me several moments to come up with a response for I was at a loss for words – well, ones which could be printed in a family newspaper like the 'Yorkshire Post'! When I had gathered my thoughts, I said that it was a "shabby decision" from which neither the Government nor British Rail emerged with any credit. It was probably as well that no one else got through as my response might have been less temperate. The more the significance of it all sunk in, the more furious I became. My wife, Muriel, felt just the same.

In a nutshell, David Mitchell's statement was to the effect that his Secretary of State – what's the betting that Paul Channon would have been addressing the House had it been decided to reprieve the line?! – had agreed to British Rail pulling out of the line but that the final decision would be delayed until November to allow the TUCCs to submit further evidence on hardship and bus substitution, and to give time for a private operator to volunteer to run the Settle–Carlisle as a seasonal tourist attraction.

Mr Mitchell told an angry House of Commons that whilst the line had considerable potential for development as a tourist attraction, British Rail was not "particularly well qualified" to promote such lines. That was rich, considering the success they had recently had in promoting scenic routes. What, I wondered to myself, did British Rail's Carol Bustard – who had made great strides exploiting the tourism angle – think of this stinging rebuke?

But there was more to come. For when I tuned into the news

on the radio, there were the dulcet tones of Mr Mitchell expounding that British Rail's priority was to invest in a modern rail system for the 21st century (did he have the Pacer in mind?) rather than "provide pleasure rides for railway archaeologists." This struck me as a particularly inane remark, even for an off-the-cuff reply to an increasingly hostile House. For the tools of the railway archaeologist (and a good many railway photographers, too!) were a reliable car and a good pair of walking boots.

As for Mr Mitchell's goodies to tempt a private operator, British Rail's 'dowry' of £850,000 for the line's continuously welded track struck me as being a puerile offer as this low maintenance cost track would be required in situ if the line was to remain open. The suggestion that the 72-mile line could be run on a par with the North Yorkshire Moors or Severn Valley Railways – with a 25 mph maximum speed? – was suitably derided by Labour's Bob Cryer who said that the minister's statement should be viewed with dismay.

Bob Cryer, a founder member of the Keighley and Worth Valley Railway, said that it would be beyond the resources of the private sector to run the Settle–Carlisle line, a point later endorsed by Michael Draper, general manager of the Severn Valley Railway who dismissed such an option as being far beyond anything contemplated in the preservation movement. But Mr Mitchell would not be deterred and stuck to his theme. It was left to veteran Labour MP Eric Heffer to remind Mr Mitchell that Bob Cryer "knows more about railways than you'll ever know!" I was inclined to agree.

Nor was the outburst against the Government's decision confined to the opposition benches. The unease on the part of many Conservatives was encapsulated by former Cabinet Minister Leon Brittan who said the matter had been handled "disappointingly" by the Government. Garsdale was being increasingly used as a park-and-ride station by his Richmondshire constituents and he made the valid point that the £500,000 the local authorities had agreed to contribute was on the basis that it would lead to retention of the line by British Rail as part of the national network. He was critical, too, of the apparent 'last-minute' nature of the appeal for the private sector to step forward.

The following morning the 'Yorkshire Post' really went to town and did the Settle–Carlisle line proud. In addition to leading with the story under the bold headline: 'Sentence of Death', Alan

Whitehouse had contributed a background piece tracing the saga from the 1981 decision to re-route the Nottingham–Glasgow service. There was also an interview with David Mitchell in which the minister for public transport confided that he did not expect the reference to the TUCCs to lead to any dramatic developments. "It is being done to prevent a legal challenge if we decide to close the line," he said. In another piece headed: 'Sell-off decision is shock for protesters', I was faintly amused to find myself sandwiched between photographs of Leon Brittan and Michael Jopling – confirmation indeed that I had joined the ranks of 'yesterday's men'!

Then, to cap it all, there was a splendid editorial under the heading 'Signal failure' which I reproduce in full:

"Running the Settle to Carlisle line is a specialised task 'for which, quite properly, British Rail is not particularly well qualified' according to the Transport Minister Mr David Mitchell. Quite properly by that analysis, attention should be focused on routes with generalised appeal rather than on tourist links. Yet at this moment BR money is being lavished on rural lines in Scotland and Wales which are to a great extent used for tourism. Settle to Carlisle enthusiasts meanwhile have proved that they can meet many vital alternative local transport needs. Their reward has been to hear Mr Mitchell not so much auctioning off the family silver as proposing to sell the bricks, mortar, wood and steel which they have sought for five years to defend.

Yesterday's statement in the House of Commons could be seen as little more than a blatant trailblazer for widespread railway privatisation. Leaked Ministerial letters last month showed that Mr Nicholas Ridley, Environment Secretary had neatly compartmentalised rural rail services in his own mind into a picturesque-amenity slot which ultimately could be paid for by private enterprise. Mr Mitchell rubbed the message home, both in the Commons and during media interviews.

It can only be a matter of time before this philosophy is extended to the trimmed trunk of basic rail services which the Government would like to see. When Mr Mitchell talked about BR having to face the challenges of the 21st Century he did not stipulate that this would happen under State ownership. The bald fact of the matter seems to be that the Government is spending money on lines which it thinks can be fattened up for privatisation, while refusing to recognise its social obligations even when local people as in the Settle to Carlisle instance are prepared to support their services with cash and custom.

If the Government's plan made actuarial sense, it could be defended for all its shabbiness. But it runs counter to the principles of self-help on which the Conservatives in particular pride themselves. It ignores the point that estimates for repair costs along the line have varied over the years. And it completely overlooks the practical reasons which kept the line in being for so long, plus the revival of local commuter trade. Thousands of people in Scotland for example have lost a useful direct train route via Carlisle and Settle to the English Midlands and London, yet all that concerns Ministers seems to be the number of tourists visiting the Dales and Lake District.

Mr Mitchell was unwise to sneer at 'pleasure routes for railway archaeologists' yesterday. Though distinctive, the Settle to Carlisle is not a museum piece but an active part of the economy. Railway enthusiasts alone could not have kept the line going for so long, but plain economics have proved it deserves a chance. The Government's plan is both a betrayal of honest enthusiasm and an abdication of social responsibility. It stinks."

Other papers were equally scathing at the Government's decision. An editorial in the Bradford 'Telegraph and Argus' headed 'A cop-out that settles nothing' opened:

"Those who have fought long and hard to save the Settle–Carlisle rail link are right to feel betrayed by yesterday's cop-out announcement that it must be axed unless a private company takes it over.

As the chairman of West Yorkshire's Passenger Transport Authority has pointed out, there was a firm understanding that if the authority and consortium of local councils could raise enough money to put the Ribblehead Viaduct in good order, the line would be spared. They have kept their part of the deal but the Government has now changed its mind."

After questioning the Government's case for writing-off the line as all but a tourist attraction and dismissing the idea of bus substitution, the leader writer continued:

"It is particularly shortsighted, though, to ignore the long-term commercial potential of the line which it has been suggested could be revitalised as a main-line route between West Yorkshire and Glasgow or incorporated into a vital freight-transport artery running the length of the country from the Channel Tunnel. Such potential is hardly likely to be fulfilled by a private company dedicated to running a sort of Disneyland-on-wheels across some of the most spectacular scenery in Britain.

There is no doubt that tourism is an important factor. The Settle–Carlisle railway is one of the North's major attractions and brings people – and their money – to the region.

But tourism is only one factor. The railway's future is surely not as a mere fun-run – assuming, of course, that someone could be found to operate it on that basis, which is far from certain. Its future is as a working railway, a key part of the country's transport network.

As those campaigning for the line's survival fight on, which they surely must, that is the point they must keep on stressing."

And 'The Northern Echo', which described the Government's "fudged statement" as "tantamount to a slap in the face for those who have worked so hard to preserve this piece of English heritage", made the valid point that:

"Procrastinating until November, supposedly to consider new evidence, while hoping for a multi-millionaire fairy godmother does not fool anyone. The Government has made it plain that it is not interested in spending money to preserve the railway, has not listened to the logical, economic and passionate arguments, not least from within its own party, and is determined to allow the line to fall into private hands... or into ruin."

There was no doubt that the Government's decision had come as an enormous shock to all those who had been fighting to save the line and who were confidently anticipating a famous victory, tempered only, perhaps, by one or two face saving conditions to get British Rail and its senior management off the hook. FOSCLA chairman Brian Sutcliffe described it as a "disgraceful decision", a view echoed by former Joint Action Committee chairman Dr John Whitelegg who remarked: "If we are going to continue to play snakes and ladders with the future of the line, we should go right back to the beginning and have another public hearing. The case for the line is now totally different."

The local authorities were equally upset. For Cumbria, Peter Robinson said the decision represented a body blow to hopes of saving the line. "The local authorities have extended themselves well beyond what is expected of them in financial terms and everyone is unpleasantly surprised by the minister's decision," he said. Carlisle's director of economic planning, Mr John Bell, added: "The Government has completely failed to grasp the groundswell of public opinion."

An even more forthright condemnation came from Councillor Michael Simmons, chairman of the West Yorkshire Passenger Transport Authority. He called for the immediate resignation of public transport minister David Mitchell who should not have been put in the position of working with the local authorities and setting targets which they had met, and then letting them down in this way. "He should resign and take the consequences for misleading those who had worked so hard to protect the line," exclaimed Councillor Simmons.

After that there was little more to be said. The first battle for the Settle–Carlisle line appeared to be over. But another looked likely to begin.

23

'SHARP PRACTICE' AND 'THE SMELL OF ROTTEN FISH'

"Reading between the lines, it seems the Secretary of State for Transport has 'instructed' the two TUCCs concerned to report only on the hardship to the commuter user. The investigative nature of the hearings is much too narrow and savours of sharp practice."

Bill Butler in a letter to the 'Yorkshire Post' published on 27th August 1988.

This is the chapter I'd have given anything not to have written. Instead of celebrating a well deserved victory, those who had fought long and hard to save the Settle–Carlisle line had received a mighty Ministerial body blow. In such circumstances there is only one thing to do: pick yourself up, dust yourself down and start all over again. Even so, it was easier said than done and I had every sympathy for those who, weeks after David Mitchell's announcement to the House of Commons, seemed punch-drunk by it all.

In many respects the Secretary of State for Transport's decision that he was 'minded' to consent to British Rail's proposal to close the line was the worst outcome of all. Had he opted for closure there and then, everybody would have known where they stood. But by deferring the decision until November, ostensibly to allow the TUCCs to undertake a further investigation on the hardship to day-to-day users, but largely to allow time for some Lady Bountiful, or as David Mitchell was to put it a 'Mr Big', to turn up and save the line was simply tempting providence.

Meanwhile, there was work to be done. First I wrote a perfunctory letter to Mr Mitchell expressing our – for I was writing on behalf of the Yorkshire area of the Railway Development Society – disappointment and, indeed, anger at the Government's decision. I also wrote to my MP. Then I turned my attention to British

Rail. Here, surprisingly, I felt the prospects might be more prom-
ising – thanks to the new local service introduced in July 1986.

The possibility of a daily service calling at all the Dales Rail
stations but designed largely for commuters travelling to and from
Carlisle had been raised at the Public Hearing in April 1986. Then
British Rail had emphasised that such a service, should it come to
fruition, would be run on a charter basis so as to avoid the requirements of the Transport Act 1962 should it ultimately be decided
to close the line – a point confirmed by their legal representative,
Mr Michael Harrison QC. Ron Cotton had even gone so far as to
explain how integrated ticketing between the British Rail and charter services would work. However, as the projected service was
purely speculation at the time of the hearing, it was only mentioned
in passing in the TUCCs December 1986 report.

Nevertheless I was surprised that when the new service was introduced during the summer of 1986 it wasn't a charter service at all.
Indeed, British Rail went to considerable lengths to promote it as
a new local service. This struck me at the time as something that
might be worth banking for a rainy day. Now that rainy day had
arrived with a vengeance.

So I wrote to the Secretary of the British Railways Board, pointing out that the new service had been introduced two years after
publication of the last closure notice in 1984. Therefore, as users
of it were unable to object to a proposal to discontinue it before
it had ever been thought of, let alone introduced, it would be
necessary for British Rail to issue a new closure proposal taking
into account the changed circumstances. In other words, it was a
case of 'Return to Go' and start all over again!

Then I put my case to the TUCCs and sought their support, but
with little success. Whilst the North Western committee had "every
sympathy" with users of the new local service, their interpretation
of the statute was that the new service was "an extension, albeit a
very significant extension, of the Dales Rail service." This was
utter bunk and I told them so. As for the North East TUCC, they
felt it was "primarily an issue for British Rail and the Secretary of
State to sort out." Frankly, I was disappointed as I'd expected
more from the official rail users watchdogs.

True, the TUCCs had been placed in a cleft stick. Having already
been told that the Secretary of State considered "guaranteed substitute bus services would cater adequately for the majority of those
who now use the line for day-to-day essential transport purposes",

the committees were now required to provide a supplementary report on whether there had been any changes in the use of the line that would lead them to modify their original advice. They were also asked to quantify the number of daily commuters and state how many would find substitute bus services an inadequate alternative. Then, to turn the knife still more, the TUCCs had to advise on the "route, frequency and timing" of the buses.

As David Mitchell was on record as having said this was all being done "to prevent a legal challenge if we decide to close the line," it was tantamount to asking the TUCCs to dig their own graves. Above all, it represented a new height in cynicism regarding the role of the official rail users watchdog in railway closure proposals.

What then would I have done had I still been chairman of the North East TUCC? The answer is simple. I would have had no truck with it and resigned there and then. As it was several members privately expressed their dismay and concern at the Government's decision and a number considered resignation. Nevertheless, I was appalled to learn that the minutes of my old committee didn't record a single word of disappointment or regret at the turn of events.

Nor did the TUCCs help themselves by seeming to reject requests from the local authorities, myself and others for their new round of deliberations to include some form of Public Hearing. A spokesman for the committees told Alan Whitehouse of the 'Yorkshire Post': "As far as we are concerned we are not in the realms of a new Public Hearing." This did not impress Councillor Michael Simmons, chairman of the West Yorkshire Passenger Transport Authority, who remarked: "It sounds as though the TUCCs have been got at." Sadly, I was inclined to believe this was true.

Fortunately the local authorities were made of sterner stuff. Councillor Bill Cameron, who headed the consortium of councils striving to save the line, vowed the fight would continue even though tactics would have to be changed to meet the new circumstances. First, it was accepted that some form of privatisation was probably inevitable; so the condition regarding the line remaining in British Rail ownership if it were to receive local authority support was withdrawn. However, the councils remained insistent that any financial backing from them was dependant on the provision of services throughout the year with train frequencies and journey times being at least as good as those offered at present. They also stressed that the Settle–Carlisle line should remain part of the national network and that trains must have access to both Leeds and Carlisle stations.

On 18th June, a 'Metro Pullman' steam excursion headed by A4 Pacific 'SIR NIGEL GRESLEY' left Leeds for Carlisle with a party of local MPs, civic dignitaries, media representatives and several hundred ordinary enthusiasts. What had originally been envisaged as a 'celebration' journey to mark the line's reprieve turned out to be more akin to a funeral cortege-cum-council of war. The irony of it all was that David Mitchell had been invited as guest of honour. Nor, to his credit, did he chicken out. Apart from a little mild heckling when he opened the refurbished waiting room at Garsdale, he was politely if coolly received. Nevertheless, there was an undercurrent of hostility, directed not so much at the Minister as to those above him responsible for the about-turn decision.

Neither Bill Cameron nor Michael Simmons pulled any punches at a news conference held in Carlisle. Councillor Simmons claimed that David Mitchell had wanted to save the line but had been overruled by "a political advisor at No 10" (Mr Greg Bourne). The Minister put on a brave face but refused to be drawn on whether he'd been got at, other than to say that had he found the decision unacceptable he would have resigned from the Government. As to the future, he saw the line's salvation in the hands of a 'Mr Big' but, failing that, he would consider proposals from a consortium of local authorities and interested private sector parties. A prospectus for the sale of the line was being drafted and should be ready at the end of July.

A fascinating incident took place during the buffet lunch that followed. I was sitting in a corner quietly tucking into my salad when Mr Mitchell sidled up. Frankly, I was not anxious to engage in conversation for fear I might say something rude! He said he'd noted I was still active in the campaign to save the line and then warned me to steer clear of the legal argument, adding that he had received advice on the validity of the Government's stance.

This puzzled me. Obviously he was aware of the contents of my letter to British Rail putting the case for a new closure proposal. And should this case be tested in the courts, it could undoubtedly put back his timetable for privatisation or closure. But why should he lean on me? I hardly felt he was concerned I might incur considerable litigation costs. Therefore, was it because my case for a new closure proposal was even stronger than I had thought? Whatever the reason, it only strenghtened my resolve to pursue the legal tack. Quite apart from anything else, I don't like being leaned upon.

On 1st July the North Western and North East TUCCs published a joint notice inviting Settle–Carlisle line users to submit written evidence for consideration in the preparation of their supplementary report. Much of the notice, which appeared in the 'Yorkshire Post' and a number of local papers and was displayed at stations on or near the line, comprised of text from a letter the TUCCs had received from the Department of Transport setting out their 'marching orders'. After describing in detail the advice sought from the TUCCs regarding substitute bus services, the notice concluded:

"Accordingly, to assist in fulfilling their obligations under Section 56(10) of the Transport Act 1962, the Committees request any user of any service affected, and any body representing such users who wish to offer any evidence relevant to change in usage or use of the trains for essential day-to-day transport purposes, to write to either of them by 1 August 1988."

What was one to make of this? The Joint Action Committee and FOSCLA were in no doubt. It was yet another opportunity to 'carry on objecting'! They quickly ran off some pro formas and started working the trains. By the end of the month a team of volunteers headed by Peter Shaw had collected almost 8,000 'new objections', the only difference being that neither they, nor the 2,000 or so letters submitted directly to the TUCCs, ranked as valid objections in accordance with the Transport Act 1962. Nevertheless, it was a commendable and worthwhile effort which underlined that interest and concern regarding the future of the line had not diminished.

For my part I felt it important to stress that this latest round of consultations was not an adequate alternative to a new closure proposal. For a start the grounds for submitting evidence were restricted. So I went through the notice, word for word, and came up with a draft which pressed the TUCCs to urge the Secretary of State to refuse consent to closure. Should he discard this advice – as seemed likely – then the TUCCs should use all their authority and influence to seek a new closure proposal.

After going over the draft with David Pickersgill, who compiles and edits the Yorkshire RDS annual reports and added a useful paragraph regarding the Government's attitude towards the Public Service Obligation (PSO) grant, it was sent to both TUCCs as evidence.

The Government changes on 25th July were to produce a ripple of excitement when it became known that David Mitchell had been dropped. Was he yet another casualty of the Settle–Carlisle closure saga? 'Yorkshire Post' political correspondent Phil Murphy reported:

"The moves add one Minister to the Cabinet, involve five promotions, allow three MPs to leave office voluntarily – two with knighthoods – and mean two sackings ... Mr Michael Portillo replaces the hapless Mr David Mitchell at the Department of Transport. Mr Mitchell is said to have requested a switch to the backbenches for family reasons, but there has been sustained criticism of his performance at the Department of Transport."

Of Mr Portillo, I knew little. Young – he was only 35 – and a former Parliamentary Private Secretary to John Moore when the latter was at Transport, the new Minister for Public Transport entered the Government from the Whips office. Before entering Parliament he had been an oil industry consultant. Michael Portillo was considered to be to the right of the Conservative Party and something of a high-flyer. One political pundit had him down as the next Prime Minister but one. If so, I hoped he didn't want to go down in history as the chap who closed the Settle–Carlisle line.

At the beginning of August, Lazard Brothers – the merchant bankers – issued a glossy 48-page brochure 'Settle–Carlisle Railway – Background Information'. Prepared by British Rail and Lazards, it was not the prospectus I'd expected in that it was singularly short on information. Indeed, it blandly explained it did "not purport to give a comprehensive description of the line" whilst there was the usual 'health warning' that it did not "constitute an offer or an invitation for the public to subscribe for or purchase any securities." And whilst stating further details would be available to prospective purchasers, what little information it did provide was sufficient to frighten off all but the financially naive.

But for the disclosure that the sale included the freehold of the Midland Hotel at Lazonby, I could see little to tempt prospective railway operators and much to deter them. For a start, they would not be allowed to run trains to and from Leeds, services having to start or terminate at Hellifield! As a sop, British Rail would allow them to "charter trains to convey passengers from Leeds to Hellifield, where they will change trains. These trains will not stop at intermediate stations." So much for the Bradford traffic which, together with that from Keighley and Skipton, would have to rely on the infrequent Leeds–Morecambe trains which "normally consist of two cars only and therefore are not capable of taking large numbers of people to Hellifield." You can say that again!

Even more serious was the absence of any information relating to costs and revenue. The brochure simply stated that as the Settle–Carlisle line was operated as an integral part of the British Rail network, it was "not possible to establish the traffic or revenue directly attributable to the line." Likewise, when it came to costs, we were told that the line "has been managed as an integral part of the Provincial Sector and, as a result, separate historic cost data for the line is not available." Frankly, this was priceless and could be discarded to a bottom drawer.

Also in August, Michael Portillo sensibly agreed to put the closure timetable back a month. The final date for offers for the line was now 31st October, the TUCCs had until the end of November to file their supplementary report, whilst the Government's decision would now be made early in 1989. Even the line itself got a stay of execution should no one from the private sector take it on. For instead of closing in March, it would now remain open until 13th May to coincide with the conclusion of the 1988–89 timetable.

The TUCCs also bowed to public pressure and agreed to hold "joint meetings in public" – Public Hearings by any other name. I warmly welcomed the apparent change of heart. There would be two days in Appleby chaired by the North Western's Mrs Olive Clarke on 23rd and 24th September, and two days in Settle under my successor, Professor Paul Fairest, on 30th September and 1st October. However, the TUCCs announcement that the meetings were being held so those who had responded to their notice could "add any points to the information you have already supplied" struck me as unduly restrictive.

Needless to say I was anxious to have my say and planned to speak at both venues; as an individual user at Appleby and on behalf of the Yorkshire RDS at Settle. Although I had already sampled Public Hearings following my switch in role from TUCC chairman to objector, I was conscious that when it came to Settle–Carlisle I had to present a strong, well structured case. Then, being aware of my limitations as a speaker, I knew I could not rely on getting by on eloquence alone. My submission would require much research and need to be drafted into a text which would stand on its own account.

My position was complicated by the fact that I had no wish to give the impression of having a chip on my shoulder following my 'sacking' from the official watchdog job; not least because there was no chip, save perhaps at the manner in which my departure from the North East TUCC was effected. Indeed, I was rather enjoying my new role as a 'privatised' watchdog for the RDS.

Nevertheless, I would be less than frank if I were to withhold my disappointment at the somewhat muted and detached approach that Professor Fairest appeared to have adopted as chairman of the North East TUCC. In extended correspondence with him on Settle–Carlisle and other matters, I had gained the impression that, rather than seeing himself as a champion of rail users, he was more anxious to protect British Rail from the criticism of people like myself. Therefore, whilst I sought neither favour nor privilege as a former TUCC chairman, I knew I had to tread carefully. And while not wishing to antagonise former colleagues and friends, I was not prepared to pull my punches when it came to presenting my case.

Until I received a tip-off two days before the Appleby meeting, I didn't know that British Rail would be represented at what I termed the supplementary hearings. Therefore, I'd not drafted any questions to put to them via the chair. This was just as well for the redoubtable Olive Clarke made it quite clear in her opening statement that the British Rail team – Mr Hugh Donovan, a barrister; solicitor Timothy Reardon, making a return visit; Mark Causebrook, the route manager based in York; and a Mr Dennis from Provincial Sector headquarters in London – were there to assist the TUCCs "by providing any factual information" but they "would not answer any questions from the floor."

Although this was par for the course, I saw no reason why British Rail needed to be shielded from its customers by the protective skirts of the TUCC. So whilst waiting my turn to speak, I scribbled out something which, if able to penetrate the formidable shield of Mrs Clarke and Mr Donovan, might cause a bit of a stir.

My Appleby submission was as a user of the new local service since July 1986. I dismissed the North Western TUCC's contention that it was an extension of Dales Rail which, of course, had continued to operate as a separate service after the new local trains were introduced. As for the claim that the procedures adopted by the TUCCs would enable new users to "effectively communicate their views", I said this was countered by the restrictions placed by the TUCCs in their quest for new evidence and did not compensate users for the loss of their statutory rights of objection.

On completing my set piece, I asked Mrs Clarke if I could put a question to British Rail through the chair. After looking to her secretary John Moorhouse who smiled and nodded, she replied: "Yes, most certainly." I referred first to the Lazard Brothers brochure which stated that, as the Settle–Carlisle line was operated as an integral part of the British Rail network, it was not possible to establish the revenue or costs attributable to the line. Recalling how British Rail's 'Financial Case for Closure' stated an annual revenue of £1 million against costs of £1.9 million, I asked: "In light of the statements in the Lazard Brothers brochure, how does British Rail explain its use of the figures in its case for closure which we now learn they are not able to provide?"

Mrs Clarke turned to the British Rail table and asked if they were prepared to explain the apparent contradiction. "No madam, we are not," replied Mr Hugh Donovan. His response was greeted with derisive laughter and won him pride of place in the following morning's 'Yorkshire Post' which described British Rail's closure case as lying "in tatters."

Later, Bradford Grammar School master Dr Robin Sisson, who had enlivened the proceedings with a number of interjections, returned to the question of the line's finances. He fared no better than me, save that he prompted Sir Reginald Sheffield, one of the North East TUCC's new intake of members, to draw Mrs Clarke's attention to a Government statement made by the Earl of Caithness in 1986 to the effect that British Rail should make financial information available so objectors could judge whether it had made its case for closure. Sir Reginald had undoubtedly done his homework.

However, the most telling contribution that day came from FOSCLA secretary Peter Shaw. Speaking in a personal capacity, he strongly rebuked the TUCCs for restricting representations to 'change in usage' or 'use of the trains for day to day essential transport purposes.' There was, he said, an analogy between the current hearings and those held in 1986. Then it was British Rail who tried to restrict the evidence, now it was the TUCCs themselves. A good point.

He had also unearthed a letter British Rail chairman Sir Robert Reid had written to Sir Nicholas Bonsor MP on 2nd August 1988. This blandly asserted: 'Now that the Minister has announced his decision on the Settle and Carlisle railway, I am sure you will agree that it serves no useful purpose to rake over the numerous arguments for and against the line's retention that have been put forward in recent years.' To this, Peter Shaw retorted that Sir Robert knew full well that the Minister had not yet announced his decision about the line, yet he was trying to dissuade an MP from becoming involved by relaying false information to make him think the issue was closed. Another good point.

To round off a good innings, Peter Shaw was able to answer the question North East TUCC member Fred Fieldhouse had put to British Rail asking how many trains had been diverted over the Settle–Carlisle line. Needless to say, the railway representatives hadn't a clue; so Peter obliged: since the last Public Hearings there had been 218 diversions over 18 days during the 1986–87 fiscal year, 311 on 21 days during 1987–88, and 89 on 4 days during 1988–89.

The following morning Bill Cameron led for Cumbria County Council and the Joint Councils Steering Group. He said that by not accepting the conclusions of the original TUCC's report, the Secretary of State for Transport had done the committees a "grave disservice" by implicitly challenging their painstaking work and the validity of their findings. This had cast doubts on the value of the whole closure procedure under the Transport Act 1962. The only virtue Councillor Cameron saw was that the TUCC's supplementary report could only reinforce their original conclusions. He warned that should the final outcome prove unsatisfactory, the shortcomings of the proceedings would be tested in the courts.

The other star performance was undoubtedly that of Michael Shrimpton, the barrister who had advised the Joint Action Committee during the 1986 hearings but who, on this occasion, was speaking as an individual user. Recalling his earlier encounters with British Rail's silk, Michael Harrison QC, Mr Shrimpton modestly described himself as "a mere polyester!" He then proceeded to deliver a scintillating legal submission in which, among other things, he claimed that the Secretary of State for Transport had acted illegally. Warming to his theme, Mr Shrimpton painted a scenario of thousands of objectors seeking legal aid in order to obtain a judicial review of the Settle–Carlisle closure. Indeed, the whole issue could end up at the European Court of Justice. This was swashbuckling advocacy at its best.

By contrast, my second and more extended innings at Settle the following Friday, although also geared to the legal argument, was a more stolid affair. Nevertheless, I pulled out all the stops and was more confident than ever of the validity of my case.

I stressed the grounds for a new closure proposal because the new local service had been introduced two years after publication of the last closure notice. As it was not possible to use a service prior to its introduction, nor object to its closure at a time when it did not exist, users of the new local service had been deprived of their statutory rights of objection.

In expressing my disappointment that the TUCCs had declined to support the case for a new closure proposal, I reminded them that it was following the stand taken by the Yorkshire TUCC in 1984 that British Rail had re-issued closure proposals for Goole–Gilberdyke, Huddersfield–Denby Dale, Goose Hill–Wath Road and, of course, Settle–Carlisle. Given that British Rail had recently published a new closure proposal for Altofts, where since the original notice was issued in 1985 the service had been cut by 75 per cent, it was illogical not to issue a new proposal for Settle–Carlisle where the number of trains had more than doubled, as had the number of people using the line.

Turning to the Government's role, I quoted from a letter published in the 'Yorkshire Post' on 27th August from former TUCC member Bill Butler who had written:

"Reading between the lines, it seems the Secretary of State for Transport has 'instructed' the two TUCCs concerned to report only on the hardship to the commuter user. The investigative nature of the hearings is much too narrow and savours of sharp practice."

"Sadly," I continued, reverting to my own text, "sharp practice has been the hallmark of the Settle–Carlisle closure saga ever since 1981 when British Rail maintained that it had no plans to close the line. But if sharp practice is something we have come to expect from British Rail with regard to Settle–Carlisle – with the honourable exception of Colin Driver, Ron Cotton and one or two others – it is not something which I, in my innocence, anticipated from the Government; no doubt encouraged by the Department of Transport."

Why, I asked, had David Mitchell come down so firmly on the side of British Rail in rejecting the case for a new closure proposal? "No doubt for the same reason as his attempt to get British Rail off the hook by invoking Section 56(10) of the Act to – and I quote – 'prevent a legal challenge if we decide to close the line.' And who is he using to do his dirty work? Why, the TUCCs of course

– the statutory bodies set up to represent the views of rail users. Not only does this stamp of 'sharp practice', it also evokes more than a smell of rotten fish about it! Not least, it undermines the credibility of the TUCCs."

My second legal tack was at British Rail's failure to publish particulars of alternative services as they were required to by the Act. This was because neither they nor anyone else knew what those services might be should the line be privatised. Nor were there any particulars of the alternative bus services on which the TUCCs had to advise the Secretary of State on the routes, frequency and timing.

Taken together we had a situation where users of the new local service were unable to exercise their statutory right of objection and British Rail had not provided particulars of any alternative services – other than the rail service via Carnforth – because they had no idea what they would be. As a consequence the closure proposal was fatally flawed. Therefore, when it was decided what the alternative services were to be, British Rail would have to issue a new closure proposal to take into account all the changed circumstances.

I concluded: "It is only by returning to go and starting all over again, that it will be possible to eradicate the stamp of sharp practice and dispel the smell of rotten fish, not to say the elements of utter farce that have surrounded this closure proposal from the very beginning. Therefore, British Rail should do the decent and honourable thing and cancel the closure proposal forthwith." My effort which had lasted a good twenty minutes won a round of applause from the body of the Victoria Hall.

During the afternoon session, Councillor Eddie Scott, who was chairman of the West Yorkshire PTA's rail working group, took up my legal theme. Describing the requirements of the TUCCs to submit a supplementary report as an "unnecessary charade," he said Ministers at the Department of Transport had "misinformed themselves on the correct way to deal with closure proposals of such complexity." Whilst he anticipated the TUCCs would "reinforce and strengthen" their original conclusions, Councillor Scott warned that should the Secretary of State's response prove unfavourable the "shortcomings of these proceedings will be tested more fully in the courts."

Throughout the supplementary hearings I could not help feeling that I'd been cast in the role of Banquo's ghost! Certainly I'd seen and heard nearly all of it before, albeit from a different vantage point; for it had been a re-run of the 1986 hearings. Far from being concerned with the frequencies and timings of alternative bus services, the question of bus substitution seldom arose. And when it did, it was invariably dismissed out of hand; most notably by Richard Watts whose case was backed by his own booklet 'Bustitution – The Case Exploded!' (RDS, £1.80) – a title that says it all.

As for British Rail, they lacked the advantage someone of Ron Cotton's calibre would have added to the proceedings. True, Mark Causebrook did his best. But his oft repeated response that he'd been advised "not to answer the question" provided a clear indication of the reason behind the presence of Mr Hugh Donovan, the barrister. As for Mr Donovan, his moment came when he delivered an eloquent vote of thanks to the TUCCs.

For myself, I felt my role in the long running Settle–Carlisle drama was all but over. Certainly, there was little more to be said. Quite what former TUCC colleagues made of my submission was difficult to assess. Therefore I was pleased when, a couple of days later, I received a note from one congratulating me for my effort and for saying "all the things that needed to be said."

. Notwithstanding the doubts surrounding their legal propriety, the supplementary hearings proved worthwhile; not least because they enabled objectors to top-up their submissions of over two years ago and reaffirm their commitment and support for the Settle–Carlisle line. This mood was captured by Olive Clarke at the conclusion of the final session at Settle when she told users that it was now up to the TUCCs "to prove ourselves worthy of the splendid job you've all done." Certainly, seasoned campaigners like Ruth Annison, Beata and Andrew Connell, Graham Nuttall (and Ruswarp), David Smith, Oliver Lovell, and Messrs Hodgkins, Tardiff, Regardsoe and Little are but a few of the names that belong to any Settle–Carlisle role of honour.

So, too, does Bill Butler MBE who wrote the 'report within a report' on tourism in the original TUCCs document. He had retired from the North East committee but had retained his interest in railway matters and I had been pleased to see him at Settle on the Friday morning. Wearing, as always, his tourism hat, he was covering the hearing for the Yorkshire and Humberside Tourist Board. I was most upset to learn afterwards that later that day he had become ill and admitted himself to the local hospital where he died the following day. Bill Butler's positive proposals for the future development of the whole concept of Settle–Carlisle remain a legacy which should not be allowed to go unnoticed.

Following the supplementary hearings it was largely a waiting game. British Rail came out with a revised financial case for closure towards the end of October. Annual revenue was now assessed at between £1 million and £1.7 million against costs of £2 million. Not even the marked reduction in the cost of repair for Ribblehead Viaduct – down from £4.3 million to £2.7 million – could persuade them not to re-affirm their decision to close the line. This came as no surprise. Nor did the fact that the figures appeared to have been massaged to show the line in the worst possible light. Indeed, they were hardly worthy of scrutiny and were lambasted by the Joint Council Steering Group and FOSCLA. Even Ron Cotton said the figures had not been fairly presented.

There was a flurry of interest on the 31st October – the last date for receipt of 'offers' for the line at the offices at Lazard Brothers – when it became known that amongst the contenders was a company trading as Settle and Carlisle Ltd who had plans for the Venice–Simplon Orient Express to run on the line. There was speculation, too, that the line might also be used by freight traffic generated by the Channel Tunnel. If some agreement could be made with the local authorities for the provision of a local service, I felt that the line might still be in with a chance. Failing that, it would probably all end up in the High Court. In the meantime we would simply have to wait and see.

The TUCCs duly submitted their supplementary report to the Secretary of State for Transport at the end of November and at the beginning of December published their conclusions. These only ran to two pages of A4 and, if representative of the remainder, struck me as a rather lack lustre effort. But, then, perhaps I was prejudiced! The important thing was that they had reiterated that closure would cause hardship for those who used the line for leisure and essential purposes and "therefore again strongly (albeit not emphatically!) recommend that consent to closure be refused and the lines (Settle–Carlisle plus Blackburn–Hellifield) be developed jointly with local authorities and other interested groups." Attached was a complex timetable of substitute bus services. Perhaps it had been designed to put the Secretary of State off the idea of 'bustitution'!

Of greater interest and probably far more significant was the 'Case for Retention' drawn up by the Joint Councils Steering Group, headed by Cumbria and Lancashire County Councils together with the West Yorkshire Passenger Transport Authority. This submission provided the most comprehensive update of the whole situation and was presented to Michael Portillo, the Minister for Public Transport, at a meeting in Carlisle on 12th December.

The Joint Councils case made it quite clear that British Rail's closure proposal related to a service which no longer ran, following the introduction of the new local service; emphasised that the Settle–Carlisle line was one of the Provincial sector's most financially successful routes; dismissed British Rail's updated financial case for closure as inconclusive; and emphasised that the line should be retained and developed within British Rail's national network.

Needless to say, I was particularly interested to see what the report said about the legal aspects of the closure proposal, which had formed a large part of my submission at the supplementary hearings even though they were not mentioned in the conclusion to the latest TUCC report. I was not disappointed.

In the summary to their report, the Joint Councils stated:

"If the Government accepted that the case for approval of even the 1983 closure proposals could not be determined without fresh evidence, then the Councils believe it should have required British Rail to institute fresh proceedings based on current levels of service. The request to the TUCCs for further evidence and specification of substitute bus services was inappropriately timed and went beyond their normal remit. In addition, the Secretary of State's own position has been compromised by the announcement that he was 'minded' to consent to closure and his directive to British Rail to seek a buyer for the line in advance of determination of the closure application."

This was music to my ears, especially as in the body of the report the Joint Councils developed the case that "the procedures followed in this case by both the British Railways Board and Secretary of State for Transport have been fatally flawed, and that any result other than refusal of consent to closure by the Secretary of State is open to challenge in the Courts."

The report then listed the principal reasons which had made the Joint Councils arrive at this view:

- the radically different level and nature of the services operating in 1988 from those operating at the time of the original closure proceedings;
- the inadequate information supplied by British Rail on alter-

native services, both bus and rail;

● the unreasonable nature of the request to the TUCCs effectively to produce the information lacking in British Rail's own case;

● the timing of the request to the TUCCs to produce a supplementary report, given the nature of the matters they were directed to deal with;

● the inevitable confusions caused by the parallel directive to seek a private buyer;

● the prejudicial nature of the announcement on 16th May 1988 that the Secretary of State was minded to approve closure.

I was delighted with these conclusions by the Joint Councils. Not only had they taken all the points I'd made on board, they had also come up with a number of other valid conclusions themselves; not least the role of the TUCCs in providing information that should have come from British Rail, the confusion with regard to the privatisation of the line and, perhaps above all, the prejudicial nature of the role of the Secretary of State for Transport himself.

I liked it! Not least because it set the scene for proceedings in the High Court which could well be the only way the whole question of the future of the Settle–Carlisle line would be resolved. This point was stressed to Michael Portillo at the meeting in Carlisle when Councillor Michael Simmons of the West Yorkshire PTA said that the Joint Councils would seek a judicial review if the line closed or a privatisation sale ended in bankruptcy.

And what of privatisation? As the year drew to its close, the prospects seemed to be on the wane. According to Alan Whitehouse, writing in the 'Yorkshire Post', all but two of the original 12 bids had been rejected by British Rail and their advisors Lazard Brothers. I was not surprised if some of the antics British Rail were reputed to be up to were anything to go by.

Take the case of running powers into Leeds, essential for a private operator if he was to make a success of running the Settle–Carlisle line. A copy of a 'confidential' report from the Provincial Manager (Eastern) to the Co-ordinator, Private Capital of the British Railways Board at Room D414 at Paddington station landed on a number of desks, including my own. It stated that a "minimum requirement" of five drivers and five guards would be required. The private operator would be charged "the full annual cost" of not less than £155,000 for these drivers and guards who, between them, would spend only 20 hours a week actually manning trains or waiting at Leeds for their return trip to Skipton, where the private operators crew would take over. A rip off!

24

JOURNEY'S END – A FAMOUS VICTORY!

"This railway line remains a British Rail railway line. But, let's face it, it's different from most railway lines: it's historic, it's scenic, it has great tourism interests. So this is a very good railway line for a partnership between the public sector, British Rail, and the private sector who have lots of good ideas of how to make the most of it."

> Michael Portillo MP, Minister of
> State for Transport, speaking on
> BBC Radio Leeds on 12th April 1989.

By the beginning of 1989 there was no doubt that many of those campaigning against closure of the Settle–Carlisle were beginning to feel battle weary. And who could blame them? They had won the argument hands down. They had also seen their advocacy matched by results. Since the battle proper began in 1983, usage of the line had increased from 93,000 to some 450,000 journeys a year. Far from being a drain on British Rail's resources, the line was now one of the best performers in the Provincial sector.

Little wonder, therefore, that the alliance of local authorities, user groups and innumerable individuals felt frustrated. They had pulled out all the stops, yet that final victory continued to elude them. Now there was little they could do but wait.

Not that the lobbying stopped. In a valiant last ditch effort, representatives of businesses along the line under the umbrella of the Settle–Carlisle Railway Business Liaison Group made direct representations to 10 Downing Street. A nine-strong delegation, headed by the indefatigable Ruth Annison of Hawes, handed in a report drawing the Prime Minister's attention to the vital role the line played in the local economy.

There was also a flurry of activity to coincide with the Richmondshire by-election following Sir Leon Brittan's departure to Brussels.

However, the most positive idea to emerge came from Councillor Michael Simmons, the high-profile chairman of the West Yorkshire Passenger Transport Authority. He suggested to Michael Portillo, the Minister for Public Transport, that in the absence of a suitable private sector candidate to take over the line, the Government should consider a "tripartite deal" in which BR, the local authorities and a new charitable trust would take over responsibilities for the line.

By the end of February it looked as if the Government had 'missed the boat' if it really planned to have the line in the private sector in time for the summer season, if only because the deadline for British Rail to issue redundancy notices had passed. As if in recognition of this, Michael Portillo announced that the date for 'closure' would be put back until October.

When asked to comment on this by the 'Yorkshire Post', I replied that the whole issue had become a farce. "It is time for British Rail and the Government to swallow their pride and admit there is no case for closure," I added.

Meanwhile, traffic on the line was booming. During half-term and the Easter school holidays overcrowding was the order of the day. So, too, were dirty windows! Yet another example of British Rail management's couldn't care less attitude with regard to the line and its customers. Then, during March weekends there was the opportunity to travel over the line in style by InterCity. Yes, it was diversions time again.

Unfortunately, my wife and I were only able to fit in two Saturday trips. On both occasions we travelled down to Carlisle on the 08.25 from Leeds in the shabby Mark 2 stock designated to the line. I even had a go at the windows myself with some Windolene – both inside and out – to ensure a better view! A case of the 'do it yourself railway'!

Returning on the 12.20 Carlisle–Euston was like travelling in a different world, especially as we plumped for the Bargain First and travelled in one of the 'new' Buffet Open First's. These coaches have been converted with flair and imagination from Mark 2F First Class saloons to provide the nearest you'll get to a 'club car' on British Rail. Together with our Marks and Spencer cuisine it made travel over 'England's Greatest Historical Scenic Route' a real treat – especially as we were blessed with good weather too.

On one journey we were treated to an apt reminder why the Settle–Carlisle was built in the first place – for express trains to run over the hills at speed. We left Carlisle 18 minutes late yet arrived at Hellifield spot on time at 14.06. A month or so before I'd been on the 08.25 from Leeds which left Settle over half-an-hour late but was only 2 minutes down on arrival in Carlisle! A clear case that there was far too much slack or recovery time in the timetable.

When I had spoken at the Annual General Meeting of the Joint Action Committee at Settle in January, I pointed out that it would be nice to think the Secretary of State for Transport would see the error of his ways in his earlier decision that he was 'minded' to consent to closure, and that he would soon come out with a clear, unequivocal refusal of consent to British Rail's case for closure. For this would be the only solution that would be really acceptable.

Of the two alternatives, one would be for him to consent to closure - full stop. No doubt there would also be some crackpot 'bustitution' solution but, with the possible exception of an educational service between Appleby and Carlisle, it would be doomed to failure. Consent to closure would not necessarily be such a dire decision as it would probably lead to the Joint Councils seeking a judicial review in the High Court.

The other option would be some sort of fudge – and whilst I am not a betting man, if I were I would be inclined to place money on this. I continued: "In many respects it would be the most unsatisfactory result. Yet, unless there were cast iron guarantees relating to the continued future of the line, and a firm commitment to issue a new closure proposal should it be desired to close it in the future, I can see little alternative to reference to the High Court."

I added that users should be on their guard against any fudge in which Ministers sought to twist arms and buy people off against taking legal action so as not to prejudice the future of the line under a private operator. Yet, given British Rail's ineptitude in running the line – with the honourable exception of Ron Cotton and a few others – there was undoubtedly a case for letting someone else have a go.

Therefore, I wasn't altogether surprised at the flurry of speculation at the beginning of April suggesting some sort of a deal was imminent between British Rail and Cumbrian Railways Ltd, a company headed by East Yorkshire businessman Michael Heathcote and Driffield fish farmer and steam locomotive owner Kenneth Ryder. The plan, as reported, was that a new company would be formed split 51–49 per cent between British Rail and Cumbrian

Railways but that, after a year or so, British Rail would pull out altogether. As for the local authorities, they were expected to maintain their financial input.

Needless to say this did not go down well with Bill Cameron and Michael Simmons, not least because no one had taken the trouble to consult them on the issue. FOSCLA, too, felt they had been ignored. Increasingly concerned at the way things appeared to be moving, solicitors had already approached David Keene QC, the silk who had so ably disposed of British Rail in the High Court in the Wortley Curve case. This struck me as a most prudent move.

And so to events of Tuesday 11 April which certainly caught me and most others unaware. I'd a number of business appointments in Leeds that morning and was actually deep in conversation over coffee with a colleague in the lounge of the Queen's Hotel when I was paged to the telephone. It was Roy Holland of the 'Yorkshire Evening Post'. He said they had been tipped off by their London office that Secretary of State Paul Channon would be making a statement on the line that afternoon.

No sooner had I returned to my coffee and I was called to the 'phone again. This time it was Yorkshire Television. They had a crew lined up to interview Michael Portillo in London and asked me to call at the Leeds studio to do a piece. Things were undoubtedly beginning to move.

Moreover, from what the media had gleaned it looked as if the line was going to be saved. But whether it was to be straightforward refusal to consent to closure, as I hoped, or some sort of fudge, as I expected, nobody seemed sure. So we would just have to wait for the Ministerial statement that afternoon.

In the event I wasn't kept in suspense for too long for just after I'd returned to my office I took a call from Chris Ryan, secretary of the Joint Action Committee. He had just been alerted by the Department of Transport that the Secretary of State was going to announce that consent to closure had been refused. In other words, after a battle lasting almost eight years, we had won!

I have to confess the news was almost an anti-climax. Perhaps I was suffering from shell-shock after years of argument and rancour with British Rail over the future of the line. Then, in the past, there had been so many raised hopes which were later dashed. This made it hard to believe that the line had been saved. And on our own terms, too, rather than in the form of some complex fudge. It was almost too good to be true.

Yet there was no doubt about it. One simple sentence in the formal letter dated 11 April from the Department of Transport to the Secretary of the British Railways Board said all that was required:

"The Secretary of State has carefully considered all relevant factors and has decided to refuse consent to the Board's proposal."

We really had won. It was, as Yorkshire Television's Richard Whiteley said to FOSCLA's Brian Sutcliffe and myself on 'Calendar' that night, a "famous victory!"

In Settle, the Union flag was hoisted at the town hall while Councillor Beth Graham cracked a bottle of champagne with railman Ken Keen at the station. No doubt, in Appleby they'd be ringing the church bells to mark the line's reprieve, just as they did in 1866 when the Bill to build it received the Royal Assent.

Michael Simmons hailed the decision as "exceptionally good news", whilst Cumbria's Bill Cameron said he was "over the moon." Bob Cryer MP expressed pleasure that the Government had listened to public opinion. "The case for retaining the line was irrefutable," he continued. "The decision means British Rail must now stop their sabotage by neglect and get down to promoting the line. How they operate it will now be under very close scrutiny."

Overall, my feeling was not so much of jubilation but rather of quiet satisfaction that at long last the right decision had been made, albeit not necessarily for the right reasons. Indeed, it was difficult to fathom just why the Secretary of State had made such a U-turn. It certainly didn't appear to be on the strength of the report I'd spent so much time drafting, let alone the supplementary report submitted by the TUCCs at the end of 1988.

For whilst the Secretary of State accepted closure of the Settle–Carlisle line would cause "some hardship to local residents who now rely on it for day-to-day essential transport purposes", he considered "provision of guaranteed substitute bus services could cater adequately for many such travellers" and added that he did not believe that "hardship in itself" justified retention of the line.

In a stinging rebuke to the TUCCs, the Department of Transport's letter continued:

"The Secretary of State does not accept that closure would cause serious hardship to other categories of users. In particular, the Secretary of State does not agree with the TUCCs view that closure would cause considerable hardship to tourists and rail enthusiasts who would be deprived of the pleasure of using the line."

That struck me as rich, especially as it was said the Secretary of State had never travelled on the line. Perhaps he might have felt differently if he had, or if he had read some of the thousands of eloquent letters of objection to the proposal to close the line. Larry Elliott of 'The Guardian', was nearer the mark when he said the Government had "failed to recognise the deep, almost religious feelings" that surround the line.

Now, I don't know what Paul Channon's pleasures in life are. However, I have little doubt he would consider himself the subject of considerable hardship were he to be deprived of them.

It was left to his deputy, Michael Portillo to get to the heart of the matter. Speaking on BBC Radio Leeds, he stressed that the Settle–Carlisle line was "different from most railway lines: it's historic, it's scenic, it has great tourism interests." How sad that his Secretary of State, no doubt backed by the mandarins at the Department of Transport, seemed unable to grasp the significance of 'England's greatest historical scenic route'.

As for British Rail, they put on a brave face and blandly "welcomed the decision as it would end the uncertainty"! But this was something they could have done by simply withdrawing the closure proposal two or three years earlier when business on the line really took off. Yet, as recently as January 1989, chairman Sir Robert Reid had told Sir Peter Horden MP that: "The current position on the Settle–Carlisle line is that the Secretary of State has agreed to the closure but has deferred it in an effort to find a private purchaser." I'd have liked to have been a fly on the wall when Sir Robert learnt his plans had been thwarted.

However, at the end of the day, those fighting to save the line owed much to Sir Robert and his senior managers. It was British Rail's arrogance, its inclination for being "economical with its interpretation of the statistics" – as a 'Yorkshire Post' editorial put it – and its penchant for scoring 'own goals', which continually undermined its credibility, not least with regard to the cost of repairing the Ribblehead Viaduct.

As the Department of Transport's letter refusing consent to closure pointed out, estimates of costs had changed, "notably those for repairing the Ribblehead Viaduct which have been reduced." It also made an interesting point with regard to the proposed Leeds–Carlisle service when it stated the Secretary of State would not have required British Rail to provide the alternative service via Carnforth had he consented to closure. Perhaps he'd got the message regarding the 'attractions' of Carnforth Down Goods Loop!

Reference to this suggests the Government was ready to consent to closure of the Settle–Carlisle line prior to its transfer to the private sector. If so, why the sudden right-about turn?

Soundings I took the day after the announcement indicated that the legal position played a big part in arriving at the decision. Briefly, the situation was this. Before the line could be privatised, British Rail had to receive the Secretary of State's consent to closure – even if it were just a case of closing it one night so it could 'reopen' under 'new management' the following morning.

Was it that British Rail and the Government were hoping such an arrangement could go through on the nod? I recalled the incident at Carlisle the previous June when the then Minister of Public Transport, David Mitchell, had gone out of his way to urge me not to take up the legal cudgels on behalf of the line. At that time I was ploughing a lonely legal furrow. However, by the time of the supplementary TUCC hearings in the autumn, the Joint Councils had arrived at the same conclusion: simply that the closure proposal was fatally flawed and if British Rail wished to close the line they would have to start the statutory closure procedure all over again.

Nor was this all. For whilst the Joint Councils, Joint Action Committee and FOSCLA now had David Keene QC on standby and were raring to go, sources within British Rail privately indicated that they doubted if their defence would be sustainable in the High Court. Officials at the Department of Transport were also said to be inclined to take a similar view. Given, too, that British Rail's financial case for closure became less plausible with each succeeding year, the Government presumably decided enough was enough. Moreover, it would go down well with public opinion at a time the DOT was under considerable pressure. As for British Rail, the fact that they "welcomed the decision" was a clear indication that they had thrown in the towel.

What, then, of the future now that the Settle–Carlisle and Blackburn–Hellifield lines have been saved? The Secretary of State made it clear that he wished British Rail to work with the local authorities, the private sector, user groups and others "to ensure that the line has a successful future and so the case for closure will not re-emerge."

The scope is enormous. For a start, whilst the line now enjoys an acceptable local service, there is a need to bring back express

trains – and I don't mean Sprinters! Refurbished Mark 2 stock in
Midland Railway red livery is the least one could expect. A Nottingham–Glasgow service for starters, with prospects of a St Pancras–
Glasgow HST service geared towards long distance tourist travel
in the future would be a stride in the right direction.

Then the private sector could play a vital role in the provision
of steam specials and excursions. The once elegant but now sadly
neglected Hellifield station could be developed as the base for
steam operations on the Settle–Carlisle line. Nor should one ignore
the important contribution the largely overlooked Blackburn–Hellifield line could play. A scenic route in its own right, its potential
is not just as a feeder into the Settle–Carlisle line but, with the
reopening of stations in the Ribble Valley, also for use by commuter
services to and from Manchester.

Two days after the announcement of the reprieve, my wife
Muriel and myself set off on what we hoped would be the first of
many celebration journeys. Weather-wise, we could not have chosen a worse morning. It was raining heavily as the 08.25 pulled out
of Leeds. But by the time we reached Settle the rain had stopped
and the patch of blue in the sky over Ribblehead Viaduct seemed
an indication of better days ahead.

Looking back over eight exhausting years of fighting to save the
line, I reflected on the triumphs and disappointments, the laughter
and tears. I particularly recalled the early days, when the campaign
consisted of little more than two enthusiasts, a dog, and a sceptical
TUCC chairman; I remembered the support I'd received from two
MPs, John Watson and Bob Cryer, who paved the way for the
advent of the Joint Councils and Joint Action Committee and the
best organised and financed operation ever mounted to save a
railway. Then there was British Rail's Ron Cotton who, thankfully,
proved more adept at promoting railways than closing them.

During the course of those eight years, thousands of people took
part in the campaign in one way or another. Each played a vital
role. For myself, there were a couple of contributions which, in
retrospect, were probably of some significance. The first was when,
in June 1981, I blew the gaffe about the decision to re-route the
Nottingham–Glasgow service. This lit a long fuse, and it was the
reverberations of the subsequent explosions which ultimately saved
the line.

Second, was my refusal to be brow beaten and intimidated by
British Rail. When, in early 1984, John Moorhouse noted the 'any

user of any service affected' clause in the 1962 Transport Act, I was not prepared to accept British Rail's interpretation of the Act that, to be a valid objector, one had to actually use the section of the line proposed for closure. Standing firm on this and other issues proved a useful delaying tactic and provided more time for the Joint Councils and Joint Action Committee to get their acts together.

But, at the end of the day, it had been a team effort. It was the continual persistance of a hard core of 100 or so people – MPs, Councillors, local government officials, user group members, plus a handful of hardy freelancers – who won the day. Throughout they were encouraged by a largely sympathetic media.

As the train was pulling out of Appleby, I spotted railman Paul Holden on the platform. "Did they ring the church bells?", I called as the train was picking up speed. "No," he replied with a smile, "they don't work!" Which just goes to show that you cannot win 'em all. But we *did* win the battle for Settle–Carlisle. That it was such a hard fight made the victory all the more worthwhile.

DRAMATIS PERSONAE

plus full supporting company of hikers, gricers, businessmen, railway personnel etc.

ABBREVIATIONS USED

APT	Advanced Passenger Train
ASLEF	Associated Society of Locomotive Engineers and Firemen
BTC	British Transport Commission
CBI	Confederation of British Industry
CTCC	Central Transport Consultative Committee
DMU	Diesel Multiple Unit
FOSCLA	Friends of the Settle–Carlisle Line Association
HST	High Speed Train
LMS	London Midland & Scottish Railway
LNER	London & North Eastern Railway
NATO	North Atlantic Treaty Organisation
PSO	Public Service Obligations
PTA	Passenger Transport Authority
PTE	Passenger Transport Executive
QC	Queen's Counsel
RDS	Railway Development Society
TUCC	Transport Users Consultative Committee

NOTICE OF INTENT TO WITHDRAW RAILWAY PASSENGER SERVICES
SECTION 56(7), TRANSPORT ACT 1962

BRITISH RAILWAYS BOARD
PUBLIC NOTICE
TRANSPORT ACT 1962
WITHDRAWAL OF RAILWAY PASSENGER SERVICES

The LONDON MIDLAND REGION of British Railways hereby give notice in accordance with Section 56(7) of the Transport Act, 1962 that they propose to discontinue all railway passenger services between Settle Junction and Carlisle (Petteril Bridge Junction) and from the following stations:—

SETTLE
APPLEBY

It appears to the Board that the following alternative services will be available:

Existing Services — By rail:

The passenger service currently operating between Leeds and Carlisle via Settle and Appleby will be diverted via Giggleswick, Carnforth, Oxenholme and Penrith.

Existing Services — By road:

Ribble-Pennine-Lancaster City Transport Joint Services 580 and 581 between Settle and Lancaster, Hellifield and Skipton.

Ribble Services 620, 621, 623, 624 and 625 between Appleby and Penrith.

Scott's Greys Service 38 between Appleby, Penrith and Carlisle.

Any users of the rail service which it is proposed to discontinue, and any body representing such users, may lodge an objection to the proposal in writing within six weeks of 24th December, 1983, i.e. not later than 4th February, 1984, addressing the objection to:

The Secretary,
Transport Users's Consultative Committee
for the North Western Area,
Room 308, Royal Exchange,
Cross Street,
Manchester M2 7BR.

or

The Secretary,
Transport Users' Consultative Committee
for the Yorkshire Area,
Record House,
Bootham,
York YO3 7DQ.

If any such objection is lodged, the service cannot be discontinued until the Transport Users' Consultative Committees have considered the objection and reported to the Secretary of State for Transport and the Secretary of State has given his consent to the closure under Section (56(8) of the Transport Act, 1962.

The Committee may hold a meeting to hear objections. Such a meeting will be held in public and any persons who have lodged an objection in writing may also make oral representations to the Committee. The Committee's report will be published.

If no objections are lodged to the proposal, the service will be discontinued on 14th May, 1984.

The original flawed closure notice.

TRANSPORT USERS CONSULTATIVE COMMITTEES

IMPORTANT NOTICE FOR RAIL USERS

PROPOSED CLOSURE OF THE SETTLE – CARLISLE AND BLACKBURN – HELLIFIELD LINES

Including Stations at:
Clitheroe, Settle, Horton-in-Ribblesdale, Ribblehead, Dent, Garsdale, Kirkby Stephen, Appleby, Langwathby, Lazonby, Armathwaite

In connection with British Rail's proposal for this closure, the Transport Users' Consultative Committees for North Eastern and North Western England (TUCCs) forwarded their joint report to the Secretary of State for Transport in December 1986. The Committees strongly recommended that consent to close the Settle – Carlisle line be refused.

The TUCCs have now received a letter from the Department of Transport as follows:

... "the Secretary of State is minded to give consent for the lines to be closed in early 1989. But he is deferring a final decision until towards the end of 1988 to allow time for representations relating to any new matters and to give an opportunity for a private sector proposal to come forward.

The Secretary of State is grateful for the report on the closure case which was submitted jointly by the North Eastern and North Western England TUCCs in December 1986. He is not however persuaded by the report that there is a case for retaining the lines on hardship grounds. He considers that guaranteed substitute bus services would cater adequately for the majority of those who now use the line for day-to-day essential transport purposes.

As it is now some time since the Committees first considered evidence on hardship, the Secretary of State would welcome a supplementary report from them under Section 56(10) of the Transport Act 1962 on whether there have been any changes in the use of the line, or otherwise, that would lead them to modify their original advice. The report should be submitted by 31 October 1988.

It would be helpful if the supplementary report could, so far as possible:
(i) quantify the number of persons who at present rely on the train for day-to-day essential transport purposes;
(ii) quantify the numbers of those persons mentioned at (i) above for whom guaranteed substitute bus services would not provide an adequate alternative – and give reasons for that;
(iii) advise on the routes, frequency and timing of guaranteed substitute bus services."

Accordingly, to assist in fulfilling their obligations under Section 56(10) of the Transport Act 1962, the Committees request any user of any service affected, and any body representing such users who wish to offer any evidence relevant to change in usage or use of the trains for essential day-to-day transport purposes, to write to either of them at the following address by 1 August 1988.

The Secretary
TUCC for N.W. England
Room 112, Boulton House
17 – 21 Chorlton Street
MANCHESTER M1 3HY

or

The Secretary
TUCC for N.E. England
Hilary House
16 St. Saviour's Place
YORK YO1 2PL

The joint TUCCs notice issued in 1988.

APPENDIX 1

TRANSPORT ACT 1962–SECTION 56

(1) There shall be established in accordance with this Section–

(a) a Central Transport Consultative Committee for Great Britain (hereinafter referred to as the "Central Committee"), and

(b) Area Transport Users Consultative Committees (hereinafter referred to as "Area Committees") for such areas of Great Britain as the Minister may from time to time direct, but so that there is no part of Great Britain which is not within the area of an Area Committee and so that there is at all times an Area Committee for Scotland and an Area Committee for Wales and Monmouthshire.

(2) The Central Committee shall consist of a chairman appointed by the Minister, the chairman of an Area Committees and such other members (not exceeding six) as the Minister may appoint after consultation with such bodies as appear to him to be representative of the interests of persons likely to be concerned with matters within the competence of the committee; and each Area Committee shall consist of a chairman appointed by the Minister, such other members as the Minister may appoint after consulation with such bodies as appear to him to be representative of the interests of persons likely to be concerned with matters within the competence of the committee and such other members (not exceeding two) as the Minister may appoint without such consultation.

The chairman of any Area Committee may appoint another member of that committee to attend a meeting of the Central Committee in his stead.

(3) The persons appointed to be members of any committee under this section shall hold and vacate office in accordance with the terms of their respective appointments and shall, on ceasing to be members of the committee, be eligible for re-appointment:

Provided that any such person may at any time by notice in writing to the Minister resign his office.

(4) Subject to the following provisions of this section, it shall be the duty of the Central Committee and of each Area Committee to consider and, where it appears to them to be desirable, make recommendations with respect to any matter affecting the services and facilities provided by any of the Boards–

(a) which has been the subject of representatives (other than representations appearing to the committee to be frivolous) made to the committee by or on behalf of users of those services or facilities, or

(b) which has been referred to the committee by the Minister or by a Board, or

(c) which appears to the committee to be a matter to which consideration ought to be given;

and copies of the minutes, conclusions and recommendations of each committee shall be sent to the Board concerned and–

(i)   in the case of any Area Committee, to the Central Committee; and

(ii)   in the case of the Central Committee and the Area Committees for Scotland and for Wales and Monmouthshire, to the Minister.

(5) Nothing in the last foregoing subsections shall entitle any committee to consider the charges made for any service or facility, or to consider any question relating to the discontinuance or reduction of railway services except as provided in the following provisions of this section; and the Central Committee shall not be obliged to consider any representation which appears to them to be more suitable for consideration by an Area Committee or which has been previously considered by an Area Committee.

(6) Where the Minister receives a recommendation under sub-section (4) of this section he may give to the Board concerned such directions as he thinks fit with respect to the matters dealt with in the recommendation.

(7) Where the Railways Board or London Board propose to discontinue all railway passenger services from any station or on any line (hereinafter referred to as a closure), they shall, not less than six weeks before carrying their proposal into effect, publish in two successive weeks in two local newspapers circulating in the area affected, and in such other manner as appears to them appropriate, a notice–

(a) giving the date and particulars of the proposed closure, and particulars of any alternative services which it appears to the Board will be available and of any proposals of the Board for providing or augmenting such services; and

(b) stating that objections to the proposed closure may be lodged in accordance with this section within six weeks of a date specified in the notice (being the date on which the notice is last published in a local newspaper as required by this section);

and copies of the notice shall be sent to the appropriate Area Committee.

For the purposes of this and the next following subsection the appropriate Area Committee is the committee for the area in which the station or the line, or any part of the line, affected by the proposed closure is situated.

(8) Where a notice has been published under the last foregoing subsection any user of any service affected and any body representing such users may within the period specified in the notice lodge with the appropriate Area Committee an objection in writing, and where such an objection is lodged the committee shall forthwith inform the Minister and the Board concerned and the closure shall not be proceeded with until the committee has reported to the Minister and the Minister has given his consent.

(9) A committee with whom an objection has been lodged under the last foregoing subsection shall consider the objection and any representations made by the Board concerned and report to the Minister as soon as possible on the hardship, if any, which they consider will be caused by the proposed closure and the report may contain proposals for alleviating that hardship.

Where objections with respect to any proposed closure have been lodged with more than one Area Committee, the committees in question–

(a) may report to the Minister jointly, or

(b) may agree that the consideration of objections and representations relating to the closure and the making of a report to the Minister shall be delegated to any of those committees appearing to them to be principally concerned;

and copies of every report under this and the next following subsection shall be sent to the Central Committee and to the Board concerned.

(10) The Minister may require an Area Committee to make a further report; and if in the case the Minister considers that a report or further report has been unreasonably delayed he may, after consulting the committee concerned and making such enquiries as he thinks fit, consent to the proposed closure without awaiting the report or further report.

(11) In any case in which a closure requires the consent of the Minister under this section, the Minister may give his consent subject to such conditions as he thinks fit and may from time to time vary those conditions; and the Minister may in connection with the closure from time to time give such directions to the Board concerned, as he thinks fit.

Where a condition attached to a consent or a direction, requires the Board to provide or assist in the provision of alternative services, the Minister may refer to an Area Committee any matter relating to those services, and the committee shall consider and report to the Minister on that matter.

(12) Every committee established under this section shall meet when convened by the chairman thereof, but in no case less frequently than twice a year, and, without prejudice to the discretion of the chairman to call a meeting whenever he thinks fit, he shall call a meeting when required so to do by any three members of the committee and minutes shall be kept of the proceedings at every meeting.

(13) Where for the purposes of subsection (9) of this section a committee decide to hear an objector orally, or to hear oral representations made on behalf of a Board, they shall hear the objector and the representations in public.

(14) Subject to subsections (12) and (13) of this section, every committee established under this section shall determine its own procedure including the quorum at meetings of the committee; and the Central Committee may from time to time make general recommendations to the Area Committees with respect to any matter affecting the procedure of functions of those committees.

(15) The Central Committee and the Area Committees for Scotland and for Wales and Monmouthshire shall make an annual report to the Minister, and the Minister shall lay a copy of those reports before each House of Parliament.

(16) The Boards shall provide every committee established under this section with such officers and servants, and such office accommodation, as appear to the Boards to be requisite for the proper discharge of the Committees' functions or as may be directed by the Minister; and the Boards may pay to the members of any such committee allowances in respect of loss of remunerative time in accordance with a scale approved

by the Minister with the consent of the Treasury and such travelling allowances and allowances in respect of out-of-pocket expenses as the Boards
may determine.

The Boards shall contribute to the expenses incurred by them under
this subsection in such proportions as they may agree or as the Minister
may in default of agreement direct.

(17) The transitional provision in Part III of the Seventh Schedule to
this Act shall have effect for the purposes of this section.

(18) For the purposes of subsection (4) of this section, any shipping
service provided by the Caledonian Steam Packet Company Limited or
the Caledonian Steam Packet Company (Irish Services) Limited shall, so
long as the company providing the service is a subsidiary of the Railway
Board, be deemed to be a service provided by that Board.

(19) Before the vesting date references in this section to the Boards or
to any Board shall be construed, except so far as the context otherwise
requires, as references to the Commission.

APPENDIX 2

SUMMARY OF CONCLUSIONS OF THE NORTH EAST AND NORTH WESTERN TUCCS INTO BR'S CLOSURE PROPOSAL

GENERAL

S 1. This is a summary of the Committees' conclusions to their report on British Rail's proposal to close the Settle–Carlisle and Blackburn–Hellifield railway lines. The report has been prepared in accordance with Section 56 of the Transport Act 1962.

S 2. During the statutory periods, the Committees received a total of 22,150 written objections to the proposals from users of the services affected. At Public Hearings held on 16 days during March and April 1986, the Committees heard oral evidence from British Rail and 392 users or their representatives, 118 represented corporate or incorporate bodies, themselves consisting of very many people directly or indirectly affected by the closure proposal.

S 3. The proposal is to close the line between Settle Junction and Carlisle (Petteril Bridge Junction) and re-route the current direct Leeds–Carlisle service by way of Carnforth and Penrith. Settle, Appleby and the Dales Rail stations would be closed. Giggleswick halt, it is proposed, would provide an alternative to Settle whilst a special bus service would run between Appleby and Penrith station.

S 4. Following consideration of the proposal and objections to it, the Committees are of the opinion that the Settle–Carlisle and Blackburn–Hellifield lines should not be allowed to close because of the hardship that would be caused to users, the substantial increase in the use of the Settle–Carlisle line, its potential in railway network terms and its importance to the economic infrastructure of the region.

S 5. British Rail's case for closure is based on cost. It claims the Settle–Carlisle line is expensive to operate and maintain and heavy expenditure is required "on essential renewals to Ribblehead Viaduct and four other bridges." It was also stated that essential track renewals are required to maintain the line to passenger standards.

S 6. At the Public Hearings the Committees repeatedly asked British Rail to substantiate its case by providing estimates of the costs required to renovate and maintain the Settle–Carlisle line and the savings that would be effected if the line closed. This request was always declined.

hardship. However, in accordance with the Transport Act 1962, the Committees are required to consider objections made by users of services affected by the closure proposal. The grounds for objection are not restricted in the Act, nor does the Act preclude the Committees from reporting on issues other than hardship. The Committee noted, too, that the Earl of Caithness, for the Government, considered that British Rail should make financial information available so that objectors could judge whether or not British Rail had made its case for closure.

S 8.   On the basis of financial evidence submitted at the Public Hearings by objectors, most notably that provided authoritatively by the Joint County Councils (Cumbria, Lancashire, West Yorkshire), which was not challenged by British Rail, the Committees were convinced that there was no case for closing the Settle–Carlisle line. The number of passengers using the line had increased to a level which covered direct expenses whilst, compared with other Provincial sector services, the line is performing well. The Committees feel the PEIDA Report should be updated to take account of the increased use of the line and support the request by the Joint County Councils for an independent social cost-benefit analysis to be undertaken.

S 9.   The North East TUCC notes that the background and controversy regarding this closure proposal has been well-recorded. Its predecessor, the Yorkshire Area TUCC, together with a number of objectors and MPs had corresponded with British Rail over the future of the line and received assurances which, in the light of subsequent events, were capable of different interpretations regarding British Rail's intentions for the line during the two years prior to publication of the 'Rail Plan' in August 1983.

S 10.   This apparent lack of candour on the part of British Rail, whilst not attributable personally to its representatives at the Public Hearings was felt by the North East TUCC to undermine the credibility of much of British Rail's evidence, such as it was, not least that relating to assurances regarding proposals designed to alleviate hardship. However, such are the characteristics of the Settle–Carlisle line that, even if these proposals were implemented, they would only be of limited benefit to a tiny proportion of those users who would suffer hardship if the line were to close.

HARDSHIP

S 11.   In this summary, the Committee's evaluation of the hardship that would be encountered if the Settle–Carlisle line were to close is presented in an abbreviated form. Moreover, the degree of hardship varies. For example, very severe hardship would be caused to disabled passengers resident in Settle and Appleby if the line were to close, whilst the degree of hardship for the occasional traveller on a steam charter service would be rather less. A more comprehensive and detailed assessment as to how closure would affect different categories of users is provided in the body of the report.

S 12.   The Committees are fully satisfied that varying levels of hardship would occur with respect to:

a) Settle and Appleby

S 13. These are the two principal stations proposed for closure. Whilst both towns are relatively small, they act as important regional centres and this highlights the importance and significance of the railway to them, especially as their economy is very dependent on tourism both for day excursions and for visitors for a longer period to North Yorkshire and Cumbria. The railway itself is one of the main attractions for visitors whilst providing access to and within the area.

S 14. If the line were to close it would have grave effects on the communities over a wide area. Residents would suffer severe hardship from difficulties in gaining access to major centres such as Leeds and Carlisle from an area greatly deprived, partly by geography, of public transport. Also of great consequence would be the loss to the economics of Settle and Appleby of the vast majority of visitors who currently arrive by train and make a significant contribution to the economic well-being of both towns. Much indirect hardship would be caused in an area of significant unemployment.

S 15. British Rail's proposal that Giggleswick halt will provide an alternative to Settle, a staffed station near the centre of the town, is unacceptable. Giggleswick is unstaffed, ill-equipped and situated over a mile from both Settle and Gigglesiwck is what John Watson MP described as "the middle of nowhere." Access is by exposed, unlit roads and will become even more hazardous when its approach is traversed by the Settle by-pass.

S 16. The prospects for alternative bus services are not good, particularly as evidence from the Joint County Councils and Dr. Mayer-Hillman for the Joint Action Committee shows that rail users would not use such services in great numbers. Journey times would be longer, costs generally higher, frequencies uncertain and the future of rural bus services unpredictable.

S 17. Appleby would be particularly badly hit. Evidence suggests that British Rail's proposed sponsored bus service to Penrith would attract little local support, especially from the elderly. Moreover, as the predominant traffic flow on the Settle–Carlisle line is from Leeds northwards, Appleby's attraction as a destination for a day out would be drastically reduced by the increased fares and extended travelling time which allows less time to be spent in the town.

b) Through Services

S 18. Regular travellers over the Settle–Carlisle line have witnessed a decline in the standards of service during recent years. Many objectors equated this with 'closure by stealth'. Through trains to Glasgow and the East Midlands were discontinued in 1982. With them went the buffet cars whilst the quality of the coaching stock on the residual service has left much to be desired.

S 19. Journey times have become progressively longer. The morning journey from Leeds to Glasgow via the Settle–Carlisle line takes 17 minutes longer than 10 years ago, whereas that to London has been reduced by

15 minutes over the same period (since 12 May 1986 a further 15 minutes have been added to the Leeds–Glasgow journey). This together with the recent removal of the advertised first class facility from the Settle–Carlisle route, is hardly conducive to retaining, let alone attracting new business and other long distance travellers.

S 20. Given this decline in service standards, which in itself can be said to represent a degree of hardship, British Rail's proposal to add an extra 45 minutes to the journey from Leeds to Carlisle by re-routing the service via Carnforth will add considerably to this hardship.

S 21. Over half-an-hour of the additional journey time on the proposed alternative route is to be spent waiting in Carnforth Down Goods Loop to gain access to the West Coast Main Line. This, more than any other single factor, illustrates and underlines the difficulty in obtaining paths for additional services on this route and the need to retain the Settle–Carlisle line as an integral part of the national rail network.

S 22. Evidence submitted by the Joint County Councils indicates that there would be little public support for the re-routed service and the Committees do not believe that it will survive for long as a through service.

c) Diverted Services

S 23. At the Public Hearings, British Rail revealed that it did not intend to discontinue all railway passenger services from the Blackburn–Hellifield line as it would continue to be used for diverted services, whilst Clitheroe would remain available for charter services (other than Dales Rail). As a consequence the Committees agree with the Joint Action Committee that the closure proposal for this line should be withdrawn. Should British Rail, at some future date, wish to discontinue all railway passenger services from this line, a further statutory closure proposal should be instituted.

S 24. The Committees share the sceptism voiced by the Joint County Councils, the Joint Action Committee and many individual and corporate objectors that the Cumbrian coast line would provide an adequate diversionary route for the West Coast Main Line services re-routed for engineering or other purposes. There was concern that such a proposal should have been suggested by British Rail.

S 25. Significantly longer journey times, the necessity of long sections of single line operation to permit the use of Mark 3 coaches (and concern regarding the safety of their use), the virtually hourly existing local passenger service and important freight traffic would all give rise to difficulties in accommodation diverted trains without extended delays. In addition the diversion of main line trains would lead to local services being cancelled or retimed . Varying levels of hardship would be caused to users of all the passenger services affected.

d) Dales Rail and Local Services

S 26. Dales Rail is a success story of which British Rail, the sponsoring Local Authorities, the Yorkshire Dales National Park, the Countryside Commission, and its users can be proud. It is unique and whilst largely geared to the leisure market, it also provides a vital link for those living in the remote areas served by Dales Rail stations who seek access to Leeds and Carlisle.

S 27. The new local service introduced in July 1986 between Skipton and Carlisle serving all Dales Rail stations (except Clitheroe) is proving very popular. It has added a new dimension to the Settle–Carlisle line and severe hardship would be caused if it were discontinued, as alternative public transport in the vicinity of the Dales Rail stations is minimal or non-existent. Hardship would also be caused to those using the Dales Rail and local services for recreational pursuits.

e) Steam and Other Charter Services

S 28. Those wishing to travel behind steam locomotives, or on trains hauled by diesel locomotives of special interest (eg. Class 40 D200), consider the Settle–Carlisle line as one of the finest railways in England. The line was built in 1870-76 to high standards: no gradient more than 1 in 100, with curves taken at 90 mph. Its closure would represent some hardship for users of these services.

f) Red Star Parcels and Freight Traffic

S 29. It was convincingly demonstrated at the Public Hearings that users of British Rail's Red Star Parcels service at Settle and, to a lesser extent, at Appleby, would suffer severe hardship if the facility was discontinued. The alternatives suggested by British Rail did not satisfy existing users.

S 30. Apart from diverted trains, freight traffic has been re-routed away from the Settle–Carlisle line, although some residual business remains between Appleby and Carlisle. British Rail intend to retain this section as an extended siding. The Committee cannot understand the logic of re-routing traffic away from the line whilst it remains open when alternative routes involve longer journeys and presumably higher operating costs.

g) 'England's Greatest Historical Scenic Route'

S 31. The above words, frequently quoted at the Public Hearings, are taken from the heading of British Rail's current leaflet describing highlights of the Settle–Carlisle line. A great users travel on the line because it passes through an area of outstanding scenic beauty and represents an incomparable example of Victorian Engineering. To quote British Rail again, it is 'The Most Spectacular Main Line in England' and, in railway terms, is as important as Hadrian's Wall and York Minster. All are unique.

S 32. Closure of the line would cause unquantifiable hardship to these users. For many the line is part of the National Heritage and its loss in aesthetic terms would represent hardship every bit as severe as that felt by those who primarily use it to get from one place to another. Its tourist potential is enormous.

h) Tourism

S 33. The report includes a comprehensive appraisal on the relationship between tourism and the Settle–Carlisle line. As Britain's largest and fastest growing industry, tourism is a vital factor in consideration of the future of the line. It passes through and provides access to the Yorkshire Dales

National Park and the Eden Valley. Both are areas of outstanding beauty.

S 34. British Rail's declared intention to close the line is clearly out of step with the recently announced policies and intentions of the Government to foster tourism and the leisure industry as a major contributor to a region's economic growth. Government policy appears to have been overlooked as far as the Settle–Carlisle line is concerned.

S 35. Over the last two years Government Departments and Local Authorities, the English and respective Regional Tourist Boards, the Countryside Commission, the Development Commission and those engaged in the commercial sector of the tourism industry (including agriculture) have been identifying problems, formulating proposals and their implementation, to provide a thriving and viable economy for the area. The co-operative success of all these actions will depend largely upon the continuation, maintenance and development of the Settle–Carlisle line. It could validly be said that the linchpin of the future prosperity of the area is largely dependent on the line's continuance.

S 36. The Committees dwell in considerable detail on the relationship between tourism and the Settle–Carlisle line in the body of the report. Since British Rail announced its closure proposal interest in the line has increased, as have the number of passengers using it. The initial argument that this has been due to people making a last journey over the line before it closed now clearly seems to be fallacious. The sustained increase in the number of people travelling and the increase in the number of services provided during 1986 indicates a growing demand. It is evident that many of those engaged in the tourist industry in North Yorkshire and Cumbria would suffer varying degrees of hardship if the line were to be closed.

THE FUTURE

S 37. One of the most striking aspects of this closure proposal is that it is the only one the Committees can recall where the number of passengers using a line proposed for closure has significantly increased following the announcement of the proposal. This does suggest that the Settle–Carlisle line has a positive future. Indeed, the Joint County Councils, Joint Action Committee and hundreds of individual objectors convinced the Committees that there is an overwhelmingly strong case for its retention.

S 38. The Committees feel that, on the basis of the evidence presented at the Public Hearings, the full potential of the line has yet to be tapped. It offers an opportunity for sustained growth and with it increased efficiency and profitability. British Rail's Project Manager, Mr Ron Cotton, has proved that, with only a minimum of promotion, the market clearly exists. The Committees consider that the existing Eastern and Scottish Regions' policy of sending long distance passengers by more extended routes, rather than the Settle–Carlisle line, has reduced the potential of the line and if this were reversed the patronage would be increased further. Effective marketing on a national and international basis could lead to still further gains.

S 39. However, the Committees do not look upon the Settle–Carlisle as being exclusively geared to the leisure market. It remains the direct route between West Yorkshire and South West Scotland and should have an InterCity service commensurate with this. It also has a strategic role as part of the national rail network, not least at times of national crisis.

S 40. In addition to future potential for passenger services, the opening of the Channel Tunnel will lead to an increase in rail freight traffic to and from Scotland. Limitations on West Coast Main Line and East Coast Main Line capacity are likely to necessitate the existence of an alternative route.

S 41. British Rail is on record as stating that the Settle–Carlisle line is, in relative terms, one of the Provincial sector's most financially successful lines in that it more than covers its operating costs. It is true that the infrastructure may be expensive to maintain, but essential maintenance has to be undertaken whether the line is open or not and increased use will result in this expenditure being spread over a greater amount of traffic.

RECOMMENDATIONS

S 42. On the basis of the undoubted hardship that closure of the line would cause, together with the strength of the commercial case presented for its retention – based on the sustained increase in use and the wealth of evidence for potential growth – the Committees strongly and emphatically recommend that consent to British Rail's proposal to close the Settle–Carlisle line be refused.

S 43. As a result, Dales Rail services could continue to operate and, as it is understood British Rail intend to use the Blackburn–Hellifield line for passenger and freight services, there would appear to be no reason why Dales Rail services should not use this line. The Committees accordingly recommend that consent to the proposal to close the Blackburn–Hellifield line also be refused.